The METROPOLITAN ECONOMY

THE PROCESS OF EMPLOYMENT EXPANSION

By THOMAS M. STANBACK, Jr.

AND RICHARD V. KNIGHT

Foreword by ELI GINZBERG

COLUMBIA UNIVERSITY PRESS 1970

New York and London

This report was prepared for the Manpower Administration, U.S. Department of Labor, under research contract Number 81-34-67-25 authorized by Title I of the Manpower Development and Training Act. Since contractors performing research under government sponsorship are encouraged to express their own judgment freely, the report does not necessarily represent the department's official opinion or policy. Moreover, the contractor is solely responsible for the factual accuracy of all material developed in the report.

Reproduction in whole or in part permitted for any purpose of the United States government.

To our children

MARGARET, TOM, MAX, ROB, BILL,

AND FLORRIE STANBACK

AND

DIERDRE AND ERIC KNIGHT

FOREWORD

BY ELI GINZBERG

THIS PIONEERING STUDY of the dynamics of employment expansion in the United States has multiple roots. It is directly related to earlier, current, and future work of the Conservation of Human Resources Project at Columbia University, which has been concerned with analyzing structural changes in the American economy with particular reference to their relevance for manpower policy.

The Pluralistic Economy by Ginzberg, Hiestand, and Reubens (1965) reviewed the extent to which the American economy is being transformed from the production of goods to services and how this transformation is related to the growth of the not-for-profit sector, particularly education and medical services. The present investigation has one of its roots in the growing importance of services, a subject that was further explored by Harry I. Greenfield in *Manpower and the Growth of Producer Services* (1966).

The present effort of Thomas M. Stanback Jr. and Richard V. Knight is also related to the shift which the Conservation Project began to make in the middle 1960s from an exclusive concern with macro-problems to an approach which focuses increasingly on the urban condition. Thomas Stanback was the co-author with Boris Yavitz of a study on *Electronic Data Processing in New York City: Lessons for Metropolitan Economics* (1967), which attempted to explore in detail the factors facilitating and retarding the growth of a major new industry in the largest of the nation's cities. The problems of the cities have continued to be of major concern to the Conservation staff. In 1968 it published *Manpower Strategy for the Metropolis* and *Business Leadership and the Negro Crisis*. It hopes to complete in 1970 an investigation of *Urban Health Services: The Case of New York*. A related study of employment expansion at a sub-national level is the monograph of Alfred S. Eichner: *State Development Efforts to Expand Employment* (1970).

The third influence on the shape and direction of the present research effort was our desire to go beyond the dominant Keynesian approach of dealing with the economy exclusively in monetary and fiscal terms and to explore the dynamics of economic growth in terms of employment at a subaggregate level. Although we do not deny that the aggregate demand for goods and services is of critical importance in determining the level of employment, in light of the differences among regions and cities, it appeared desirable to probe beneath the surface of demand in the hope of uncovering new insights into the dynamics of employment. A shorthand description of the present study is that it is a partial retreat from Keynes' preoccupation with an aggregative static model of underemployment developed in money terms to a dynamic model of employment expansion in an economy of multiple labor markets. Whereas both classical and Keynesian theory treats the economy as being localized at a single point, Stanback and Knight consider the spatial dimension and thus explicitly recognize that the economic activity takes place at many different points, and further that any study of the national economy must recognize such spatial organization.

This particular approach has a long and honorable history; it has been the center of interest of those who are called regional economists. For several decades students have sought to explain the growth of different regions of the country. However, this work of Stanback and Knight differs from most of these earlier efforts at regional economic analysis in several significant regards. First, its primary emphasis is not on the region but on the metropolitan labor market. This represents a shift from an analysis of a limited number of heterogeneous regions to one that is predicated on a typology of cities in terms of size and primary functions. Next, it is concerned with analyzing the dynamics of growth in terms not of a few aggregations but with reference to the wealth of detail reflected in a classification of thirty-two industries. Finally, the several measures developed by Stanback and Knight have been shaped and refined to reveal as much as possible about the "dynamics" of the way in which job creation in one sector of the metropolitan labor market is correlated with growth in other sectors.

The authors eschewed certain analyses. For instance, they did not attempt an occupational analysis which might have some value in accounting for differential rates of growth among metropolitan labor markets. The analysis of how the supply of labor might quantitatively or qualitatively affect the rate of growth of different cities is left for later study. Moreover, they do not study unemployment. Nevertheless the authors go far in breaking new ground.

In appraising their work it may be helpful to distinguish three contributions: their methodology for studying the expansion of employment; their important substantive findings; and the relevance of their findings for economic and manpower policy.

With regard to their methodology, some of the important building blocks out of which they erected their edifice are outlined here. These basic data consisted of the Census materials for thirty-two industrial groupings for 1940, 1950, and 1960, supplemented by a finer breakdown of 113 industries. Their focus was on the metropolitan labor market as the unit of analysis rather than on states or regions as had most, if not all, of their predecessors. Students of manpower do not need to be persuaded of the rationale of this decision; they have long recognized that the labor market is the most useful unit for subaggregate analysis.

The authors did much more. They organized the 368 labor markets according to two distinct criteria—size and dominant economic function. They organized their data into nine categories of metropolitan labor markets—three large, three medium, and three small, which resulted in the following distribution: 13 large cities (1.6 million to 8 million); 114 medium (200,001 to less than 1.6 million); and 241 small (25,001 to 200,000). Throughout, the authors compare these several metropolitan labor markets to the remaining 2,541 counties, which they designate as nonmetropolitan.

They developed a new typology of metropolitan labor markets in which they distinguish among the following types: nodal, mixed, manufacturing, recreational, medical/educational, and governmental. Specialized cities were grouped into one or another of these categories depending on whether a particular function accounted for a relatively large proportion of all employment. The last four terms are more or less self-explanatory. A "nodal" city is one which presumptively provides a range of business and consumer services for the hinterland in which there is no city of larger size. A city was classified as "mixed" when employment was distributed among several functions with no one predominating and when the city did not serve as a nodal center for the area. In compressing 368 cities into this sixfold schema the authors understandably, of course, encountered difficulties with respect to some whose characteristics were blurred. The important point, however, is that this category schema repeatedly revealed dimensions of growth and decline of employment that otherwise would have remained obscured.

The authors distilled additional findings by analyzing their data simultaneously in terms of size and function. And they went considerably further in developing useful constructs. Among the most important was their recognition of the need to avoid the "netting out" of employment change, which had been the approach followed by most of their predecessors. Concerned with learning more about the dynamics of employment expansion, they distinguished between job creation and job destruction which the netting out process obscured. Clearly net changes are important. But so is a finding that in certain labor markets or regions or even in the nation at large, a net addition of 100,000 jobs within a decade might be the result of the creation of 500,000 new ones and the destruction of 400,000 existing jobs or might reflect only the addition of 100,000 new jobs. Further, studying the "job increase/decrease offset" (JIDO), the authors gained new insights into the employment impact of industrial relocation.

To develop their typology they found it necessary to devise a new analysis of employment structure. The share of employment in each industry was analyzed for 368 cities and broken into quartiles. It was the distribution within these quartiles which revealed the essential structural characteristics of cities. The authors borrowed additional measures from statistics and economics and modified some, such as the multiplier and acceleration principle. But the strength of their work is not in the elaboration of such measures but in the strength of the underlying matrix, particularly their classification of cities.

Their second contribution is their substantive findings. The first points out that cities of different sizes grew at different rates and that medium-size labor markets experienced the largest net gains in employment between 1950 and 1960. Moreover, these different rates reflected different experiences with job increases and decreases. For instance, the largest metropolitan labor markets experienced a slower rate of net growth than the other size categories of metropolitan labor markets as a result of their having a somewhat higher rate of destruction of nonagricultural jobs and a lower rate of job creation. The medium group had the fastest rate of growth because it had both the highest rate of job creation and a relatively modest rate of job destruction.

Another interesting finding emerging from the study of size of city relates to industrial composition. For instance, with only minor exceptions, business services grew more rapidly in larger cities. Consumer services, on the other hand, grew fastest in small cities and slowest in large cities.

Another important finding emerging from the city-size analysis is that there is a regional pattern for all except the largest cities. The greater the role of manufacturing within a region, the smaller are the roles of business and consumer services.

During the past years, much has been made of the crucial role that services have played and probably will continue to play in the growth of employment. While the findings of the Stanback–Knight study do not contradict this, they do raise questions. For instance, the authors find that the expansion of services and the general level of employment are closely correlated in certain types of cities: nodal, medium-size mixed, and resort cities. But in others—manufacturing, government, medical/educational, small-size mixed, and large metropolitan labor markets—the relationship is much less consistent. Apparently the response of the service sector in these latter types of cities to other forces leading to expansion was much less strong. There is, then, no generalized relationship between total expansion in employment and the expansion of services: in nodal, resort, and medium-size mixed cities, general employment and service employment tended to expand in unison; this was not true of other types of cities, such as manufacturing, medical/educational, government, and small-size mixed cities.

The authors suggest the need for modifying the conventional wisdom not only about employment in the service sector, but also with regard to manufacturing employment which they find, at least in some cities and some regions, continue to be the bellwether of employment expansion. And much of their data is suggestive about the difficulties that cities dependent on government employment, particularly military employment, have in expanding because of the absence of an adequate infrastructure.

The Conservation Project believes that the test of significant research in the social sciences is its contribution to the improvement of public policy. As noted above, much of the efforts of Stanback and Knight were directed to developing a more relevant and improved approach for the study of employment expansion. This effort is particularly meritorious since the nation's future depends more and more on the viability and prosperity of its cities. If the authors had done no more than advance the discipline of metropolitan economics they would have made a contribution, since progress must be phased. They would have left to their successors the task of making the linkages to policy. But they themselves have made a first contribution by noting how their findings relate to current policy and how they might be used to improve it.

The whole of their analysis is a warning about the limitations of a national manpower policy, especially one geared to training and retraining, that fails to be sensitive to local and regional differences. The programs that are appropriate for Atlanta are not likely to fit Detroit, and the requirements of New York are different from either. While the authors cannot put forward the specifications that should guide local manpower programing, an application of their analysis will prove constructive if the planners use and refine the model they have developed.

The authors note the extent to which cities must recognize that they are in competition with one another and that their futures will be determined not only by their tax rates, but perhaps even more by the amenities they are able to offer companies who are considering locating or relocating. The American economy has become fluid; fewer and fewer industries are rigidly tied to one particular location. In the future, their location will largely be determined by where their executives and work force prefer to live.

The authors therefore place heavy stress on a central business district which can provide both the range of business services that can help to generate new enterprises and employment and that can help to attract and retain customers through the amenities which it offers. There may be some comfort here for the mayors of our largest cities when they confront the pull to the suburbs. Clearly they must keep their central business district vital.

It is a regrettable trait of men and nations to recognize problems after their ability to deal with them effectively has atrophied. The plight of many cities reflects in large measure the uncontrolled migration during the past two decades of millions of people from farms and rural areas who came to the city because they had everything to gain and nothing to lose. But the city proved much less hospitable for many than they had hoped or expected. Now there are only small numbers still on farms who must sooner or later leave. But there are still millions who are living in small places (rural non-farm) where their prospects of employment are bleak and the services available to them and their children are so meager that they will be unable to improve their circumstances unless they relocate.

If we are to learn from our mistakes in the past and if we are to avoid compounding the difficulties in our large cities which have brought many of them to a point of explosion, we must make use of the knowledge and insights offered by Stanback and Knight to multiply and expand the many centers of growth that dot the map so that those who must still relocate can be guided effectively rather than left to their own devices with untoward consequences both to themselves and the communities to which they move. Herein lies the greatest potential for studies such as this one. We hope that many students will be stimulated to pursue the important pathways which they have marked.

Columbia University
April, 1970

PREFACE

WHEN WE BEGAN our study of subnational labor markets in the American economy, it became immediately clear that the metropolitan labor market should be the basic unit of analysis. We were confronted by two major problems: First, how could 368 metropolitan areas that varied widely in terms of size, function, geography and social characteristics be examined? Could the concept of metropolitanism alone be regarded as sufficient or should a typology be developed? Second, how could widely diverging trends in employment change in these metropolitan places be represented in such a way that offsetting changes would not be netted-out (as is the case when using orthodox methods of aggregation).

Our solution to these problems was to develop a typology of metropolitan places and to devise new measures of employment change consistent with the theory of urban and regional development. Once this methodology was established it was possible to move rather readily to an analysis of employment structure and change. The fundamental observation which emerged was that both size and economic function significantly influenced the character of urban labor markets. Metropolitan places differ substantially and such differences must be recognized before effective policy and programs can be established.

We feel that knowledge of basic economic processes is essential to an understanding of urban problems. Accordingly, we believe this book should be of interest not only to economists but also to regional and urban planners, geographers, urban sociologists, and state and city developmental officers.

It is a pleasure to have this opportunity to thank a number of persons who helped us. Our greatest debt is to Dr. Eli Ginzberg who urged us to take on this research initially and who supported us throughout with many useful suggestions and with his warm enthusiasm and confidence. We are grateful also to Dr. Lowell D. Ashby, Chief of the Regional Economics Division, Office of Business Economics, U. S. Department of Commerce, who directed the preparation and publication of the data which are analyzed here. It would not have been possible to carry out the study in its present form without this material. We wish to thank also Dr. Ruth T. Mack, Dr. Victor R. Fuchs and Dr. Richard P. Brief who read substantial portions of the manuscript and offered construction criticism. Dr. Herman F. Otte provided a geographer's evaluation of the classification of metropolitan places.

A number of persons assisted us in the course of our work but our greatest debt is to Athanasios Kavgalakis, Norman Knight, Tadek Korn, Herman Melzer, and Jim Suarez. These men helped us through the various stages of data preparation, programming, analyses, and readying the material for publication.

Columbia University   Thomas M. Stanback Jr.
June, 1970   Richard V. Knight

CONTENTS

TABLES

The METROPOLITAN ECONOMY

THE PROCESS OF EMPLOYMENT EXPANSION

ABBREVIATIONS USED
IN THE STUDY

CBD   central business district
FIRE   finance, insurance, real estate
INR   industry not reported
JIDO   job increase/decrease offset
MLM   metropolitan labor market
NMC   nonmetropolitan county
SMSA   standard metropolitan statistical area

1 THE NATURE AND PLAN
OF THE STUDY

BEHIND THE AGGREGATED national statistics which present in capsule form the story of growth in the American economy is a complex and fascinating story, a story of employment shifts to metropolitan areas, of variations in the industrial structure of employment, and of changing patterns in metropolitan labor markets.

In this study we focus attention on metropolitan economies because we feel that they hold the key to an understanding of what has taken place in the economy as a whole. There is both empirical and theoretical justification for such emphasis.

In the first place, there has been a tendency for growth to center in the cities. During the twenty-year period from 1940 to 1960 employment in metropolitan labor markets increased by 19 million jobs, an increase equal to 91.1 percent of the *net* rise in employment for the nation as a whole.

The process by which this has taken place is a complex one, however. Jobs have opened up in certain industries and in certain labor markets and have closed out in others. Net measures of change in employment understate the extent of change which has taken place. We have estimated the number of job increases and job decreases for the national economy as follows:

	1940-50	*1950-60*
Job increases	15,101,000	14,640,000
Job decreases	3,002,000	5,743,000
Net change in employment	12,099,000	8,897,000

Approximately three-quarters of the jobs that opened up were in metropolitan places whereas most of the jobs that closed down were in nonmetropolitan areas (figures in parentheses are percent):

	1940-50		1950-60	
	Job increases (000)	Job decreases (000)	Job increases (000)	Job decreases (000)
MLM's	11,533(76.4)	1,190(39.6)	11,150(76.2)	2,375(27.2)
NMC's	3,568(23.6)	1,812(60.4)	3,490(23.8)	3,368(73.0)
Total U. S.	15,101(100)	3,002(100)	14,640(100)	5,743(100)

Unless we consider employment changes taking place in local (metropolitan) labor markets we will not be able to understand the dynamics of employment expansion.

Second, the metropolitan economies play a highly strategic role in the growth process. Although growth is most often discussed in macroeconomic terms with the national economy viewed as a single point in space, regional and urban economic theory indicates that metropolitan growth and change are at the very heart of economic development. The increase in market size and the economies of agglomeration which spark growth tend to occur largely in metropolitan economies. They, in turn, lead the way toward further growth in surrounding areas. We find evidence of such agglomeration in the tendency for a variety of business services to spring up together in certain relatively fast-growing "nodal" metropolitan places. These places act as growth centers and figure importantly in the location of new enterprises and additional facilities for firms in expanding industries.

Finally, the metropolitan economy comprises the most logical unit for analysis. In contrast to states, which are political rather than economic units, and regions, which are large and somewhat arbitrarily defined, the metropolitan economy is a commonly accepted, well-defined economic organization which is meaningful in terms of labor market analysis.

It is important to note, however, that metropolitan areas are closely linked together into a national system of metropolitan places and must be considered in the context of regional or national systems of places. National trends or changes in output, demand, and technology will have a differential impact on individual metropolitan areas, and change in one area will lead to further changes in other (linked) areas. Consequently, we have tried to retain a national–regional perspective when analyzing metropolitan places. Our emphasis, however, has been placed on finding similarities among metropolitan economies so that a meaningful typology of metropolitan places could be derived. By classifying metropolitan economies according to type of economic activity and size, it is possible to observe both similarities and variations which would, of necessity, go undiscovered if more aggregative units were studied. Moreover we are able to develop an understanding as to how a particular place will respond to a particular growth stimulus and how the national system of metropolitan places adjusts to overall national growth.

The metropolitan units to be studied are, in most instances (214 out of 368), standard metropolitan statistical areas (SMSA's).[1] The remaining metropolitan units are counties which contain cities of more than 25,000 population, but which are not a part of an SMSA as

[1] In determining the counties which comprise an SMSA we adopt the 1965 Bureau of the Budget definition and use this definition for each of the three census years. In this way we observe the employment changes which took place in a geographically unvarying reporting unit over a period of two decades.

Specifically, each SMSA must include at least: one city with 50,000 inhabitants or more; or two cities having contiguous boundaries and constituting, for general economic and social purposes, a single community with a combined population of at least 50,000, the smaller of which must have a population of at least 15,000. In determining whether or not counties adjacent to the central county are metropolitan in character, the Bureau of the Census applies certain detailed criteria. A minimum of 75 percent of the labor force of the county must be engaged in nonagricultural work. In addition, "it must have 50 percent of its population living in contiguous minor civil divisions with a density of at least 150 persons per square mile . . . radiating from a central city in the area." Finally, its nonagricultural work force must equal at least a tenth of the nonagricultural workers living in the central county, or it must be the place of residence of a nonagricultural labor force of 10,000 or more.

As regards the requirement that an adjacent county be economically and socially integrated, an adjacent county is usually considered to be so integrated if it meets either of the following criteria: 1) "15 percent of the workers living in the county work in the county or counties containing central cities . . . ," or 2) "25 percent of those working in the county live in the county or counties containing central cities of the area." See U.S. Bureau of the Census, *U.S. Census of Population 1960*, Size of Place, pp. X-XI.

usually defined. We have chosen to include these counties with the SMSA's rather than to group them among the large number of non-metropolitan counties (NMC's). Both personal observation and pre-liminary analysis of the data indicated that in terms of industrial composition and change within their labor forces these counties are essentially metropolitan and resemble the smaller SMSA's.

There is reason to regard these metropolitan units as an accept-able first approximation of a labor market, and we shall henceforth refer to them as metropolitan labor markets (MLM's). The clusters of counties which are officially designated as SMSA's by the Department of Commerce were selected in accordance with criteria designed to insure that each member county is both economically and socially integrated with the county containing the central city. It is highly likely that a person changing his job will do so within the SMSA. Yet the SMSA is, of course, a compromise. For some types of employment (e.g., the executive or professional man commuting from a consider-able distance), the SMSA underbounds the labor market. For other types (e.g., the unskilled worker residing in the central city who is unaware of job opportunities in the suburbs or unable to commute to such employment except at high cost in time and money), it over-bounds. The latter is very probably the most important limitation. Its significance is that the SMSA employment data do not disclose dif-ferences between the structure of the labor force in the central city and in the suburban fringes, nor do they indicate the shifts which occur between them. The analysis of urban labor markets in such detail requires different source material.[2]

Counties with cities of more than 25,000 population which are not SMSA's would also appear to be acceptable as approximations of MLM's. Cities in these counties are rarely larger than 40,000 in popu-lation, and their commutation areas tend to be more restricted than for the official SMSA's. Most persons live in or close to the city in

[2] Such an analysis is currently being carried out by Stanley Friedlander of the Conservation of Human Resources Project utilizing material for 30 SMSA's published in *County Business Patterns*, U.S. Department of Commerce, for the period 1950-67.

which they work—when they do not, they usually live within the county's boundaries. In most instances, therefore, the county's boundaries encompass the relevant urban labor market. They may, however, also include a limited amount of additional employment associated with rural or semi-urban economic activity on the periphery.

OBJECTIVES OF THE STUDY

The major tasks of this study are twofold: to classify metropolitan places, and to analyze employment growth patterns in each type of place. On the one hand we examine the industrial composition of the work force of MLM's in 1960 and develop a typology based on principal economic function and size. On the other hand we examine variations in the nature and extent of employment changes for the two decades 1940-50 and 1950-60. Change is measured in terms of jobs opened up (job increases) and jobs closed out (job decreases) as well as in terms of the more conventional measure, net employment change. We also try to interpret our findings both in terms of growth prospects for metropolitan places of different types and sizes and in terms of national and regional economic planning with particular emphasis on manpower planning.

There are important secondary tasks as well. In addition to studying employment structure and change in MLM's, we study NMC's to provide a basis of comparison between the metropolitan and non-metropolitan sectors of the economy.[3] Moreover, to provide necessary background for analysis of the MLM's, we examine some of the more

---

[3] The NMC is less satisfactory as a unit of study than is the MLM in that this type of place is simply a residual category. There is, no doubt, very considerable variety among these counties. Some are essentially rural, while others are comprised largely of towns where people live and work under essentially urban conditions. The analysis of these places is not, however, a major objective of this study. We examine the employment characteristics of NMC's only for regions or for the nation as a whole.

important characteristics of structure and change in the labor force for each region and for the total U.S. economy for the period 1940 to 1960.

There has been much earlier work from which we have borrowed. Economic theory lends itself fairly readily to speculation regarding the principles which guide employment structure and change in the labor force of urban economies. Considerable theoretical work has been done in recent years, although this work has yet to be synthesized into a unified theory of urban growth.[4] On the empirical side, a number of studies have been published relating to the employment structure of individual cities, but only a few efforts have been made to examine the structure of a large number of urban economies and to make comparisons among them.[5] Even less work has been done relating to employment change in these places.

There exists, therefore, a considerable gap between the somewhat scattered elements of urban economic theory and the statistical evidence. We seek to contribute to the closing of this gap by providing a more complete description of employment structure and change in metropolitan economies than has hitherto been available. This we do through the use of certain techniques of classification and measurement. The development of a methodology for analyzing MLM's we regard as, in itself, a very important objective of the study.

[4] For some leading studies of regional and urban economics, see J. R. Mayer, "Regional Economics" *Surveys of Economic Theory,* Vol. II, 1967; Walter Isard, *Methods of Regional Analysis: An Introduction to Regional Science* (Cambridge, M.I.T. and Wiley, 1960); Brian J. Berry and Allen Pred, *Central Place Studies; A Bibliography of the Theory and Application* (Philadelphia, Regional Science Research Institute, 1965); Wilbur R. Thompson, *A Preface to Urban Economics* (Baltimore, Johns Hopkins Press, 1968).

[5] The best known of these studies are Gunnar Alexanderson *The Industrial Structure of American Cities* (Lincoln, University of Nebraska Press, 1956); Otis D. Duncan et al., *Metropolis and Region* (Baltimore, Johns Hopkins Press, 1960); Edgar M. Hoover and Raymond Vernon, *Anatomy of a Metropolis* (Cambridge, Harvard, 1959); Ezra Solomon, *Metropolitan Chicago* (Glencoe, Ill., Free Press, 1960); Pittsburgh Regional Planning Association, *Economic Study of the Pittsburgh Region,* Pittsburgh, University of Pittsburgh Press, 1964).

A Description of Measures

It is one thing to develop a theoretical approach, but it is quite another to apply the approach to the real world. That this study was made possible is due in no small degree to the publication of comparable 1940, 1950, and 1960 *Census of Population* employment estimates for thirty-two industrial classifications for every county within the United States.[6] From this county data it was possible to prepare employment estimates for each MLM and for each NMC.

The accuracy and reliability of the measures are limited by the data upon which they are based. In Appendix A we discuss the comparability of the two decades, the definition of employment and method of enumeration, the appropriateness of the industrial classifications, the accuracy of the data, and the use of supplementary (more detailed) industry employment data.

Where necessary we have aggregated industrial classifications. For example, "manufacturing" includes ten manufacturing classifications; "mainly business services," seven classifications which are principally business services; "mainly consumer services," seven classifications which are principally consumer services. The final classification is industry not reported (INR).[7]

Employment data were first assembled by industrial classifications for each MLM, after which measures of structure and measures of change were computed. Measures of structure are simply percentage distributions of total employment among the industrial classifications within the reporting unit.

Measures of change are based on comparisons of employment at the beginning and end of the ten-year census interval. Rarely do we find all industries increasing at the same time; usually there is a considerable degree of industrial transition associated with growth. One industrial sector may contract while others expand. To avoid the loss

[6] Lowell D. Ashby, Department of Commerce, *Growth Patterns in Employment by County, 1940-1950 and 1950-1960* (8 volumes; Washington D.C., U.S. Department of Commerce, 1965).

[7] The thirty-two industrial classifications and the aggregated categories appear in Table 2.5.

of information change for the entire reporting unit, we record employment changes for each of the thirty-two industrial classifications within
the MLM. An absolute net increase in employment from one census
date to the next is recorded under the heading "job increases," a
decrease, under the heading "job decreases." This makes it possible
to aggregate for the entire reporting unit job increases and job decreases separately. Such an aggregation for selected industrial classifications and aggregative categories within the reporting unit Atlanta
(a medium-size MLM) is shown in Table 1.1.

In every instance we summed up job increases and job decreases
separately. With the data prepared in this manner it is possible to
examine the reporting units individually (e.g., Atlanta), or to aggregate at any level that is desired (e.g., the region, the U.S. economy).

Moreover, it was possible to compute decadal rates of job increases, job decreases, and net change for each industrial classification,
for a metropolitan labor market as a whole, or at a higher level of
aggregation. Shown below are the rates of job increase, job decrease,
and net employment change for all industry categories, aggregated
first for Atlanta, then for places of the same size category as Atlanta
(medium) in the Southeast, then for the entire Southeast region, then
for all medium-size places in the United States, and then for the total
United States.[8] (Note, that the rate of net change equals the rate of
job increase less the rate of job decrease.)

Rate of Job Change for All Industries, 1950-60

	Job increases	Job decreases	Net change
Atlanta	39.2	4.2	35.0
Medium-size MLM's in			
Southeast	37.2	5.7	31.5
Entire Southeast	29.0	16.4	12.6
Medium-size MLM's in			
U. S.	32.1	5.6	26.5
Entire U. S.	25.5	10.0	15.5

[8] Rate of job increase is the number of jobs opened up expressed as a
percentage of employment at the beginning of the decade. Rate of job decrease
is the percent of jobs existing at the beginning of the decade which have since
been closed out.

TABLE 1.1
Key Measures of Employment: The Atlanta MLM

	Employment[a]		Distribution of total employment[b]		Employment change, 1950-60[a]		Job increase/Job decrease,[c] 1950-60			
							Decadal rates[b]		Distribution[b]	
	1950	1960	1950	1960	Job increase	Job decrease	Job increase	Job decrease	Job increase	Job decrease
Primary	8.8	4.6	3.0	1.2	.2	4.4	2.0	49.9	.1	35.3
Construction	23.6	26.5	8.0	6.6	2.9	0.0	12.1	0.0	2.5	0.0
Manufacturing	58.5	87.4	19.8	21.9	33.6	4.7	57.5	8.1	28.9	37.7
Utilities	4.9	5.3	1.7	1.3	0.4	0.0	7.7	0.0	0.3	0.0
Mainly business services	63.3	89.3	21.4	22.3	29.3	3.4	46.3	5.3	25.3	27.0
Mainly consumer services	110.1	141.1	37.2	35.3	31.0	0.0	28.1	0.0	26.7	0.0
Retail	51.2	62.1	17.3	15.5	10.9	0.0	21.2	0.0	9.4	0.0
Food/dairy products	8.6	9.7	2.9	2.4	1.1	0.0	12.4	0.0	0.9	0.0
Eating/drinking places	7.6	8.7	2.6	2.2	1.0	0.0	13.7	0.0	0.9	0.0
Other retail	35.0	43.8	11.8	11.0	8.8	0.0	25.0	0.0	7.6	0.0
Recreation	15.3	15.5	5.2	3.9	0.2	0.0	1.3	0.0	0.2	0.0
Hotel/personal services	12.6	12.7	4.3	3.2	0.1	0.0	0.6	0.0	0.1	0.0
Entertainment/recreation	2.7	2.8	0.9	0.7	0.1	0.0	4.8	0.0	0.1	0.0
Private household	19.0	21.7	6.4	5.4	2.8	0.0	14.6	0.0	2.4	0.0
Medical/education	24.6	41.7	8.3	10.4	17.1	0.0	69.7	0.0	14.8	0.0
Government	22.4	26.2	7.6	6.6	4.0	0.0	16.9	0.0	3.3	0.0
INR	4.4	19.4	1.5	4.9	15.0	0.0	342.8	0.0	12.9	0.0
Total	296.1	399.7	100.0	100.0	116.1	12.5	39.2	4.2	100.0	100.0

[a] In 000's.
[b] In percent.
[c] Job increases or job decreases were computed separately for each of the 32 industrial classifications listed in Table 2.5. Only where industry categories have been aggregated will it be possible that both job increases and job decreases will be shown (example, Manufacturing).

In an individual reporting unit the rate of net change in one of the thirty-two industrial classifications is, of course, equal to the rate of job increase or of job decrease (whichever has occurred). The job increase statistic records the increase in employment in a given industrial classification in the reporting unit; the job decrease statistic records the decrease. When two or more reporting units are aggregated, however, it is possible that employment in a certain industrial classification may have increased in one reporting unit but decreased in another. In such a case we would observe for the combined reporting units both job increases and job decreases in the single industrial classification. This is the explanation of the fact that in a number of regions we find both job increases and job decreases in agriculture, an industry in which the trend has been overwhelmingly toward the reduction of employment.

Not only is it possible to compute rates of job increase and job decrease separately, but it is also possible to distribute the job increases and job decreases among the various industrial classifications and categories (i.e., to compute the share of total job increases accounted for by each classification or the share of total job decreases). The rate of job increase and share of job increases accounted for by mainly business services in Atlanta and other similar-size places in the Southeast region and in the nation are compared below:

Measures of Growth in Business Services, 1950-60

	Rate of job increases	Share of job increases
Atlanta	46.3	25.3
Medium-size MLM's in Southeast	35.6	17.4
Entire Southeast	32.8	13.5
All medium-size MLM's in U. S.	28.3	15.0
Entire U. S.	21.7	13.1

INFORMATION PROVIDED BY MEASURES OF JOB INCREASES
AND DECREASES

Measures of job increases and decreases are used extensively throughout the study and it is important to interpret them correctly. Essentially they are marginal measures—measures of increases or decreases in the employed work force over a significant period of time. Job increases arise from the expanded hiring of labor by existing firms, the entry of new firms into an established industry, or through the entry of a firm in a new industry. Job decreases arise from the closing down or transferring of firms to another location, from a declining level of activity, or from a declining reliance on labor to produce a previous or even enlarged level of output. Traces of shifts in employment between industrial classifications within a given labor market or geographical shifts within an industrial classification will be lost (netted out) unless such a procedure is followed.

Job changes associated simply with the employment turnover (people leaving a given employment and being replaced) are not included in the measures. But measures do take account of the dynamic —and more dramatic—aspects of employment change.

Moreover, we must recognize that these measures of employment change provide no indication of whether the change was due principally to demand or to supply forces. We are unable to establish, for example, whether a decrease in the employment in retailing in a given MLM is due to: 1) a decline in demand for workers in this classification under conditions in which factor prices (i.e., wages, interest, and rent) remain relatively the same, the decline in employment resulting from a decline in demand due to, say, a shift of the retailing function to smaller communities lying outside the MLM counties; 2) substitution of other inputs, which have become relatively cheaper; or 3) the joint result of these two types of causation.

Similarly, it is difficult to establish whether an increase in employment in manufacturing is due to: 1) an increasing demand for manufacturing employment, all input prices remaining relatively the same; 2) the effect of increased availability of labor (due perhaps to the technological displacement of farm labor) upon the relative factor price of labor; or 3) a combination of demand and supply oriented forces.

The inability to disentangle demand and supply forces in observed employment change is, of course, a limitation upon the usefulness of our method. But we find no reasonable alternative if we are to make use of this body of data to describe structure and change in labor markets. We must, therefore, proceed with caution in interpreting our findings, recognizing, in particular, the inherent limitations of the data when venturing any projections of recorded change into the years ahead.

THE RELATIONSHIP BETWEEN EMPLOYMENT STRUCTURE,
JOB INCREASES, AND DECREASES

The structure of employment (i.e., the percentages of total employment found within the various industrial classifications) measures, in relative terms, the quantities of labor inputs devoted to the production of various (industrial) classifications of goods or services. As far as labor markets are concerned, structure is a useful indicator of the importance of industries with respect to manpower requirements, at least in so far as we are dealing with *quantity* rather than *quality* of labor inputs.[9]

Moreover, from the standpoint of manpower strategy relating to the training and placement of people in the work force, it is important to know in what industrial classification new jobs are opening up and in what classifications jobs are being closed out. Such knowledge is provided by the job-increase and job-decrease measures.

A careful examination of the arithmetic of job increase and job decrease is of importance for the understanding of the dynamic nature of changes in the demand for labor. Let us take the simple example of a labor market in which there are no job decreases, and job increases are occurring in a single industrial category—manufacturing. If during an initial period, manufacturing employment increases from 100 to 105 persons, job increases will amount to 5 persons. If during a second period manufacturing employment continues to increase, rising to 115

---

[9] It is important to observe once again that these measures tell us nothing of the extent to which changes in relative factor prices have resulted in factor substitution. Accordingly, the changes in employment do not necessarily reflect simply the changes in the demand for labor without regard to quality or to the prices of other factors of production.

persons, job increases will double, rising to 10 persons. But if, in a third period, the number of persons in manufacturing continues to rise but at a slower rate, say, to 117 persons, job increases in this period will total only 2 persons. In the labor market during the third period, the demand for *additional* workers (i.e., the second difference in employment) has *decreased,* not increased, even though the total number of jobs has risen.

We can now understand more readily the relationship between the change in structure and job increase and decrease. For a given industrial classification, an increase in the percentage of total employment accounted for by that classification proceeds from any of the following: 1) an increase in employment in the industry with no change in employment in any other industry; 2) a higher rate of job increase in the given industry than in the other industries taken as a whole (assuming no job decreases in any industries); 3) no job increases in any industry including the industry in question, but job decreases in one or more industries other than the industry in question; and 4) job decreases at a higher rate in other industries (taken as a whole) than in the given industry (assuming no job increase). In short, we see that an increase in percentage of total employment found in a given industry stems from a higher job-increase rate than that found in the other industries taken as a whole and/or from higher rates of job decrease in other industries.

A corollary to the above is that where there are no job decreases within the economy in question (i.e., total U.S., region, MLM), an industrial classification will retain its share of total employment only if its rate of job increase is equal to the overall rate of job increase. In this case the role of job increase is equal to the role of net employment change. It follows that where very little change occurs in the industrial composition of a city or region, the share of job increases during a period will approximate the share of total employment at the beginning and end of the period (assuming that job decreases are small). On the other hand, if the percentage of employment in a given classification increased significantly, the share of job increases accounted for by that classification will be even larger.

THE VOLATILE NATURE OF JOB INCREASES
AND DECREASES

These elementary observations focus attention on the great sources of difficulty in matching people and jobs in a changing economy: changes in employment structure take the form of *marginal* increases or decreases in the demand for labor and such marginal changes may be quite volatile.

Where there are shifts from primary to manufacturing or service employment, where growth is rapid and there is a strong tendency for growth to occur in new places or regions, and where the industrial composition of older regions and cities is undergoing rapid change, job opportunities for persons entering the work force will be to a large extent those which appear in our statistics as "job increases." The replacement demand (which our "job decreases" data do not reveal) will play a relatively small role in the market place. Where structure is changing relatively little and growth rates are low, replacement demand for labor will play a more critical role.

An inspection of Table 1.1 shows that relatively small changes in structure are, indeed, very frequently reflected by shares of job increases which are far larger than the proportion of total employment accounted for by the industrial classification at the beginning of the period. Thus, the medical/educational services classification increased its share of total employment in Atlanta from 8.3 to 10.4 percent between 1950 and 1960, while accounting for 14.8 percent of total job increases during that period.

On the other hand, the retail services classification showed a decline in its share of total employment between 1950 and 1960 from 17.3 to 15.5 percent. Its share of job increases, 9.4 percent, was, therefore, much smaller than its share of total employment in either 1950 or 1960.

The lesson is clear: the marginal impact of changes in the structure of labor markets will often take the form of sharp changes in the demand for additions to the labor force. Analysis of the existing composition of the work force provides a very unreliable guide for projection of manpower requirements.

REPLACEMENT DEMAND

We are not entitled to treat replacement demand as unimportant, however. Even if employment in a given industrial classification is maintained at a constant level, a number of workers will leave employment as a result of normal processes of attrition such as marriage, child raising, retirement, or death, and will need to be replaced. Furthermore, observed declines in employment in a given industrial classification within a labor market (i.e., job decreases) do not necessarily mean that people have been discharged or even that they have moved to other employment. It is quite possible that no hiring of new workers is taking place and that the observed job decreases simply reflect normal attrition. The conclusion to be drawn is that if we are to know for a given labor market the number of workers for which training and placement in a specified industry is required during a period, we must know not only the net change in the number of workers during the period but also the extent of attrition.

Unfortunately, detailed information relating to attrition is difficult to secure. Certain of the major factors contributing to attrition, such as marriage (applicable to the female labor force), retirement, or death, are likely to be fairly constant for given age groups in the various MLM's and their effects can be estimated. On the other hand, the participation rates of women, and the age composition of the labor force will vary considerably among industrial classifications and among MLM's, and these variations will influence attrition rates. For example, attrition rates for nurses may be expected to be high due to the age–sex composition of this segment of the work force (frequently nurses leave the work force to marry or to have children). Further, in declining industries such as railroad transportation, attrition due to age and retirement will tend to be high due to the relatively large number of older workers in this segment of the labor force. On the other hand, in growing industries such as air transportation, attrition from such causes will be low, particularly where there has been a tendency to hire new entrants into the labor force from among those recently graduated from high school or college. Finally, rapidly growing metropolitan areas that have experienced considerable in-migration will usually have a relatively large percentage of the work force in the younger age brackets, so that attrition due to retirement or death will be below average.

In spite of the variety of factors influencing attrition, it is possible to make crude estimates of attrition from retirements and death which provide an indication of the possible magnitudes of attrition rates in the metropolitan labor market.[10] For the population as a whole deaths average 26.7 per 1,000 between the ages of 20 and 45 during a decade or about 2.7 percent per annum. Further, roughly 2.2 percent of the population between the ages of 20 and 65 attain the age of 65 each year. If the age distribution of the labor force in a given industrial classification were the same as that of the entire population between those ages, we would expect the attrition rate in a labor force of constant size to be about 5 percent per year (2.7 percent plus 2.2 percent). This would mean that the "concealed" rate of job decreases (covered up by replacement) might be as high as 50 percent for a ten-year period without any workers having been released involuntarily.

We see, therefore, that job replacement of workers lost through attrition may be of considerable importance and that it is likely to vary among industrial classifications and among MLM's, being less important in the faster-growing classifications and labor markets and increasing in importance as the rate of growth decreases.

The present research treats only one aspect of labor force changes —those changes which occur in the labor force as a result of the processes of growth and change. Replacement of workers lost through attrition represents a different problem—the maintenance of the labor force through time. Replacement is a matter of importance and is deserving of careful research. New knowledge in this area should be placed alongside information gleaned from measures of job increases, job decreases, and employment structure to fully assess the nature and scope of the recruitment and training task.

[10] Hugh Folk and Donald E. Yett, "Methods of Estimating Occupational Attrition," *Western Economic Journal*, Vol. VI, No. 4. (September 1968), pp. 297-301.

The Plan of the Study

This study proceeds in four stages. The first (chapter 2) is principally a national and regional analysis of the industrial composition of the work force and the extent of employment change in the various industrial classifications. The findings from this analysis provide background and demonstrate the need for subsequent analyses of the MLM's and NMC's.

The second stage (chapter 3) is a brief presentation of the principal theoretical concepts bearing on employment structure and employment expansion in urban economies. Here we show, first of all, how cities vary in function and why it is reasonable and desirable to classify them both according to function and size. Second, we show how tendencies toward employment expansion in a city may be amplified and how the growth process can feed upon itself.

The third stage (chapters 4 to 9) includes the entire analysis of employment structure and change for the MLM's and NMC's of the American economy. In chapters 5 and 6 we examine employment structure (i.e., the distribution of employment among industrial classifications) and employment change for each size-of-place category of MLM's (i.e., small, medium, large) and for the NMC's. This analysis is carried out for the nation and by regions in terms of a classification scheme for MLM's based on size alone.

Chapter 6 marks the beginning of what we consider to be the most significant part of the analysis. In this chapter, the industrial composition of employment in individual MLM's is examined in greater detail and a typology based on both size and function is developed. Each MLM is then classified. Chapters 7 and 8 present the analysis of employment change. Two areas are treated: first, how closely is employment change in one industrial classification associated with change in employment in the MLM as a whole and with change in the other classifications? second, of all the job increases (or decreases), what share is typically accounted for by a given industrial classification? The answers to these questions are sought for the various type–size groups of MLM's based upon the classification system developed in chapter 6.

In chapter 9 the nature and extent of geographical redistribution of employment among the industrial classifications are studied. Attention centers on those industries likely to export goods or services from the metropolitan economy and, therefore, most sensitive to changes in the importance of locational factors. Here we discuss how urban growth may affect the competitiveness of an export industry and trace through for selected industries and for several MLM's the developments which have taken place.

The final stage consists of chapters 10 and 11. In chapter 10 we leave the data to speculate on the factors which appear to play increasingly important roles in the growth and development of metropolitan economies, with particular emphasis being given to amenities and the urban form. In chapter 11 the major findings are summarized and implications for public policy are discussed.

2 EMPLOYMENT CHANGE AND EMPLOYMENT COMPOSITION: NATIONAL AND REGIONAL

IN THE PRESENT CHAPTER we study national and regional data. National data include Alaska and Hawaii; regional data do not. A recognition of national and regional employment trends in the various industrial classifications is an important first step toward understanding the employment changes which have occurred within the urban economies.

EMPLOYMENT CHANGE: NATIONAL

TRENDS WITHIN SIZE-OF-PLACE CATEGORIES

The trend toward increasing importance of metropolitan counties noted in the previous chapter was by no means of equal significance for all sizes of place or for all regions. As shown below it was strongest for the medium-size MLM's, where the percentage of total national employment rose from 27.6 to 32.8 percent during the two decades; somewhat weaker in the small and large MLM's, where it rose only slightly from 12.0 to 13.2 percent and from 28.2 to 29.1 percent respectively. In the remaining counties, the NMC's, the percentage declined, falling from 32.2 percent of total U.S. employment in 1940 to 24.9 percent in 1960.

Size of place[a]	Employment change, 1940-60	Percent of total U.S. employment change, 1940-60	Percent of total U.S. employment 1940	1960
Large-size MLM's	(6,524,244)	(31.0)	(28.2)	(29.1)
Medium-size MLM's	(9,284,933)	(44.2)	(27.6)	(32.8)
Small-size MLM's	(3,308,507)	(15.8)	(12.0)	(13.2)
Total MLM's	19,117,684	91.0	67.8	75.1
NMC's	1,879,150	9.0	32.2	24.9
Total U. S.	20,996,834	100.0	100.0	100.0

[a] Size of MLM's was based on 1960 population.

Small-size MLM's	SMSA's with 50,001-200,000 population plus non-SMSA counties with a city of 25,000 or more
Medium-size MLM's	SMSA's with 200,001-1,600,000 population
Large-size MLM's	SMSA's with 1,600,001 or more population

SHIFTS IN REGIONAL SHARES OF EMPLOYMENT

Later we shall examine the differences in regional rates of growth and the conflicting forces of employment expansion and contraction which lay behind them. For the moment it is sufficient simply to establish the extent of the redistribution of total U.S. employment which took place among the regions from 1940 to 1960. (See list of states which comprise each region.) Only the regions of the Southwestern and Western United States experienced an increase in share of national employment. The Far West region made especially large gains, increasing from 7.8 to 11.9 percent of national employment. The Southwest and Rocky Mountain regions rose from 6.8 to 7.6 and 2.1 to 2.4 percent respectively. The largest proportionate loss was suffered by the Plains region which declined from 10.1 percent in 1940 to 8.8 percent in 1960.

These shifts must be seen in perspective. At the end of twenty years the older industrial regions of New England, the Mideast, and the Great Lakes had lost only 2.1 percent of their combined share of the nation's total employment, the Southeast only 1.8 percent. Dynamic, but clearly not revolutionary, changes occurred.

*Regions and States**

New England
  Maine
  New Hampshire
  Vermont
  Massachusetts
  Rhode Island
  Connecticut

Mideast
  New York
  New Jersey
  Pennsylvania
  Delaware
  Maryland
  District of Columbia

Great Lakes
  Michigan
  Ohio
  Indiana
  Illinois
  Wisconsin

Plains
  Minnesota
  Iowa
  Missouri
  North Dakota
  South Dakota
  Nebraska
  Kansas

Southeast
  Virginia
  West Virginia
  Kentucky
  Tennessee
  North Carolina
  South Carolina
  Georgia
  Florida
  Alabama
  Mississippi
  Louisiana
  Arkansas

Southwest
  Oklahoma
  Texas
  New Mexico
  Arizona

Rocky Mountains
  Montana
  Idaho
  Wyoming
  Colorado
  Utah

Far West
  Washington
  Oregon
  Nevada
  California

Noncontinental States
  Alaska
  Hawaii

* Definitions of regions are those used by the Office of Business Economics, U.S. Department of Commerce.

CHANGES WITHIN GOODS AND SERVICES SECTORS

Recent writers who have concerned themselves with the changing composition of the American labor force have noted that the goods sector taken as a whole has virtually ceased to contribute to employment expansion and that such expansion as has occurred has been accounted for by the services, largely in the not-for-profit sector of the economy.[1]

In general, the Census of Population data bear out this finding:

Employment Change

(in thousands)[a]

	1940-50	1950-60
Goods Sector[b]		
Job increases	6,215 (41.2)	4,833 (33.0)
Job decreases	2,059 (68.6)	4,418 (76.9)
Net employment change	4,156 (34.3)	415 (4.7)
Services Sector[c]		
Job increases	8,651 (58.8)	7,987 (67.0)
Job decreases	860 (31.4)	1,269 (23.1)
Net employment change	7,791 (65.7)	6,718 (95.3)
All Sectors (including INR)		
Net employment change	12,099	8,899

[a] Percent of total jobs increases, decreases, or net change in parentheses. INR is excluded from totals in the calculation of percentages.

[b] Includes primary, construction, and manufacturing.

[c] Includes consumer, business, and government services and utilities.

We must recognize that changes in employment reflect both changes in demand for an industry's output and changes in output per employee. It is not possible to match output and employment data

[1] Cf. George J. Stigler, *Trends in Employment in the Services Industries* (Princeton, Princeton University Press, pp. 5ff; Victor R. Fuchs, *The Growing Importance of the Service Industries,* occasional paper 96 (New York, National Bureau of Economic Research, 1965), pp. 1ff; Eli Ginzberg et al., *The Pluralistic Economy* (New York, McGraw-Hill, 1965).

TABLE 2.1

Trends in Output, Employment, and Output per Man in Selected
Industrial Classifications
Total U.S., 1950-1960

	Annual rates			Decadal rates	
				Percent change in employment	
	Output[a]	Employ-ment[b]	Output per man	1950-60 NID	1950-60 Census
Primary	1.3	[c]	2.2	—9	—38
Construction	3.0	1.8	1.2	20	10
Manufacturing	2.9	0.9	2.0	10	17
Utilities	7.7	1.1	6.5	11	14
Mainly business services					
Transportation	1.3	[c]	2.1	—7	—7
Communications	6.8	1.5	5.2	16	15
Wholesale	4.2	2.0	2.1	22	12
FIRE	4.6	3.7	0.9	44	40
Mainly consumer services					
Retail	2.5	2.2	0.4	23	11
Total U.S.	3.2	1.7	1.5	18	16

[a] Measured in 1958 dollars.

[b] Full-time employment equivalent as estimated by National Income Division (NID).

[c] Negative rates of change.

[d] Based on change in GNP.

Source: First four columns, *Survey of Current Business;* fifth column, *Census of Population.*

relating to the various industrial sectors for the three census years, but comparable data have been prepared by the National Income Division (NID) of the Department of Commerce for a limited number of classifications covering both output and employment for the period

1947 to the present.[2] Table 2.1 presents these measures for 1950 and 1960.[3]

The primary industry data reveals clearly the development which took place in agriculture: output grew at a rate far below that of GNP and consumer expenditures; and output per worker increased at a rate substantially above the average for the economy as a whole. The net result was an absolute decline in number of workers. In manufacturing, output increased at a rate somewhat less than for the nation as a whole; output per employee at a rate substantially above. For this very large category the net result was a relatively low rate of growth of employment during the 1950s.

Within the service sector there are very great differences in trends in total output and in output per worker. In communications, the relatively low rate of increase in employment reflects principally the effect of very large increases in output per worker, total output having risen very rapidly. In the transportation classification the rate of increase in total output was well below that for the nation as a whole (largely the result of the shift from rail transportation into private motor vehicle transportation whose output is not included in the national product estimates) but there was a substantial increase in output per worker. The absolute decline which we note in employment reflects the joint influence of both factors.

For wholesaling and retailing, rates of increase in employment do not differ greatly. The rate of increase in output was much higher in wholesaling, however, 4.2 percent per year as compared to 2.5 percent in retailing. This, of course, indicates that rates of increase in output per worker were substantially greater in wholesaling than in retailing.

Finally, the business service FIRE (finance, insurance, and real

[2] The employment estimates differ somewhat from the census estimates for two reasons: 1) They are expressed as full-time employee equivalents whereas the census estimates include part-time workers; 2) They are based on establishment reports rather than place-of-domicile enumeration, resulting in a difference in classification of type of work in some instances.

[3] It will be seen in Table 2.1 that in some cases the rate of change is roughly the same as it would have been if census employment data had been used.

estate), showed very high rates of increase in output and relatively low rates of increase in output per worker. The high rate of increase of employment reflects, therefore, the joint influence of these two factors.

Among the remaining two categories we find, again, dissimilar forces at work. In construction, rates of increase in both output and output per employee are below the national average. The tendency for the effect of one rate to offset the other results in a rate of increase in employment not substantially different from the overall national average. In utilities, rates of increase in both output and output per worker are extremely high. The net effect is a relatively low rate of increase in employment.

It is apparent from the above that within the service sector relatively rapid employment growth was confined to a restricted number of classifications. This may be seen in greater detail in the employment measures presented in Table 2.2. Among the mainly business services classifications we note that during the second decade only the FIRE and business repair services show rates of net employment change above the national rate, and among the mainly consumer services classifications only the medical/educational services and private household services employment grew at greater than the national rate. These four business and consumer services, which grew more rapidly than total employment, accounted for 36.7 percent of combined business and consumer services in 1950 and 43.7 percent in 1960. If we add the two government services, administration and armed forces, which also grew more rapidly than the nation, the six classifications combined accounted for 44.3 percent of combined business, consumer, and government services in 1950, 51.3 percent in 1960.

SOURCES OF EMPLOYMENT CHANGE

BY JOB INCREASES/DECREASES

Job increases. When we examine the contributions of the various industrial categories to employment expansion measured in terms of percentages of total job increases (Table 2.3) we find that during the most recent decade the largest share was attributable to consumer

TABLE 2.2

*Rates of Job Increases, Job Decreases, and Net Employment Change
in the U.S., 1940-1950, 1950-1960,
by Selected Industrial Classifications*

	Employment change		Job increases		Job decreases	
	1940-50	1950-60	1940-50	1950-60	1940-50	1950-60
Primary	—15.7	—37.3	3.2	1.9	18.9	39.2
Construction	67.2	10.3	67.7	14.0	0.5	3.7
Manufacturing	37.8	20.0	40.3	27.8	2.5	7.8
Utilities	44.3	14.4	44.6	17.6	0.3	3.2
Mainly business						
services	44.9	13.5	45.5	21.7	0.6	8.2
Transportation	35.2	—7.3	36.5	11.3	1.3	18.6
Communications	80.0	15.5	80.2	19.4	0.2	3.9
Wholesale	63.9	11.7	64.3	14.7	0.4	3.0
FIRE	30.6	40.3	30.7	40.6	0.1	0.3
Business/repair	51.4	22.7	51.5	29.1	0.1	6.4
Mainly consumer						
services	23.3	23.7	28.9	26.3	5.6	2.6
Retail	35.4	11.3	35.8	14.3	0.4	3.0
Recreation	13.0	3.7	15.2	9.8	2.2	6.1
Private						
household	—29.9	17.0	0.5	20.4	30.4	3.4
Medical/education	44.0	58.0	44.3	58.0	0.3	0.0
Government	97.7	39.5	99.5	42.0	1.8	2.5
Administration	69.3	27.4	69.6	28.3	0.3	0.9
Armed forces	235.6	69.0	244.7	75.5	9.1	6.5
INR	22.0	209.6	34.1	216.2	12.1	6.6
Goods sector	18.3	1.5	27.4	18.0	9.1	16.5
Services sector	35.4	22.5	39.3	26.8	3.9	4.3
Total	26.7	15.5	33.3	25.5	6.6	10.0

services (31.3 percent) followed by manufacturing (27.7 percent), business services (13.1 percent), and government (10.2 percent).[4]

The share of job increases due to consumer services rose from

[4] INR accounted for 12.4 percent from 1950 to 1960 versus 1.6 percent the preceding decade. See Appendix B for discussion.

TABLE 2.3
Distribution of Employment in 1940, 1950, and 1960, and Share of Job Increases/Job Decreases, 1940-1950,
1950-1960, in the U.S., for Selected Industrial Classifications

	Employment 1940	1940-50 Job increases	1940-50 Job decreases	Employment 1950	1950-60 Job increases	1950-60 Job decreases	Employment 1960
Primary	20.8	2.0	59.5	13.9	1.0	54.4	7.5
Construction	4.6	9.3	0.4	6.0	3.3	2.2	5.8
Manufacturing	23.3	28.3	8.7	25.4	27.7	20.0	26.4
Utilities	1.2	1.6	0.1	1.4	0.9	0.4	1.4
Mainly business services	13.5	18.5	1.2	15.4	13.1	12.6	15.2
Transportation	4.8	5.3	1.0	5.1	2.3	9.6	4.1
Communications	0.9	2.1	0.0	1.2	0.9	0.5	1.2
Wholesale	2.7	5.2	0.2	3.5	2.0	1.0	3.3
FIRE	3.2	3.0	0.0	3.3	5.3	0.1	4.1
Business/repair services	1.9	3.0	0.0	2.3	2.6	1.5	2.4
Mainly consumer services	31.1	27.0	26.4	30.3	31.3	7.9	32.4
Retail	14.0	15.1	0.9	15.0	8.4	4.4	14.4
Recreation/entertainment	4.6	2.1	1.6	4.1	1.6	2.5	3.7
Private household	5.2	0.1	23.6	2.8	2.3	1.0	2.9
Medical/education	7.3	9.8	0.3	8.4	19.0	0.0	11.4
Government	4.0	11.8	1.0	6.2	10.2	1.6	7.4
Administration	3.3	6.8	0.1	4.4	4.9	0.4	4.8
Armed forces	0.7	5.0	0.9	1.8	5.3	1.2	2.6
INR	1.5	1.6	2.8	1.5	12.4	1.0	3.9
Total U.S.	100	100	100	100	100	100	100
Rates of:							
Job increases		33.3			25.5		
Job decreases			6.6			10.0	
Net employment change		26.7			15.5		

the first decade to the second. The share due to manufacturing was roughly the same during both decades, and the shares accounted for by business services and government declined in the second compared with the first decade.

In the mainly consumer services category, job increases were dominated during the 1950-60 decade by the medical/educational services classification. This classification accounted for 19 percent of total job increases during the second decade (almost two-thirds of the total job increases within the mainly consumer services).

Since the classification of medical/educational services is of such importance it is well to learn what we can of its components from a sample of 113 MLM's which provides greater industry detail.[5] According to these data, the shares of employment in 1950 and 1960 and of job increases during the intervening years were as follows:[6]

	% 1950 Employed	% 1950-60 Job increases	% 1960 Employment
Medical & other health services (incl. hospitals)	3.3 (37)	6.1 (34)	4.2 (35)
Educational services (govt. and private)	3.3 (37)	8.3 (46)	4.8 (41)
Welfare, religious, & non-profit organizations	1.2 (13)	1.7 (9)	1.4 (12)
Legal, engineering, & misc. professional services	1.2 (13)	2.0 (11)	1.4 (12)
Medical/educational & related services, total (113-MLM sample)	9.0 (100)	18.2 (100)	11.8 (100)
Medical/educational & related services, Total U.S.	8.4	19.0	11.4

Numbers in parentheses indicate shares of total medical/educational services employment.

[5] For description of the 113-MLM sample, see Appendix A.

[6] Shares of job decreases have not been shown because of their relative unimportance. They are one-half of 1 percent or less in each classification.

In short, the sample data indicate that about four-fifths of job increases within the medical/educational services classification was accounted for by medical and educational services combined, with the educational services being somewhat more important than medical.[7]

As we examine Table 2.3 once again, the only other important source of job increases within the consumer services category during the 1950s was the retail classification, but here, as noted earlier, the share of total job increases was far less than the proportion of total employment accounted for by retailing in either the 1950 or 1960 census.

It is interesting to note how very small was the share of job increases due to the consumer services classification of recreation/entertainment. In the most recent decade when both per capita income and the amount of leisure time available to the average citizen reached record heights, this classification accounted for less than 2 percent of total job creation. One can only surmise that the increased expenditures for leisure-time activities found their way largely into leisure-time goods (e.g., automobiles, gasoline, sports clothes, athletic equipment, cameras, lawn mowers, television, books, and boats) rather than leisure-time services, and/or that the labor component of recreational/entertainment services output declined (e.g., reduced labor requirements with the shift from hotels to motels, from theaters to drive-ins; the decreased demand for labor in bowling due to the use of pin-setting equipment).

In the manufacturing category, the largest shares of job increases were found in the electrical/other machinery equipment, other miscellaneous manufacturing, and other transportation equipment (largely aircraft) classifications:

[7] The reader will note that one of the four component types of services which comprise the medical/educational and related services is entitled "legal, engineering, and miscellaneous services." This classification would appear to be largely a business rather than consumer service.

Shares of Job Increases, in Manufacturing, 1950-60

Electrical/other machinery	25.4
Other misc. mfg.	25.0
Other transportation equip.	12.5
Food products	10.7
Printing/publishing	7.2
Remaining classifications	19.0
Total manufacturing	100.0

The electrical/other machinery equipment and the other transportation equipment classifications showed the highest rates (1950-60) of job increases within the manufacturing sector (49.5 and 105.3 percent, respectively). It is unfortunate that the detail for the national economy is not available for the important other miscellaneous manufacturing classification. The 113-MLM sample shows almost two-thirds of the job increases in this classification accounted for by a subclassification entitled "other primary metals and fabricated metals industries," which also showed a job-increase rate (47.3 percent) well above that for the entire manufacturing category (27.8 percent). Important contributions were also made by the food products and printing/publishing industry classifications, where growth rates were lower (30.9 and 34.3 percent, respectively) but still well above the average for manufacturing as a whole.

The point here is that the major share of job increase in manufacturing occurred within a relatively restricted number of industry classifications in which rates of job increases were well above the average for both the sector and the economy as a whole.

As regards the business services, a relatively small share of total job increases was accounted for within this industry category—13.1 percent during the 1950-60 period, down from 18.5 percent in the preceding decade (Table 2.3). This decline reflected principally the lessened importance of transportation and wholesaling as sources of new jobs, but communication and business repair services also declined in importance to some extent. Only FIRE shows a larger share of total job increases in the second decade than in the first.

Finally, the category of government accounted for a tenth or more of job increases in the United States in both decades. Moreover, it should be borne in mind that the industrial classification system is such that the government category excludes persons employed in governmental institutions other than state, local, and federal administrative agencies and in the armed forces. Substantial shares of employment in a number of other industrial classifications are, in fact, government employment. Bureau of Census estimates of the proportion of government employment in each industrial classification in 1950 indicate that government employment comprised 74 percent of the employment in education and 27 percent in medical services in that year.[8]

If we make use of these percentages of government employment to estimate job increases within these two subclassifications using the 113-MLM sample, we find that 43 percent of total job increases within the medical/educational service classification (almost 8 percent of all job increases) were accounted for by government-type employment.[9]

Job decreases. Although the primary sector was the major source of job decreases, manufacturing became a significant source of job decreases during the second decade, its share of total job decreases going from 8.7 percent (1940-50) to 19.9 percent (1950-60). Among the four industries accounting for a large majority of manufacturing job decreases there appear to have been two types of processes at work. The first is represented by the textile mill products and lumber/furniture products industries, which were largely declining segments in the economy from the standpoint of employment. The second is represented by the motor vehicle equipment and apparel industries where growth and decline were occurring simultaneously.[10]

[8] U.S. Department of Commerce, *Census of Population, 1950*. Vol. II, Part 1, Table 133.

[9] See page 28 above for estimated shares of job increases in these two subclassifications based on the 113-MLM sample. The estimated share of 1950-60 job increases due to government associated employment in medical services was 9.2 percent (.27 × 34.0 percent), of educational services, 34.0 percent (.74 × 46.0 percent).

[10] A detailed analysis of the census data reveals that in the case of the motor vehicle industry increases were occurring largely in the fast-growing regions, whereas decreases were occurring in the areas which had traditionally specialized in this type of manufacturing (almost 9 out of every 10 job decreases

Job Increases/Job Decreases in Manufacturing, 1950-60

	Job increases (000's)	Job decreases (000's)	% of job decreases	% of manufacturing job decreases
Textile mill prod.	77.7	364.0	6.3	32.0
Lumber/wood prod.	97.8	220.7	3.8	19.0
Motor vehicle/allied prod.	123.0	129.0	2.6	13.1
Apparel mfg.	223.6	128.4	2.2	11.3
Remaining mfg. classifications	3,535.5	303.3	4.9	24.6
Total manufacturing	4,057.6	1,145.4	19.9	100.0

Among the service categories, the share of job decreases was largest for the mainly consumer services during the first decade, for the mainly business services during the second. In both instances the share of job decreases was accounted for largely by a single industrial classification. During the first decade 23.6 percent of total job decreases originated in the private households classifications as domestic servants found more profitable employment in the booming war and postwar economy. During the second decade 7.8 percent of total job decreases was accounted for by the railway and railway express classification (not shown in Table 2.3).

The shares accounted for by the remaining classifications (contract construction, utilities, and government) were of only secondary importance in both decades.

Taken as a whole the evidence afforded by the measures of job increases and job decreases does not lend itself to easy generalization regarding the role of the goods and services sectors in employment growth. It is clear that the greater share of job decrease occurred in the goods sector (due principally to the decline of the primary indus-

---

occurred in the Great Lakes regions). In the case of the apparel industry, job decreases were confined almost entirely to the Mideast and Great Lakes regions, the job increases occurred largely in the Southeast. See chapter 9 for an analysis of geographical redistribution of employment in those industries.

tries), but it is also clear that significant sources of both growth and decline are to be found within the manufacturing category.

More important, the component classifications of the service categories exhibit such a variety of trends that there appears to be little support for the popular notion that rapid growth is occurring in a wide spectrum of services. We find that while growth is impressive in a limited number of services it is quite unimpressive in others. Roughly half (51 percent) of 1960 service employment (including administration and armed forces) were in categories that grew faster than the nation during the period 1950-60. The following evidence must be considered in any assessment of the role of the services as a source of employment expansion:

1. The business services, no doubt of great significance in the growth process, constitute a relatively small share of total job increases for the nation as a whole. This will be found not to be the case for a number of medium- and large-size MLM's, however.

2. The rise in the share of job increases due to consumer services from the 1940s to the 1950s was accounted for almost entirely by medical/educational services. There is no evidence that for the nation as a whole higher consumption spending for goods and leisure-time activities resulted in a larger share of total job increases being accounted for by the two service activities which it would seem should be most closely associated with higher per capita disposable income— retail services and recreation-type services.

3. Government employment in administration and armed forces combined did not show a larger share of job increases during the second decade than during the first. Perhaps of greater interest, the administration classification actually showed a smaller share of job increases and a slightly larger share of job decreases in this period.

These remarks must not be viewed as denying the importance of the role of the service sector in employment growth. The fact remains that the service sector as a whole did show very substantial net employment increase, whereas the manufacturing sector showed very little, and the primary sector showed a sharp decline. Moreover, there is evidence, to be presented in later chapters, that employment expansion in certain of the business services was strongly associated with growth in certain size and type of MLM's. If the direct employment effect of employment change in the business services has been modest there is good reason to suspect that the contribution which these services have made by acting as some sort of catalyst or agent of growth is quite significant.

EMPLOYMENT CHANGE: REGIONAL

In Table 2.4 we observe that rates of net increase in employment declined from the first to the second decade for the nation and for every region in the continental United States. Moreover, rates of job increase declined and rates of job decrease rose except in the Southwest (where rates of decrease were slightly higher during the first decade). In short, a higher rate of employment expansion during the first ten-year period was broadly diffused throughout the economy and manifested itself both in terms of higher rates of job increase and lower rates of job decrease than those which were to prevail in the following decade.[11]

SHARES OF JOB INCREASES WITHIN REGIONS

Manufacturing.   During the first decade the share of job increases accounted for by the manufacturing classifications ranged from 42.4 percent in the Great Lakes to 13 percent in the Rocky Mountain region (Table 2.4). During the second decade they ranged from 33.7 percent in New England to 19.7 percent in the Southwest. Perhaps a more interesting observation is that the share of job increases accounted for by manufacturing was larger during the second decade than during the first in every region except the older established industrial regions of New England, the Mideast, and the Great Lakes:

[11] Of course, these observations must be assessed in the light of any distortions in the shares of job-increase/job-decrease measures which may result from the large increase in the industry not reported category in 1960. It is highly unlikely that the general finding is due to the excessive classification in INR. In the case of job increases the bias acts to raise the rate during the 1950-60 period, rather than lower it. See Appendix A.

	1940-50	*1950-60*
New England	34.2	33.7
Mideast	34.7	27.9
Great Lakes	42.4	31.4
Plains	24.9	26.7
Southeast	21.3	27.0
Southwest	15.2	19.7
Rocky Mountains	13.0	20.3
Far West	21.3	30.1
Total U.S.	28.3	27.8

Business and consumer services. It has been observed that shares of job increases accounted for by certain business and consumer services tended to decline in the second decade. For the nation as a whole this was true of transportation, communications, and wholesaling among the business services; and retailing and recreation among the consumer services. Together these classifications accounted for 30 percent of total job increases in the economy during the first decade, only 15 percent during the second. Shares of job increases declined in all eight regions for the transportation, wholesale, and retail classifications, and in seven of the eight regions for the communications and recreation classifications. Although there was considerable interregional variation, in none of these regions did the total share of job increases accounted for by these five important service classifications exceed 22 percent during the second decade and in half of the regions it was less than 15 percent:

	1940-50	*1950-60*
New England	25.2	7.2
Mideast	29.7	9.1
Great Lakes	26.7	13.1
Plains	32.3	14.2
Southeast	31.4	19.6
Southwest	31.5	20.2
Rocky Mountains	34.7	21.5
Far West	29.5	16.1
Nation	29.7	15.2

TABLE 2.4
Job Increases, Job Decreases, and Net Employment Change in
Selected Industrial Classifications, Regional and National,
1940-1950, 1950-1960

	New England		Mideast		Great Lakes		Plains	
	1940-50	1950-60	1940-50	1950-60	1940-50	1950-60	1940-50	1950-60
Net change	19.6	13.0	22.9	11.4	28.9	12.3	19.2	5.7
Rate of increase	24.3	21.5	27.2	18.5	33.2	20.6	25.4	19.0
Rate of decrease	4.7	8.5	4.3	7.1	4.3	8.3	6.2	13.3
Distribution of JOB INCREASES								
Primary	0.6	0.1	0.5	0.2	0.6	0.3	2.6	1.1
Construction	8.2	1.8	7.5	1.2	6.9	2.8	11.4	2.7
Manufacturing	34.2	33.7	34.7	27.9	42.4	31.4	24.9	26.7
Utilities	1.5	0.3	0.9	0.5	1.4	0.7	2.2	1.1
Mainly business services	18.7	10.2	22.3	13.7	16.7	11.1	20.6	11.3
Transportation	3.8	0.9	5.9	2.0	5.2	2.0	7.0	2.2
Communications	2.3	0.9	2.8	0.8	2.0	0.7	2.0	1.1
Wholesale	5.4	1.1	7.7	1.2	4.4	1.5	5.1	1.6
FIRE	4.0	5.5	2.8	5.8	2.4	5.0	2.8	5.4
Business/repair	3.2	1.8	3.1	3.9	2.7	1.8	3.7	1.1
Mainly consumer services	24.6	26.7	23.1	28.1	24.3	33.1	28.0	35.7
Retail	12.7	4.0	12.2	4.7	13.6	8.1	16.9	7.9
Recreation/hotel	1.0	0.3	1.1	0.4	1.6	0.7	1.3	1.4
Private household	0.0	0.6	0.0	0.3	0.0	2.0	0.0	3.1
Medical/educaton	10.9	21.8	9.8	22.7	9.1	22.4	9.8	23.3
Government	11.7	9.9	10.5	7.5	6.1	5.2	6.7	11.0
Administration	6.6	2.9	7.7	5.2	4.9	3.7	5.1	3.7
Armed forces	5.2	7.0	2.8	2.3	1.3	1.6	1.5	7.2
INR	0.4	17.2	0.4	20.9	1.5	15.4	3.7	10.5
Distribution of JOB DECREASES								
Primary	15.9	16.8	27.1	30.1	51.3	43.4	54.3	61.2
Manufacturing	22.8	57.3	12.8	32.4	11.4	28.8	5.8	8.6
Mainly business services	0.9	12.2	0.9	16.8	0.9	16.1	2.5	16.2
Transportation	0.9	9.8	0.8	14.2	0.8	12.6	1.6	9.4
Mainly consumer services	50.3	11.6	48.4	17.0	33.5	8.1	34.3	6.7
Private household	47.4	2.1	42.1	3.1	30.5	0.5	26.9	0.4
INR	8.1	0.0	9.6	0.0	1.9	0.6	1.6	2.5
All otherb	2.0	2.1	1.2	3.7	1.0	3.0	1.5	4.8

a Alaska and Hawaii not included.

b Includes government and construction.

	Southeast		Southwest		Rocky Mtns.		Far West		U.S.[a]	
	1940-50	*1950-60*	*1940-50*	*1950-60*	*1940-50*	*1950-60*	*1940-50*	*1950-60*	*1940-50*	*1950-60*
	20.6	12.6	32.5	23.6	36.0	23.2	57.6	40.3	26.7	15.5
	32.4	29.4	44.4	34.5	41.7	34.3	59.7	44.3	33.3	25.5
	11.8	16.1	11.9	10.9	5.7	11.1	2.1	4.0	6.6	10.0
	3.2	1.3	5.0	3.7	4.1	3.7	2.1	0.7	2.0	1.0
	10.2	5.3	13.5	3.8	12.8	4.6	9.6	3.2	9.3	3.3
	21.3	27.0	15.2	19.7	13.0	20.3	21.3	30.1	28.3	27.8
	1.8	1.3	2.5	1.7	2.2	1.3	1.6	0.7	1.6	0.9
	16.3	13.5	17.3	15.4	21.0	14.3	18.1	14.3	18.5	13.1
	4.8	2.8	5.0	2.6	7.6	2.7	4.5	2.2	5.3	2.3
	1.5	1.1	2.1	0.8	2.1	1.2	2.2	1.1	2.1	0.9
	4.3	2.2	4.2	3.5	4.5	2.8	4.6	2.2	5.1	2.0
	2.9	5.2	3.3	5.4	3.4	5.6	3.7	5.3	3.0	5.3
	2.8	2.1	2.7	3.1	3.4	1.9	3.1	3.5	3.0	2.6
	30.2	32.3	29.5	32.1	31.8	37.4	29.6	29.5	27.0	31.3
	17.6	11.1	17.0	10.9	17.1	12.2	15.7	8.3	15.1	8.4
	3.2	2.3	3.2	2.3	3.3	2.6	2.6	2.3	2.1	1.6
	0.1	4.0	0.3	2.4	0.2	3.3	0.2	2.2	0.1	2.3
	9.4	15.0	9.0	16.5	11.2	19.3	11.1	16.7	9.8	19.0
	14.5	11.8	15.1	13.9	13.4	12.6	16.7	11.4	11.8	10.2
	6.6	5.1	7.3	6.3	8.7	7.3	8.6	5.1	6.8	4.9
	7.9	6.7	7.8	7.6	4.7	5.3	8.1	6.2	5.0	5.3
	2.4	7.6	2.0	9.7	1.6	5.8	1.0	10.2	1.6	12.4
	74.5	73.6	80.3	63.9	67.2	57.8	64.0	43.0	59.5	54.4
	6.8	12.3	3.4	8.7	5.4	4.8	13.1	13.9	8.7	20.0
	1.0	6.9	1.2	11.7	3.5	19.3	2.6	16.6	1.2	12.6
	0.9	5.5	0.8	8.2	2.6	13.3	2.4	13.1	1.0	9.6
	16.1	3.7	12.9	7.4	15.8	6.4	17.9	6.5	26.4	7.9
	15.5	0.5	11.2	0.8	10.5	0.4	16.1	0.1	23.6	1.0
	.8	1.2	.6	1.0	2.7	1.1	.9	.6	2.8	1.0
	.8	2.3	1.6	7.3	5.4	10.6	1.5	19.4	1.4	4.1

On the other hand, in the two service classifications which showed sharp upward trends for the nation, FIRE and medical/educational services, the share of job increases rose during the second decade in every region. Moreover, the combined share of total job increases accounted for by these two service classifications during the 1950-60 decade was not less than 20 percent in any region and was 25 percent or more in five of the eight regions:[12]

	1940-50	1950-60
New England	14.9	27.3
Mideast	12.6	28.5
Great Lakes	11.5	27.4
Plains	12.6	28.7
Southeast	12.3	20.2
Southwest	12.3	21.9
Rocky Mountains	14.6	24.9
Far West	14.8	22.0
Nation	12.8	24.3

EVIDENCE OF CHANGING INDUSTRIAL STRUCTURE

Examination of the job-increase and job-decrease rates provides evidence of a changing industrial structure within the regions. The Plains, Southeast, Southwest, and Rocky Mountains regions, characterized by a heavy commitment to the production of primary products, showed rates of overall job decrease of 5.7 to 11.9 percent during the first decade and 10.9 to 16.1 percent during the second. Since job decreases in these regions occurred largely (57.8 percent or more) within primary-type industrial classifications (Table 2.4), it is clear that here jobs were being closed out in agriculture (and, in some instances mining, forestry, and fisheries activities) at the same time that they were being opened up in manufacturing, service, and governmental employment.

[12] The two remaining services, not treated in the above paragraphs, were business/repair services and private household services. Combined, these two services accounted for no more than 3.7 percent of total job increases during the first decade and 6.1 percent during the second.

The transition was particularly marked in the Southeast, where the overall regional job-decrease rate for the second decade was 16 percent and the job-increase rate 29 percent.

In the Far West region, however, very few job decreases took place in either decade. This would seem to be due in considerable measure to the fact that agricultural production in this region had tended for many years to be more heavily capitalized than elsewhere. The region had also experienced rapid growth in demand for certain of the particular types of agricultural output in which the region specialized (e.g., citrus fruits, wines, flowers). Under such conditions there was less opportunity for declines to occur in agricultural employment as a result of increased mechanization and shifts in demand.

In the more heavily industrialized regions of New England, the Mideast, and the Great Lakes, the economic structure was changing at a slower pace during the 1950s than in the South and West, but by no means at an insignificant rate. The job decreases which took place in these older industrialized regions were concentrated to a much larger extent in manufacturing than was true of the other regions. During the second decade manufacturing accounted for major shares of job decreases in New England, the Mideast, and the Great Lakes (57 percent, 32 percent, and 29 percent, respectively) compared with 13.9 percent or less in the other regions (Table 2.4). Clearly changes in these three most industrialized regions involved to an important extent losses as well as gains in urban-type employment, and tended for this reason to be different from that which was occurring in much of the rest of the nation.

INDUSTRIAL COMPOSITION OF THE EMPLOYED WORK
FORCE: NATIONAL AND REGIONAL

The process of job increases and decreases brought about significant changes in the industrial composition of regional employment. Table 2.5 presents for each region the industrial composition of the employed work force "normalized" in terms of the employment structure of the

TABLE 2.5

Comparisons of Regional and National Employment Structure and Measures of Convergence

(Distribution of total employment among selected industrial classifications: for U.S., 1940, 1950, 1960; for regions, 1960, normalized)[a]

	All U.S. Distribution of total employment			Number of regions approaching the norm[b]		Regions 1960 (normalized)							
	1940	1950	1960	1940-50	1950-60	New England	Mideast	Great Lakes	Plains	South-east	South-west	Rocky Mtns.	Far West
Primary	20.8	13.9	7.5	4½	4	31	35	73	221	155	155	184	71
*Construction	4.6	6.0	5.8	3	4	91	89	84	96	116	130	121	105
Manufacturing	23.3	25.4	26.4	7	8	136	117	132	69	84	56	51	86
*Food/kindred products	2.4	2.5	2.8	5	6½	78	100	107	148	89	78	100	100
*Textile mills	2.5	2.2	1.4	3	3½	214	86	14	7	307	14	7	14
*Apparel	1.8	1.9	1.8	5	5	118	218	41	53	118	47	18	47
*Lumber	2.1	2.1	1.6	3	5½	81	50	75	44	194	56	94	169
*Printing/publishing	1.4	1.5	1.7	5	3	112	135	124	100	59	65	76	88
*Chemicals	1.0	1.2	1.3	5	4	62	146	108	54	115	77	46	54
*Electrical/other machinery	2.4	3.6	4.6	3½	6	172	120	183	67	35	41	24	74
*Motor vehicle equip.	1.3	1.5	1.3	5	6	15	54	354	46	15	15	8	31
*Other transportation equip.	0.7	0.8	1.4	5	4	180	87	67	73	53	80	40	253
*Other misc. mfg.	7.9	8.3	8.5	8	8	163	127	143	62	62	56	64	77
*Utilities	1.2	1.4	1.4	5½	4	92	100	100	108	100	131	123	100

				b	b								
Mainly business services	13.5	15.5	15.2	4½	5	90	114	93	103	85	103	109	111
*Transportation	4.8	5.1	4.1	5½	5½	68	110	100	115	93	100	124	95
*Railroad/railway express	2.5	2.4	1.4	3	2½	50	100	114	157	93	86	179	79
*Trucking/warehousing	1.1	1.2	1.4	5½	5	79	93	114	114	86	107	121	86
*Other transportation	1.2	1.5	1.3	6	3½	77	146	69	69	100	100	69	115
*Communications	0.9	1.2	1.2	4½	5½	108	117	92	100	83	100	117	125
*Wholesale	2.7	3.5	3.3	6	5½	88	109	91	112	88	115	109	112
*FIRE	3.2	3.3	4.1	5½	7	110	125	90	95	80	98	98	115
*Business/repair	1.9	2.3	2.4	5	4	92	112	92	87	83	112	100	125
Mainly consumer services	31.1	30.3	32.4	5	4½	95	97	95	103	102	109	110	111
Retail	14.0	15.0	14.4	5	4	92	95	100	106	99	112	111	99
Recreation	4.6	4.1	3.7	3	5	81	97	86	89	103	116	114	119
*Private household	5.2	2.9	2.9	2	4	66	76	69	79	176	124	79	83
*Medical/education	7.3	8.4	11.4	5	6	109	103	97	108	88	98	116	105
Government	4.0	6.2	7.4	3	2	92	91	59	78	116	134	127	138
*Administration	3.3	4.4	4.8	4	3	90	115	81	85	96	110	135	117
*Armed forces	0.7	1.8	2.6	4	6	96	46	23	65	154	177	112	177
*INR	1.5	1.5	3.9	3	4	110	121	103	85	79	100	69	103
Total U.S.	100	100	100										

a Figures for regions are normalized percentages of total employment. Figures for U.S. are actual figures. For explanation of normalizing technique see footnote 13.

b These columns indicate the number of regions for which the normalized value rises or declines toward 100. Regions in which normalized value remains unchanged are scored as ½.

* Note: Each classification marked by an asterisk is one of the thirty-two industrial classifications from the Department of Commerce. All other classifications were prepared by totaling data for thirty-two industrial classifications. Primary includes agriculture, forestry and fisheries, and mining. Retail includes food/dairy product stores, eating/drinking places, and other retail trades. Recreation includes entertainment/recreation, and hotels/other personal services. Each of these eight component classifications is also one of the thirty-two industrial classifications for which data were available from the Department of Commerce.

nation.[13] This procedure provides an adjustment for national trends in the composition of the work force. Such an adjustment permits comparisons between two or more census years of industrial classifications, such as railroads/railway express, which declined as a percentage of total employment throughout the nation, or medical/educational services, which increased.

The measures indicate that there was a tendency for the various regions to become more alike in terms of industrial composition over the two decades. In most instances this increased similarity is evidenced by a tendency for the normalized values to rise or decline toward 100 percent in the various regions, indicating a general tendency for structure to be more like that of the nation as a whole.

Manufacturing was a major source of increased similarity. Here the normalized data moved upward or downward toward 100 percent, thereby indicating increasing similarity to the nation, in seven of the eight regions during the first decade, in all regions during the second. Among the ten manufacturing classifications seven showed more than half of the regions moving toward the national norm during the 1940s, and six during the 1950s.

For the mainly business services category, the normalized measures moved upward or downward toward 100 percent in four and a half out of eight regions during the first decade and five out of eight

[13] In each region, employment has been distributed among industrial classifications. The percentage of employment in each industrial classification is then expressed as a percentage of the norm, i.e., as a percentage of the share of total U.S. employment which is accounted for by that classification in the national economy. Thus in the Southeast in 1960 the share (i.e., percentage) of total employment in the primary category was 11.6 percent. The share of total employment in the primary category in the nation in the same year was 7.5 percent. "Normalized," the share in the Southeast is expressed as 155 percent of the share in the nation and is shown as 155 in the table. Normalized values are shown for the year 1960 only.

In interpreting these data it must be borne in mind that an extreme "overstructuring" (i.e., very high proportion) or "understructuring" (i.e., very low proportion) of employment in an industry category in one or two regions acts to raise or lower the national average, causing the other regions to tend to have relatively low or relatively high normalized values. For this reason it is wise to ignore small variations from 100 percent.

during the second.[14] Such evidence taken alone fails to indicate increased similarity, but we observe also that those regions in which the normalized values for business services increased or decreased in such a way as to make them *less* similar the changes were slight, whereas in those regions in which the increases or decreases resulted in *greater* similarity the changes were usually substantial.

Much the same can be said of the mainly consumer services category. There were five out of eight regions in which the normalized values changed toward increased similarity during the first decade, four and a half out of eight during the second. The changes making for decreased similarity were in every case slight, whereas the changes making for increased similarity were in a number of cases substantial.

Changes in the primary goods category provided the most important source of increased similarity of employment composition among the various regions even though normalized regional structure values showed about as much difference at the end of the twenty-year period as they did at the beginning. In this category the source of increased similarity lay in the widespread reduction in the importance (i.e., in the number of persons employed) of this regionally specialized industrial classification rather than a movement in the normalized values toward 100 percent. For the nation as a whole the percentage of employment within the primary sector declined from 20.8 percent in 1940 to 7.5 percent in 1960.

But in spite of these changes which made for increased similarities, the year 1960 saw the regions still characterized by important differences in employment structure. In the Southeast, although there had been very significant trends toward the national norm in the services and in many of the manufacturing classifications, employment remained relatively high in the primary sector, in the (relatively) low-wage textile, apparel, and lumber-furniture industries, in private household services, and in armed forces; relatively low in most of the other services.

The old industrialized regions of New England, the Mideast, and the Great Lakes continued to show concentration of employment in

[14] In those instances in which the normalized value remains unchanged, it is scored as one half.

manufacturing; the Plains, in primary (agriculture) activity and in the complementary food and kindred products manufacturing, in transportation services, and in wholesaling.

The fast-growing Southwest and Rocky Mountain regions also retained much of their earlier structural character. In spite of the significantly increased importance of their manufacturing sector there was not one classification within this sector in which the share of employment was above the national average in 1960 in either region. Both regions had become more specialized in those classifications relating to resort-type activities (i.e., retail and recreational services) and both had, at the end of the period, the same relatively heavy concentrations of employment in armed forces which had characterized their structure twenty years earlier.

Even the rapidly growing, rapidly transforming, Far West retained in 1960 something of its prewar character. From the outset there were heavy concentrations of employment in public administration and armed services. In 1960 the share of employment in both of these classifications was well above the national average. In manufacturing the percentage of employment had risen from 76 to 86 percent of the national norm in the two decades, but the region's share of employment was equal to or greater than the norm only in the three industrial classifications in which it had exceeded the norm in 1940: food/kindred products, lumber/wood products, and other transportation equipment manufacturing. Finally, the region retained its characteristic heavy structuring (relative to the nation) in the mainly business services and mainly consumer services categories, although the normalized measures of structure had declined since 1940 in every classification except private household services. As will be observed later (chapter 6) the industrial structure of the region influences the size and type of cities within the regional system.

SUMMARY AND CONCLUSIONS

In this chapter we have examined employment change first for the nation and then for the regions. Following this we have observed the effects of such changes upon employment composition of the nation and the regions. This analysis serves as a background against which we study employment structure and change in the MLM's and NMC's.

The analysis of the national economy leads to the general observation that changes in the industrial composition of labor markets often take the form of volatile marginal changes in the demand for additional labor in given industrial classifications. For example, the very large shares of job increases due to employment expansion in the medical/educational services during the 1950s reflect a somewhat less dramatic change in the percentage of the total labor force employed in medical/educational services from 1950 to 1960. The lesson to be drawn is that analysis of the existing or projected composition of labor markets provides a very unreliable guide for a projection of additional manpower requirements. It is the sharp *changes* in labor requirements, such as are reflected by measures of job increases and job decreases, which need to be studied.

Employment changes have varied widely both within and among industrial categories. Manufacturing has been characterized by significant tendencies toward both employment expansion and employment contraction. Job increases within the manufacturing category have been accounted for largely by a relatively small number of fast-growing industries, job decreases, by a few industries which are declining in terms of employment or which are shifting the location of their plants. For the goods sector as a whole, the net increase in manufacturing employment has been offset by decreases in the primary industries with the result that the sector appears to have ceased to grow. Viewed in this fashion, employment expansion for the entire economy appears as largely the result of growth in the service sector.

Growth of total service employment has, indeed, been impressive, but the individual service classifications have exhibited a variety of trends. There is little support for the popular notion that service employment is increasing rapidly on all fronts. Stated briefly, the major developments in the service sector were as follows: mainly consumer services accounted for 31 percent of all job increases during the 1950-60 decade; mainly business services, for 13 percent; and government, for 10 percent. Within the mainly consumer services category a majority of job increases was accounted for by the medical/ educational services classification (19 percent of all job increases). The only other important source of job increases was retail services, which contributed 8 percent, far below its share of total employment in the most recent census (more than 14 percent) and a much smaller share of job increases than was noted for the preceding decade. The remaining consumer service classifications, recreation/entertainment and private households, combined accounted for less than 4 percent of all job increases.

Among the mainly business services classifications, only FIRE (5.3 percent of total job increases) stands out as an important source of employment expansion. Each of the four other business services classifications account for well under 3 percent of total job increases.

Government's share of total job increases was about equally divided between administration and armed forces. This share of job decreases was roughly constant from the first to the second decade.

Analysis of the regional data reveals important elements of both similarity and diversity. The role of manufacturing as a source of job increases was important throughout the nation. Although shares of job increases due to manufacturing were largest in the older industrialized areas they declined from the first to the second decade. In each of the fast-growing regions of the Southwest and West, however, shares of job increases rose in the second decade—to substantial levels of 20 percent or more.

In general, the trends in job increases among the service classifications (e.g., the sharp upward trends in medical/educational services, and FIRE) which were noted for the nation are found in the regions. On the other hand, there were very considerable regional differences in job decreases in the primary and manufacturing industry classifications. In those regions characterized by a heavy commitment of manpower to the production of primary products, job decreases in agriculture and other primary classifications offset to a considerable extent expansion in other types of employment. In regions heavily committed to manufacturing, job decreases in manufacturing played an important role. In the rapidly growing regions of the Southwest and West, however, there were few job decreases anywhere. Employment expansion centered upon manufacturing, the business and consumer services, and government. Virtually no employment expansion was accounted for by the primary industries.

These changes in employment acted over the twenty-year period to bring about a greater similarity among regions. In most of the manufacturing and service classifications the percentages of employment rose or fell in the 1950 and 1960 decade in such a way as to reduce variations from the national norm. The primary industries remained geographically specialized but declined in importance. The year 1960 found the regions significantly changed from 1940 and more similar. Nevertheless, they retained important characteristics of their earlier employment structure.

3 SOME PRINCIPLES CONCERNING EMPLOYMENT STRUCTURE AND EMPLOYMENT EXPANSION IN URBAN ECONOMIES

IT IS THE PURPOSE of the present chapter to present briefly some theoretical concepts bearing on employment structure and employment expansion in metropolitan economies. In the first section an investigation of variations in an industry's employment structure (share of employment in a specified industry) among MLM's reveals that the importance of an industry varies greatly, indicating that there are differences in the extent to which products are exported. Where a relatively large percentage of employment is found within a given industry there is evidence that at least part of that particular industry's output is exported, and where the percentage is low there is evidence of import.

We then show why it is reasonable and desirable to classify MLM's both according to function and size. In the second section we show how employment expansion in MLM's may be analyzed in terms of increased activity in the export sector and amplification of these and other changes in the more residentiary industries, as well as through the acceleration principle. We also note factors contributing to or inhibiting growth in metropolitan economies.

CHARACTERISTICS OF EMPLOYMENT STRUCTURE: THE BASIS FOR A TYPOLOGY

Fundamental to any discussion of urban employment structure and change is the observation that the city is itself an economic organization. As in the case of a nation or a region, the city exports certain goods and services and imports others in turn. Moreover, its economic organization is to a significant extent engaged in the provision of goods and services to meet the needs of its own residents. Accordingly, the structure of employment of a city will tend to reflect the range and relative importance of the goods and services it produces at a given moment.

TYPES OF MARKETS: LOCAL, NATIONAL, REGIONAL, AND HINTERLAND

Each industrial activity in a city may be thought of as having its own market. On a map these different markets would be seen to overlap one another as well as the markets of other cities.

The MLM itself may be considered to represent a *local market*. As will be shown later, services such as retailing, dry cleaning, laundry, and auto repair tend to be performed predominantly for the city's own population. Other services such as retailing and banking may be performed largely for local consumption but are, at least to some extent, exported as well.

The export markets of cities vary with respect to geographic areas which they serve. The wide spectrum of export markets may be broken down into general categories. For our purposes, *national and international markets* are considered as belonging to the same category since many goods and services (e.g., wheat, jet planes, films, and even engineering services) are often produced for both of these markets. The national market needs to be distinguished from a subnational or *regional market*. In the case of the latter, certain activities (e.g., automobile-assembly plants, warehouses, and carton fabricators) are located in a particular city for the purpose of serving a limited portion of the country. (Here the term "regional market" is used to signify a major subnational market rather than the regional divisions used elsewhere in the study.

The final category is the *hinterland market*. Such a market consists of an outlying area which a city "structures" by providing it with services. Hinterlands are not important to all cities; in fact, as we shall see later in this chapter, the existence of this type of market implies a special type of city, the *nodal city*. In thinking of the relationship between a city and its hinterland market, it should be noted that there may be other cities in a particular city's hinterland but none of the other nodal-type cities will be larger. The services which a city exports to its hinterland make it possible for the hinterland to function as an economic organization. Evidence of hinterland export activity would be a telephone exchange, a bank, a courthouse, or legal offices.

Determining the degree of export activity. One method of approximating the extent to which an industry serves the local market is to study the structure of industry employment in each MLM, measured in terms of percentage of employment accounted for by each industrial classification. If an industry's production is primarily geared to local demand, we expect that industry's employment to be distributed in proportion to local demand in each of the various MLM's. The measure we use as a proxy for local demand is the size of the metropolitan labor force. Thus, if there are only minor variations among MLM's in the structure of an industry's employment (i.e., in the percentage of total employment accounted for in that industry) then the industry may be considered to be "residentiary," or local. If the variation in the structure is large there is evidence that the output of the industry is important only in certain places and we presume that in such places it is largely exported. Accordingly, it is considered to be essentially "basic," or an export-type industry.

Evidence of variations in structure. Variations in employment structure can best be observed if the percentages of employment accounted for by a given industrial classification in the MLM's are arranged in the form of an array (i.e., from lowest to highest). In Table 3.1 the highest and lowest percentages along with values for selected percentiles are shown. Analysis of these data shows wide variations in the ranges of percentages among the industrial classifications. For example, in manufacturing percentages range from 53.9 percent to 2.6 percent; in armed forces, from 50.2 percent to zero; and in transportation, from

21.4 percent to 1.1 percent. In contrast, in utilities percentages range only from 4.6 to .5; in food and dairy product stores, from 3.9 to 1.4 percent; in communication from 3.6 to .4 percent.

We note, further, that for some industrial classifications a relatively large percentage of employment is limited to a relatively few cities whereas in other classifications it is found in a much larger number. Thus the highest-ranking city in hotels and other personal services has roughly 20 percent of its work force employed in this classification; the city which represents the 95th percentile has less than 5 percent. In the case of the manufacturing category, however, the percentage of employment declines relatively slowly as we move progressively from the top-ranking manufacturing city toward the median. The top city shows 53.9 percent of its employment in manufacturing; the city representing the 95th percentile, 46.3 percent; the 90th percentile, 43.2 percent; the 75th percentile, 35.8 percent; the median, 24.1 percent.

The major lesson to be learned from inspection of these data is that very few of the industrial classifications are so ubiquitous that there does not exist a significant degree of employment concentration within the upper limits of the array. For example, a relatively unspecialized classification such as other retailing varies from 11 to 14 percent in the top quartile (i.e., from the 75th to the 100th percentile). This means that the share of total employment within this classification is almost 30 percent larger in the MLM which is most specialized than in the MLM representing the 75th percentile.

This preliminary analysis of variations in industry structure shows that industries are not either "residentiary" or "basic," but rather, that some industries are "more residentiary" than others. In the next section, we use a more precise measure of the extent to which an industry is residentiary—the coefficient of variation.

Coefficients of variation: Industrial structure. The extent to which the percentage of employment accounted for by a given industrial classification varies among MLM's is presented in Table 3.1. The coefficient of variation of structure for each industrial classification

TABLE 3.1

Evidence of Structural Variations among MLM's

(Percent of employment in selected industrial classifications, 1960, for indicated percentiles, and coefficients of variation)

Industrial classification	Lowest value	Percentiles[a]							Highest value	Highest-ranking MLM	Coefficient of variation[b]
		10th	25th	Median value	67th	75th	90th	95th			
Primary	.1	1.7	2.8	4.7	7.0	8.7	13.7	19.2	35.4	Carlsbad (N. M.)	0.87
†Construction	3.5	4.3	4.9	5.8	6.6	6.9	8.2	9.2	13.2	Ft. Lauderdale (Fla.)	0.27
Manufacturing	2.6	8.7	14.6	24.1	32.1	35.8	43.2	46.3	53.9	Gastonia (N. C.)	0.51[c]
†Utilities	.5		1.1	1.3	1.5	1.6	2.0	2.4	4.6	Florence (Ala.)	0.39
†Mainly business services	6.2	9.4	11.3	13.8	15.5	16.7	20.0	22.1	30.5		0.29
Transportation	1.1	2.0	2.6	3.6	4.3	4.8	6.1	8.1	21.4	Altoona (Pa.)	0.53
Railroad/railway express	.0			1.2	1.8	2.2	3.2	4.8	18.5	Altoona (Pa.)	1.08
Trucking/warehousing	.3		1.0	1.3	1.5	1.7	2.2	2.4	3.8	Odessa (Tex.)	0.41
Other transportation	.2					1.1	1.8	2.3	6.2	Miami (Fla.)	0.80
†Communications	.4			1.2	1.3	1.4	1.7	1.9	3.6	San Angelo (Tex.)	0.32
†Wholesale	.8	1.8	2.3	3.1	3.6	3.9	5.0	5.5	9.2	McAllen (Tex.)	0.38
†FIRE	1.6	2.3	2.7	3.3	3.9	4.3	5.3	6.0	9.7	Hartford (Conn.)	0.35
†Business/repair	.3	1.5	1.8	2.1	2.3	2.5	2.9	3.2	10.1	Albuquerque (N. M.)	0.36

Industrial classification										C.V.[b]	
†Mainly consumer services	22.3	28.2	30.7	33.9	36.0	37.4	43.1	48.7	62.8	0.18	Daytona Beach (Fla.)
†Retail	9.3	12.7	13.8	15.1	15.7	16.2	17.6	18.9	22.2	0.13	Butte (Mont.)
†Food/dairy stores	1.4	2.1	2.3	2.5	2.7	2.8	3.0	3.2	3.9	0.16	
†Eating/drinking places	1.2	2.0	2.4	2.7	3.0	3.1	3.5	3.8	6.4	0.24	Hot Springs (Ark.)
†Other retail	5.5	8.0	8.8	9.8	10.3	10.8	11.6	12.4	14.2	0.15	Sarasota (Fla.)
Recreation	0.1	2.7	3.1	3.7	4.1	4.4	4.9	5.6	26.9	0.49	Las Vegas (Nev.)
Hotel/personal	1.6	2.2	2.5	3.0	3.3	3.6	4.2	4.7	19.8	0.45	Las Vegas (Nev.)
Entertainment/recreation	.2						1.1	1.1	10.3	0.89	Reno (Nev.)
†Private household	.7	1.7	2.1	2.6	3.4	4.1	6.3	7.6	11.4	0.57	Selma (Ala.)
†Medical/education	6.3	8.8	9.9	11.3	12.4	13.1	16.4	20.0	41.8	0.37	Iowa City (Iowa)
Government	1.6	2.6	3.1	4.4	6.7	10.1	20.5	29.8	56.2	1.10	Washington, D. C.
Administration	1.5	2.4	2.9	3.9	4.6	5.2	8.4	10.3	25.1	0.65	
Armed forces	.0				1.14	2.7	12.7	20.5	50.2	2.12	Lawton, Okla.
INR	.9	1.8	2.4	3.1	3.7	4.0	5.2	5.8	8.4	0.38	Sarasota, Fla.

[a] The 368 MLM's have been arrayed for each industrial classification on basis of percentages of employment. Percentages shown in each percentile are for lowest-ranking MLM in that percentile except the 50th and 100th. Percentages less than 1 are not shown except for the lowest value in each classification.

[b] Coefficients of variation for each industrial classification are for the entire array of percentages of employment.

[c] Coefficients of variation in individual manufacturing categories range from .48 in printing/publishing to 3.04 in textile mill products.

† A dagger has been used to designate the more residentiary industries, those with coefficients of 0.38 or less. Private household employment is also classified as residentiary. Variations in employment structure in this industry reflect regional differences in supply conditions.

is used as a measure of the dispersion of the MLM's percentages of employment accounted for by that classification around the mean percentage for all MLM's combined.[1]

The coefficient of variation measures reveal that there is much less variation in the percentages of employment for some classifications than for others. In general, the coefficient of variation is lowest in the consumer services (for the mainly consumer services category the coefficient of variation is .18) followed by contract construction, mainly business service, and utilities (with coefficients of .27, .29, and .39). The manufacturing, primary, and government categories show much higher coefficients of variation (.51, .87, and 1.10). Such observations indicate that manufacturing, primary, and government-associated employment tend to be subject to geographical specialization and thus may be considered as basic industries.

Services are more perishable, less subject to export, and, therefore, tend to be performed in every city to some extent. We see this rule exemplified in retailing and in certain consumer services such as cleaning, laundry, and auto repair.[2] It is also true of certain business services such as commercial banking, insurance, auditing, and the provision of legal services. Therefore, services such as those mentioned above may be considered as the more residentiary industries.

Consumer services are by no means entirely destined for local markets, however. Retailing is "exported" by cities to persons who travel from smaller places to make selection from the greater variety of goods which are offered in the big retail markets. Entertainment

---

[1] The coefficient of variation is computed for each classification by dividing the standard deviation of the percentages of total employment within that classification by the average percentage (for the 368 MLM's) of employment within the classification. When the observations are normally distributed, two-thirds of the percentages fall within the limits defined by one standard deviation from the mean. The coefficient of variation expresses this standard deviation as a percentage of the average and permits comparison of variability among the various industrial classifications. For example, two-thirds of the variation in structure in mainly business services is accounted for by variations of 18 percent of the mean structure.

[2] Coefficients of variation for cleaning-laundry, and for auto repair, computed for the 113-SMSA sample, were .25 and .23.

services are exported to the vacationer who visits the resort city. Business services such as wholesaling, banking, and consulting are exported to an even greater degree.

The coefficient of variation is always greater for detailed industrial classifications than for the more aggregative category which they comprise. For example, the coefficient of variation for retailing is .13, but coefficients for the component retailing classifications range from .15 to .24. Similarly, the coefficient of variation for mainly business services is only .29, but the business services comprising this category show coefficients which range from .32 to 1.08.

These greater variations in the more detailed classifications simply point to the tendency for each city to possess a degree of uniqueness in specialization which is easily glossed over in general discussion. Structural constraints tend to increase with increased aggregation. One city may have exactly the same percentage of its employed work force engaged in retailing as another but the composition of that employment in terms of types of retailing may be quite different.

The differences observed among the coefficients of variation for subclassifications point to the need to study employment structure in considerable detail. If there is greater diversity of structure in detailed than in more general industrial classifications there may also be greater diversity in employment structure in terms of such characteristics as level of skill, age, and educational requirements.

The markets for the more residentiary industries are usually more limited than those for the basic industries. To the extent that residentiary goods and services are exported it will be primarily to nearby hinterland type markets. Here the metropolis involved has traditionally been referred to as a "central place."[3] In the case of the more basic industries, however, goods or services flow outward to national or regional markets. Cities where these industries are concentrated should not be thought of as serving a particular hinterland.

When the metropolis acts as a central place for a hinterland it will generally tend to provide many services for export. When the

---

[3] For a bibliography of Central Place studies, see Brian J. L. Berry and Allen Pred, *Central Place Studies* (Philadelphia, Regional Science Association, 1964).

metropolis exports to larger markets, however, resources will tend to be concentrated in relatively few industries. This distinction between places specializing in the basic industries and places exporting a variety of the more residentiary type industries turns out to be most helpful in the study of the structure and growth of employment in MLM's. The metropolis serving a hinterland is referred to as a nodal-type place. Other metropolises are referred to as being non-nodal or specialized.

TYPES OF MLM'S: NODAL AND NON-NODAL

Goods tend to flow through a nodal city with very little value being added as they move into or out of the hinterland. Such a city provides the junction of transport routes, as well as terminals and storage facilities. Perhaps more important, commercial, governmental, and a variety of service activities are clustered there.

Distributors and agents located in the nodal city assist the flow of goods in both directions—from hinterland to larger markets, and from cities in other areas to the hinterland. Services, however, flow mainly in one direction—to the hinterland. They may originate in a city other than the nodal city; if so, they will probably be supervised and/or customized to the hinterland's needs (e.g., insurance and bank loans) by the nodal city. The nodal city will rarely export services to cities outside its hinterland, regardless of whether they are smaller or larger, since such cities will have nearer, cheaper, or better sources available. Services originating in the nodal city may be highly specialized to meet the hinterland's requirements, such as textile consultants and mineral assayers. Some of these services may not be available even in larger cities outside the nodal city's hinterland.

The concepts of the hinterland market and the nodal city to a considerable degree are flexible. The hinterland of a large nodal city includes the peripheral areas coterminous with its local market, but is comprised mainly of the cities and towns which it serves. These cities may be at considerable distance from the nodal city and require services different from those required by the hinterland of a small nodal city. The term "hinterland" becomes synonymous with "region" when we talk about a *regional center,* since no nodal city in the region (its hinterland) is likely to be larger than the regional center.

Whether the nodal city is large or small, it may be expected to have a relatively large percentage of its employment in such service classifications as wholesale, FIRE, business and professional services, transportation, communications, and administration.

In visualizing a nodal center it is useful to note that it usually has a well-developed central (downtown) business district because the services in which the city specializes benefit by being in close proximity to each other (e.g., legal, insurance, and accounting offices, banks, consultant firms). The central business district (CBD) is the nucleus of the labor market and is like a nerve center. It is here that there is the highest degree of interaction between individuals and the greatest interdependence among firms. Each firm tends to specialize its activities and buy the services it needs from other firms rather than to provide internally all of the services it requires (i.e., it "externalizes" services).

As the number of firms in each industry increases and as the number of industries in a labor market increases, the amount of "internalized" services (i.e., the number of services which the firm provides within its own organization) should tend to decrease. The reason for this is that as the market broadens it becomes feasible for firms to be organized to supply the goods and services which previously the firms had to produce for themselves.[4] Thus the larger the number of firms and the greater the heterogenity of industrial activity in a labor market, the more important are the externalized services made possible by the CBD.

The concept of the CBD is useful in suggesting the types of industries which will comprise important segments of the labor force of nodal cities and of cities specializing in the exporting of business services. CBD-type industries place a high value on locating within the central labor market for the reasons already given. They are usually housed in multistory buildings and are specialists in the output of

---

[4] See the discussion of external economies below.

consumer, government, and producer services, or they are administrative divisions of manufacturing firms. In these industries there is a high proportion of white-collar workers and few production workers. A relatively high percentage of those employed is likely to be female.

The non-nodal city does not provide a wide range of services to a hinterland, but rather specializes in producing a limited number of goods and/or services to be exported to a regional or national market. Its activities may be classified either as goods (manufacturing) or as services. Each category could be further disaggregated into consumer or producer (final or intermediate) demand, but the distinction between these categories becomes blurred inasmuch as many firms serve both types of demand. Insurance companies, universities, and hospitals are examples of export service activities which could form a city's employment base. Indeed, Hartford, Princeton, and Rochester (Minn.) are cities so specialized. Automobiles are exported from Detroit, cigarettes from Winston-Salem, chemicals from Baton Rouge. Goods are usually shipped to the consuming market, but frequently the consumer must travel to the service, e.g., to Aspen to ski.

If a labor market is composed mainly of primary and heavy manufacturing industries, the proportion of industries found in the central business district will be smaller and the CBD will be found to be less developed and less important in the functioning of the labor market. Moreover, in cities where a few large firms dominate the labor market, such firms will tend to internalize their service requirements (i.e., to provide for such requirements from within their corporate organizations). Under such conditions there is an inadequate development of servicing facilities and, as a result, the establishment of new firms becomes more difficult. Each new firm must provide for its own requirements.[5]

Non-nodal cities can be identified most easily if they export only manufactures. A high percentage of employment in manufacturing is

[5] Benjamin Chinitz, "Contrasts in Agglomeration: New York and Pittsburgh," *American Economic Review*, Vol. 51 (May 1961). See also the discussion of the tendency for external economies to add to locational attractiveness of a city in the section on "external economies and the spawning of new firms," p. 68 below.

a good indication of such export activity. The export type employment in service activities in non-nodal cities is more elusive. A high percentage of employment in FIRE or in professional services might indicate either a nodal or a non-nodal city. In general, however, a city which is primarily nodal would be expected to be relatively highly structured in a number of services since it is providing for the needs of a hinterland, whereas a city which is primarily non-nodal would be unlikely to be a heavy exporter of more than one or a limited number of such services.

GROWTH AND CHANGES IN

EMPLOYMENT STRUCTURE

Though a particular city may be of one type or the other, it is not unlikely that it may be a combination of both. What was originally a nodal city may take on export-type activities as it grows, or what was once a non-nodal city may assume some of a nodal city's functions. It is natural that as firms grow they tend to extend their activities into wider markets. Accordingly, the city which initially serviced only a restricted hinterland may, in time, come to export specialized services to broader markets. Moreover, as a nodal center grows, the development of its labor force and the increasing size of its local market may encourage the location of specialized manufacturers or service firms serving broader markets.

On the other hand, an essentially non-nodal, goods-exporting city like Detroit may gradually modify its functions, shifting emphasis from actually producing manufactured products (e.g., automobiles) to managing (research, designing, marketing, etc.) the national industry. As an industry grows, production and assembly plants may become decentralized, while management functions remain centralized and assume greater importance in the city's economy. At the same time, the city may take on additional services for the area which surrounds it and perform increasingly as a nodal center.

Finally, economies of scale or factor substitution may tend to alter the composition of the labor force with increasing size of the city. As a city grows it is not unlikely that certain services will require fewer workers per unit of output provided. This might occur, for example, in the case of certain types of retailing, transportation, or warehousing. At the same time, a growing urban economy might require relatively more employment in governmental services because of greater need for welfare, recreational, and educational services or simply because of diseconomics of scale arising out of bureaucratic organization.

In the light of the above it seems reasonable to expect that size of place will be an important determinant of the composition of the labor force of a city. Even within a given type of city (e.g., nodal) we may suppose that as the city increases in size the employment structure will reflect the effect of growing local and external markets, changing functions, the growing importance of central business district-type activities, and both economies and diseconomies of scale.

IMPLICATIONS FOR A TYPOLOGY

All that has been said indicates that it is both logical and useful to seek to classify cities in terms of two basic prototypes: the nodal city and the non-nodal city. Moreover, the analysis suggests the criteria by which classification may be carried out. It suggests that economic function tends to be reflected in the composition of the work force. The nodal city should be identifiable by a relatively high proportion of total employment in certain types of services which it provides for its hinterland. We do not visualize a nodal city as being heavily concentrated in only one or two consumer and/or business services but rather in a group of services.

The non-nodal city should be identifiable by a relatively high proportion of its total employment in a restricted number of classifications. Although this type is perhaps most easily visualized as a city with relatively heavy concentrations of employment in manufacturing, the classification would also include cities with concentrations of employment in services (e.g., an entertainment center such as Las Vegas).

In these instances in which non-nodal cities export business services to the nation or to a region, we would not expect to find as wide a range of business services as in a true nodal center nor would we expect to find the same combination of services. The hypothesis with which we work is that the nodal center acts as the metropolitan hub of its hinterland, providing it with those services which can be provided most economically by a metropolis and services which tend for a number of reasons to be provided by firms which are in close proximity to one another. The non-nodal city is simply a city in which there is a concentration of resources, usually in a more restricted number of economic activities in which it has some locational advantages. The non-nodal city has as its prime economic function the export of goods or services to a regional or national market rather than the servicing of the needs of a hinterland.

Two additional observations must be made regarding classification of cities. The first is that we should expect to find that many cities have mixed nodal/non-nodal characteristics. The very processes of growth are such that we would expect the growing nodal center to attract firms which export goods and services to the region or nation at large. Moreover, it is not unreasonable to expect non-nodal cities to take on nodal functions as they and the areas surrounding them develop economically.

The second observation is that structural characteristics may be expected to vary with size of place. This would tend to be true because of opportunities for development of specialization arising out of economies of scale associated with larger local or hinterland markets, because of development of external economies, or because of diseconomies of scale.

THE DYNAMICS OF EMPLOYMENT EXPANSION

It is common knowledge that when a new industry locates in a community the number of jobs created will be in excess of the additional workers employed by the industry itself. Indeed, this is the basic premise of every chamber of commerce or state developmental agency which actively seeks to bring in new industry.

Moreover, anyone who has taken an interest in the economic scene over a period of years has marveled over the observation that in cities which have grown rapidly, growth seems to feed upon itself: the location of every new firm appears to add to the attractiveness of the city for still another.

The purpose of the remainder of this chapter is to describe a number of mechanisms by which any given autonomous change in employment is amplified, by which further stimulation to growth arises, and by which constraints upon growth develop.[6] Although it is not possible to identify the influence of each of these mechanisms in the subsequent statistical analysis, an understanding of the economic principles involved provides valuable insights in interpreting the results of the analysis of employment change which is carried out in chapters 7 and 8. In those chapters we shall be concerned with observing the extent to which employment in given industrial classifications responds to growth in the metropolitan economy as a whole, and with discovering what shares of job increases and decreases are accounted for by each of the industrial classifications in the various sizes and types of MLM's.

LOCAL RESPENDING OF INCOME FOR
CONSUMER GOODS AND SERVICES

When employment increases as a result of the location of a new export firm in a given city, there is a secondary or derived demand for labor which results from the respending of incomes within the city's boundaries. Persons receiving income from the firm in the form of wages, salaries, rents, interest, or profits spend a high proportion in the local consumer goods and services market thereby generating additional demand for labor. Moreover, persons receiving this second "round" of income also spend a large part locally, generating still further income from which there are additional "rounds" of spending, each smaller

6 To study autonomous changes it is necessary to consider location factors. Such factors are considered briefly in chapter 9. For additional references, see Victor Fuchs, *Changes in the Location of Manufacturing in the United States since 1929* (New Haven, Yale University Press, 1962); Edgar S. Dunn, Eric E. Lampard, Richard F. Muth, and Harvey S. Perloff, *Regions, Resources, and Economic Growth,* (Baltimore, Johns Hopkins Press, 1963); and Edgar M. Hoover, *Location of Economic Activity* (New York, McGraw Hill, 1948).

than the one preceding. If we think of the new firm as becoming established and employing its new work force month after month, and of the various successive respendings of income also occurring one on top of the other, month after month, we can visualize the amplification of demand which takes place.

It is very important to note, however, that not all of the income which is spent locally gives rise to new income within the community.[7] The reason is, simply, that not all of the sales dollars remain within the local economy. Part of the expenditure is used to bring goods into the economy, to pay wages to nonresidents, and to pay for services rendered by firms outside the city. In short, a part of the local consumer expenditure leaks out of the local economic system to pay for import components. The part which remains, however, comprises a demand for local resources including labor.

The amplification process which results from local respending is generally designated by the term "income multiplier."[8] To translate

[7] Charles M. Tiebout, *The Community Economic Base Study* (New York, Committee for Economic Development, 1962). The statements in this paragraph follow closely those of Tiebout, p. 73.

[8] The multiplier principle may be illustrated as follows:
Total income increase = Increase
in income received by exporting

$$\times \qquad \frac{1}{1 - \text{(propensity to consume locally} \times \text{local income created per dollar of local consumption sales)}}$$

Let us suppose that $1.00 of new income has been injected into the local economy and the propensity to spend locally is .50. If 40 percent of the extra income received from consumer spending is retained after payment for imported merchandise and services the multiplier will be

$$\frac{1}{1 - (.50x \ .40)} \quad = \quad \frac{1}{1 - .2} \quad = \quad 1.25$$

and the increase in local income will be $1.25.

Where the "leakages" of income due to savings, taxes, spending outside the city, and importing are large, the multiplier will be small. On the other hand, if the percentage of income spent locally is large, and imports are small, the multiplier will be large.

the income multiplier into an employment multiplier in a given metro-politan economy would be a difficult and complex task, beyond the scope of the present study. Needless to say, the size of the employ-ment multiplier would vary with the type of new export firm which located within the metropolitan economy (i.e., its tendency to generate local income in the form of wages and its wage level) as well as with the propensity to spend income locally and the number of new jobs created per dollar of local spending for consumer goods and service.[9]

THE PROVISION OF GOVERNMENT SERVICES

As usually formulated in aggregative economic analysis, the income multiplier treats only the respending for consumer goods and services. Government spending is regarded as an autonomous injection of in-come into the stream which will have its own multiplier effect. Local government services include, however, a variety of activities closely associated with consumer and business needs, such as police and fire protection, provision of recreational services, and operation of schools.

[9] As we have seen it is possible by analysis of employment structure to determine those industries which are predominantly export industries and those industries which are predominantly residentiary. Researchers have gone further and estimated the probable extent of employment engaged in export activity in each industry, and proceeded from these estimates to observe the relationship which exists between employment in the basic (export) sector and the residen-tiary sector. From such analysis it is possible to prepare estimates of the extent to which creation of employment in basic industries generates further creation of employment in residentiary-type industries. For a review of this (location quotient) approach see Richard B. Andrews, "The Mechanics of the Urban Base," a review of ten articles published in *Land Economics* (May 1955-February 1956). Important studies have been carried through for individual cities: see Katherine McNamara "Bibliography on the Economic Base," *Land Economics* (May 1954), pp. 186-91. A study which measures export and import trade activity and the relationship between these sectors for 368 MLM's, 1940-60, is being prepared by Richard V. Knight, *Employment Expansion and Metro-politan Trade* to be published in late 1970. Here it has been found that over two-thirds of the variation in employment growth rates, 1950-60, could be explained by variations in the growth of employment in the export sector, and by variations in the size of the metropolitan trade multiplier.

Changes in the level of such activities are probably not closely tied to the level of local income in the short run but over a more extended period they are likely to be rather closely associated. If such observations are correct, we may conclude that when employment increases as a result of the location of a new (export) firm in a given city there tends to be a secondary or derived demand for labor due to an increase in government services. This secondary effect is analogous to the multiplier effect due to local respending of income. Thus, in addition to the jobs generated in retailing and consumer services, there would be jobs generated in the public school system, in the parks system, and in city hall. In short, there are jobs generated for services in the local public sector as well as in the local private sector.

LOCAL INVESTMENT (PRIVATE AND PUBLIC SECTORS)

A well-known theory relating to the demand for investment goods is the acceleration principle.[10] The accelerator theory holds that the demand for *additions* to the stockpile of capital goods (i.e., net investment demand) is dependent upon the *change* in the demand for final goods or services which are produced by the capital goods in question.[11] As commonly stated the acceleration principle holds that

$$I = \alpha (D_t - D_{t-1})$$

where I represents demand for additions to the stock of capital, α represents the number of dollars worth of capital goods to produce a dollar's worth of final goods per time period, D_t and D_{t-1} represent the demand for final goods in periods t and $t-1$.

For the metropolitan economy the acceleration principle would relate chiefly to the construction industry, which is the major local

[10] John M. Clark, "Business Acceleration and the Law of Demand: A Technical Factor in Economic Cycles," *Journal of Political Economy*, XXV (1917), 217-35.

[11] In treating local investment demand (private sector) we refer only to housing and business structures. Machinery and equipment demand is not treated since it is usually purchased outside the local economy. The demand for housing is seen as the demand for the services which the house or apartment provides the resident, whereas the demand for business structures is seen as derived from the demand for the goods or services sold by the firm.

industry engaged in the production of houses, buildings and roads; according to this principle the annual demand for new construction would depend upon the *change* in annual demand for the services of houses, plants, and roads. Thus, according to the acceleration principle, the demand for construction is derived from the growth of the city.

Here again we find a route for amplification of growth tendencies within the city's economy. It must be noted, however, that according to the principle, *growth* in the capital goods producing industry requires not merely growth in final demand, but growth in final demand by increasing amounts. Repeated increments in demand of the same amount would merely sustain the existing capital goods producing industry if only the accelerator mechanism were at work. Growth by lesser amounts would reduce the level of demand for the output of the capital goods producing industry.

Expenditures for government investment are major outlays, typically involving financing through bond issues, and subject to considerable variation from year to year. Over the long run, however, such expenditures are likely to behave in a manner similar to other investment expenditures. The demand for additional public facilities such as schools and court houses is derived from the demand for the services which they provide. The demand for resources within the construction industry to produce such facilities would, therefore, appear to be strongly influenced by the change in demand for public services (i.e., the increment in demand for the service which makes necessary new facilities).

DIFFICULTIES IN APPLYING THE ACCELERATION PRINCIPLE TO EMPLOYMENT

The acceleration principle can be translated in terms of labor requirements within the construction industry but there are difficulties. The effective demand for labor can change as a result of changes in relative factor prices (i.e., interest rates, wages, profits) or productivity, as well as because of changes in final product or service demand. Moreover, an increase in demand for additions to the stock for housing and other fixed facilities may not have a full impact upon employment within the construction industry if there is unemployment at the beginning of the time period in question.[12]

The applicability of the acceleration principle may also be impaired by the fact that there may be changes in the final product "mix" (e.g., changing importance of housing demand relative to roads which will alter the demand for labor). Finally there is the difficulty that the demand for resources to be employed in the construction industry arises not only from the need to construct new fixed capital but also to maintain and renovate existing buildings and roads and to demolish old buildings prior to construction.[13]

It is clear from the coefficient of variation measures that the share of employment comprised by contract construction is, in fact, relatively stable among the 368 MLM's. This implies that there is a strong tendency for employment in construction to vary *in proportion* to employment elsewhere within the metropolitan economy. If this is the case the acceleration principle offers at best only a partial explanation for the behavior of investment. Demand for such employment would, therefore, appear to be related *both* to the metropolitan economy's level of income and employment and to its rate of growth. Later (chapter 7) we attempt to measure the extent to which the acceleration principle is operative.

GROWTH OF THE MARKET, ECONOMIES OF SCALE,
AND IMPORT SUBSTITUTION

An important concept in economics is that there are minimum efficient sizes for various types of firms. This means that the market must be of a certain size before the establishment of a firm can be justified. The size of the market required to make a firm economically viable is

[12] A more detailed discussion of the acceleration hypothesis is presented in chapter 8.

[13] The job decrease measures may provide a useful indicator of the importance of demolition.

called the "critical size" of the market. As a city grows, and the local market becomes larger, these critical sizes are reached for more and more activities and either local or nonresident investors enter the market and set up shop.

The result of establishing such new firms is, of course, to increase the output destined for use within the city, thereby resulting in import substitution. If the newly formed firm produces parts, supplies, or business services previously purchased outside the city's economy, there will be *import substitution which serves to increase local employment engaged in supplying inputs to local business.* If the newly formed firm provides consumer services or goods previously purchased outside the city's economy, there will again be *import substitution which serves to increase employment but this time in the consumer goods and services sector.*

To sum up, as growth occurs in the city, a series of critical market-size thresholds are passed which cause successive enlargements of local employment by increasing the consumer's propensity to consume locally and by increasing the volume of inputs purchased in the local market by the firms supplying the needs of local consumers or exporting goods and services to outside markets. Such import substitution has the effect of amplifying the initial employment expansion which set it off.

EXTERNAL ECONOMIES AND THE SPAWNING OF NEW FIRMS

A closely related concept is that of external economies of scale. The term was first used by Alfred Marshall to describe those cost reductions which accrued to firms in a given industry as a result of growth of the industry. The economies were seen as coming about when the industry grew large enough to justify the organization of firms to provide specialized business services, supplies, training services, or other inputs on a more efficient, lower cost basis.

In time the term has come to apply to economies which are "external" to a firm but result from the demand created by the prior establishment of other user firms, whether such firms are within a single industry or not. Firms which supply these external economies provide services or goods which the user firm would otherwise have to provide for itself. Examples of external economies are found in most of the business services (e.g., advertising agencies, accountants, data processing service bureaus) and in a number of manufacturing firms that produce on contract (e.g., producers of parts, job printers).[14]

We refer here to economies which come about when the user firm contracts-out rather than produces the good or service within its own organization (in-house). In the previous section we referred simply to substitution of goods or services locally produced for those goods or services which were previously imported. In either case the supplying firm exists because thresholds of critical market size have been overcome.

In the latter case the impetus to grow lies in the fact that the existence of the supplying firm is an attraction to firms to locate within the city. Since firms may secure basic business services and even certain component parts and materials outside of their own organizations, they may operate with a smaller investment of capital and with a less elaborate organization. Such conditions permit a city to compete with other cities for new firms and also to encourage would-be local entrepreneurs to organize new businesses.

AVAILABILITY OF FINANCE

Still another possible route by which growth in a city's economy may feed upon itself is through the increased availability of finance. In practice there are barriers to the ready flow of risk capital from one area to another, especially where small- and medium-size firms are concerned. All other things being the same, a successful business man in Houston would prefer to invest in a new enterprise in the Houston area rather than one in some small township located a great distance

---

[14] The externalizing of a service will be picked up in the data as a job shift from the externalizing industry to the external industry e.g., from banking to mainly business services. There will not be an increase in jobs, however. To the contrary, since economies have taken place it is not unlikely that there will be a decrease in numbers of persons employed.

away. As regards short-term credit, banks prefer to lend to local firms whose operations can be fairly accurately and continuously evaluated rather than to distant enterprises with whom communication is difficult.

Moreover, the existence of an atmosphere in which general growth is occurring and in which profits tend to rise from one year to the next serves to bring about a greater willingness on the part of individuals and firms to invest in new enterprises.[15]

Perhaps of even greater importance is the increased *ability* of local banks to extend loans. When new firms enter the market and begin to make payments to employees and local suppliers, demand deposits will increase in local banks and the reserve position of these banks will be improved. The result, of course, is an increased supply of short-term credit in the metropolitan economy.

The consequence of these combined tendencies is that once growth begins to occur in a city, availability of new financing may improve sharply, providing an important stimulus to still further growth.

OTHER FACTORS

The preceding sections do not exhaust the factors which cause growth to become cumulative. As the city grows its labor market broadens and tends to become more heterogeneous. Increasingly, firms find that they can readily procure the special skills they require. This ready availability of labor, along with availability of external economies mentioned above, make the city an attractive place to locate.

Moreover, the need to be close to customers, to sources of finance —and to competitors—increasingly provides a locational pull as the city grows. As more firms locate for these and other reasons examined above, the centripetal force becomes even greater.

Still an additional point is that the growth of the metropolitan economy and its ability to service the needs of the hinterland may cause firms to locate within the hinterland even if space or other factors

---

[15] We are indebted to Ruth Mack for suggesting this additional growth mechanism. Of course, an excessive tendency to make credit available could lead to a liquidation crisis in the event of some economic reversal.

rule out locating within the metropolis itself. Such location of firms increases the size of the metropolis' external market and results in still further tendencies toward economies of scale, external economies, and the spawning of new firms.

NEGATIVE ASPECTS

Needless to say, there are negative aspects. The increasing size of the city brings increasing rental costs, overhead costs, and costs of congestion and administration of the public sector. For a number of reasons, wages tend to be higher in cities. Thus firms face increasing problems, relating to the cost and availability of usable space and to the cost of a number of other inputs. These factors cause some firms to leave at the same time that others are entering. Increasingly, as the city grows, the constraints upon further growth become more numerous and severe, and only the viable firms can survive.

IMPLICATIONS FOR ANALYSIS

The preceding discussion of factors which influence the growth of a city and its employment extends beyond the limits of possible empirical verification in this study. Nevertheless, there are important implications for the analysis which follows. In general, this discussion of the factors influencing growth supports the observations made earlier when we treated the factors influencing employment structure. Cities may be expected to alter their function and structure as they grow. Significant differences in structure among the size-of-place categories would appear as a logical process of growth, with larger places reflecting the effects of external economies and economies of scale in the composition of their labor forces.

A second and closely related implication relates to patterns of job increases and decreases. From what has been said it is clear that employment expansion may be expected to be concentrated in different industrial classifications in different stages of growth of a city. As the metropolitan economy grows larger the development of external economies and increase in market size should be evident in an increasingly important role of business services in the growth process. These industrial categories may be expected to increase their share of total employment and, as they do so, their share of job increases.

There is good reason to expect that among size categories of metropolitan economies there will be a difference in the importance of industrial classifications as sources of employment change. Not only do metropolitan economies change their functions as they grow but there are both economies and diseconomies of scale which are operative. In particular, it is likely that job decreases will be relatively more important in the large metropolises where the constraints of size exert the greatest influence. It is a major objective of the empirical analysis which follows to reveal as clearly as possible the characteristic patterns of employment structure and change in MLM's of different sizes.

Size of place is clearly not the only factor which acts to shape the patterns of employment structure and change, however. A nodal city of a given size would be expected to be characterized by a different pattern of growth than would, for example, a manufacturing city. It follows, therefore, that there should be differences among types of MLM both in terms of employment structure and in terms of patterns of job increase and decrease.

Still another implication of the previous discussion is that cities should become more alike as they become larger. We have seen that as nodal cities grow, specialized "exporters" may be expected to be attracted by external economies, by the breadth of the labor market, and by other factors. On the other hand, as non-nodal cities grow they are more likely to take on nodal functions. In both instances, growth and development acts to reduce dissimilarity because the cities involved increasingly are able to take on functions previously performed only by cities located at higher levels of the hierarchy.

In the next five chapters, the analysis proceeds as follows. First, we turn our attention to the tendency of employment structure and change to vary with size of place. Analysis of structure by size-of-place categories is presented in chapter 4; analysis of change by size-of-place categories appears in chapter 5.

A second stage of the analysis begins with chapter 6 where the structural relationships which exist among industrial classifications at the MLM level are examined and a classification of the individual MLM's according to both function and size based on the evidence of the employment data is presented. Following this we examine employment change in chapters 7 and 8, making use of the dual classification system of MLM's devised in chapter 6.

4 VARIATIONS IN EMPLOYMENT STRUCTURE AMONG SIZE-OF-PLACE CATEGORIES, 1960

SIZE-RELATED CHARACTERISTICS of cities have been investigated only rather recently, and the literature on the subject is not extensive. Sargent P. Florence was the first to emphasize the role of size in a city; Duncan and Reiss examined some of the social characteristics of size; and Victor Fuchs has investigated the role of SMSA size in the differences in wage levels.[1] Since there has not been any systematic analysis of employment structure and change viewed in terms of size, we present our findings relating to size alone before proceeding to an analysis based on a more detailed classification scheme in which each MLM is classified according to both type (i.e., major function) and size.[2]

The traditional approach in examining employment composition and change has been to disaggregate the nation into regional divisions and, if further detail is desired, to divide the regions into individual states.[3] Although we do not deny the validity of the regional concept,

[1] Sargent P. Florence, *Investment, Location, and Size of Plant* (Cambridge, Cambridge University Press, 1948); Òtis D. Duncan and Albert J. Reiss, *Social Characteristics of Urban and Rural Communities, 1950* (New York, Wiley, 1956); Victor R. Fuchs, *Differentials in Hourly Earnings by Region and City Size* (New York, Columbia University Press for National Bureau of Economic Research, occasional paper No. 101, 1967).

[2] See chapter 2 for definitions of MLM's and size categories.

[3] Harvey S. Perloff, *Regions, Resources, and Economic Growth* (Pittsburgh, Carnegie Institute Press and University of Pittsburgh Press, 1961); Lowell S. Ashby, *Growth Patterns in Employment by County, 1940-1950 and 1950-1960*, 8 vols. (Washington D.C., U.S. Dept. of Commerce, 1965); Victor R. Fuchs, *Changes in the Location of Manufacturing in the United States since 1929* (New Haven, Yale University Press, 1962).

we do question the usefulness of comparing states. Our approach, therefore, is to view the economy first as a system of metropolitan and nonmetropolitan places.

The Size Hierarchy of MLM's and the Significance of the Size Variable

It has been observed that in developed economies there is a hierarchy of cities which has the characteristic that as the size of city is doubled the number of cities in the size class is halved.[4] In this study the MLM rather than the city is the unit of investigation and the size hierarchy shown in Table 4.1 for MLM's is found in general to display this tendency. This hierarchy does not conform completely to the observed size relationship for cities mentioned above, because in many instances MLM's include small cities within the cluster of counties and such cities, therefore, lose their identity. The result is that in the hierarchy of MLM's, the smaller places tend to be underrepresented (e.g., there are relatively few MLM's with a population of 50,000 to 100,000).

In part, the explanation of this tendency toward size hierarchy would appear to lie in the type of functions performed by a metropolis in the overall economy. A clustering of national financial and commercial activities in New York, of federal governmental activities in Washington D.C. or of the nation's motor vehicle manufacturing in Detroit will make for a large MLM. A clustering of regional activities and/or decentralized offices and branches of national firms or the federal government will make for a medium-size MLM, and the combination of local activities along with a narrower selection of regional or national activities, for a small-size MLM. The number of large MLM's is bound to be small since there are only a limited number of services or manufactures produced for such extensive markets.

Of course, there are other factors contributing to or limiting the

[4] Brian J. L. Berry, "City Size Distribution and Economic Development," reprinted from *Economic Development and Cultural Change*, Vol. IX (July 1961), in *Regional Development and Planning*, John Friedman and William Alonso, eds. (Cambridge, MIT Press, 1964).

TABLE 4.1

Size Distribution of MLM's, Regional and National, 1960[a]

Size of MLM by 1960 population	National	Regional								
		New England	Mideast	Great Lakes	Plains	Southeast	Southwest	Rocky Mtns.	Far West	Alaska and Hawaii
LARGE	13	1	6	3	1	—	—	—	2	—
Over 6,400,000	1	—	1	—	—	—	—	—	—	—
3,200,001 to 6,400,000	5	1	1	2	—	—	—	—	1	—
1,600,001 to 3,200,000	7	—	4	1	1	—	—	—	1	—
MEDIUM	114	7	19	21	6	32	13	2	13	1
800,001 to 1,600,000	17	—	2	3	2	3	2	1	4	—
400,001 to 800,000	39	6	6	8	1	8	5	1	3	1
200,001 to 400,000	58	1	11	10	3	21	6	—	6	—
SMALL	241	12	20	51	31	70	27	15	14	1
100,001 to 200,000	65	4	2	19	7	17	7	4	5	—
50,001 to 100,000	22	1	—	1	3	6	7	3	1	—
25,001 to 50,000	154	7	18	31	21	47	13	8	8	1
NMC[b]	2.541									

[a] All MLM's are SMSA's except the size category 25,001 to 50,000, which is comprised of single counties which are not a part of an SMSA according to Department of Commerce definition. Each of these latter counties containing a city of 25,001 or more population in 1960.

[b] Regional totals not computed.

size of metropolitan economies such as size of markets or economics of scale, which were mentioned earlier. Although we can only guess why certain activities tend to cluster in particular sized metropolises, we can identify these activities by analyzing the structure (i.e., composition) of employment by the different sizes of MLM's.

Our analysis focuses on the employment composition of various sizes of place, which may contribute to an understanding of the role of cities, and their hierarchical ordering may shed light on a number of characteristics of the labor market. For example, it is known that female participation rates are highest in the service industries, many of which our investigation will show tend to increase their proportion of total MLM employment with size of place. If employment composition varies significantly with size of place, we have reason to expect that other important characteristics such as the occupational skill mix or income per household will also tend to vary.

The Importance of NMC's and MLM's in the Determination of Regional Employment Structure

It is important to observe that the functions performed by metropolitan economies will be affected by their relationship to the NMC's and that, therefore, their employment structures will vary. The type of activity carried out in a region's metropolitan centers will reflect the amount and type of services which it is necessary for them to provide to other MLM's and NMC's in their hinterlands. Thus where the NMC's are important in a region, they will play a major role in determining the structure of the economies of many (if not all) of the metropolitan centers.

In 1960 the NMC's accounted for 25.4 percent of the nation's employment and for 69.8 percent of its employment in primary (i.e., agriculture, forestry, fisheries, mining) activities. The importance of these counties varied greatly by region, ranging from 51.5 percent of employment in the Plains to 10.2 percent in the Mideast region.

We observe in Table 4.2 that where agriculture plays a major role in the entire region's economy (i.e., where percentage of regional employment in agriculture is high) the percentage of regional employment in the NMC's is large.[5] Moreover, the industrial composition of the NMC's, themselves, is predominantly agricultural.

Since agriculture is a very dispersed activity, these metropolitan places supplying the necessary goods and services tend to be small and to be dispersed geographically.[6] This scattering of small cities

[5] Table 4.2 shows measures for 1950 rather than for 1960. The year 1950 was chosen because it marked a midpoint during the period 1940-60.

[6] Some manufacturing, such as textiles in the Southeast, is also dispersed.

TABLE 4.2
Percent of Employment in NMC's, by Region

Region[a]	NMC's	Agriculture		Manufacturing		Large MLM's
		Region	NMC's	Region	NMC's	
Plains	51.5	24.6	41.7	15.3	7.5	10.5
(excluding St. Louis)	(57.5)	(27.2)	(41.7)	(13.3)	(7.5)	—
Rocky Mountains	51.1	18.3	29.4	10.3	7.0	—
Southeast	50.7	21.7	35.6	19.3	17.1	—
Southwest	38.3	16.4	31.0	11.7	8.1	—
Great Lakes	22.1	8.1	26.0	35.0	22.5	35.6
Far West	14.4	7.9	20.2	19.2	19.3	44.7
New England	11.8	3.5	13.0	38.0	34.1	32.7
Mideast	10.2	3.4	13.6	31.4	26.2	59.3

[a] Regions arranged according to percentage of regional employment in NMC's.

over the rural landscape seems to place a limit on the size of the largest metropolis in a region. As can be noted in Table 4.2 (last column) there were no MLM's with a 1960 population of over 1,600,000 in the four regions where the NMC's were most important (i.e., Plains, Rocky Mountains, Southeast, Southwest).[7]

Where manufacturing tends to be important a larger share of the region's total employment is located in the MLM's (a smaller share in the NMC's). At the same time, manufacturing also comprises a relatively large share of hinterland activities. Not unexpectedly, this concentration of manufacturing employment in both metropolitan and nonmetropolitan places forms the basis for larger MLM's than would otherwise be possible, since economic activity is less dispersed. Large-size MLM's are found mainly in regions where manufacturing dominates.

A further observation is that the presence or absence of a large

[7] This statement excludes the population which lies within the three counties of the St. Louis SMSA that are technically within the Plains region. The St. Louis SMSA lies at the Southeast corner of the Plains region and two of its five counties are in the Great Lakes region.

metropolitan center may, in turn, have an important impact on the development of a region. If certain business services are found only in large metropolises then regions with no such metropolises have to import these business services, get along with inferior services, or do without them altogether. Therefore, there are certain costs for a region which are incident to remoteness from major metropolitan centers. Moreover, the importation of specialized services represents an income leakage from the region.

Regions seeking to encourage the development of business services face the problem that such services tend to require highly skilled manpower, very often of professional grade. Such persons prefer to reside in those centers offering a variety of amenities. The dilemma faced by regions that have no large metropolitan centers is that they not only have difficulty attracting specialized business services firms, but that without them, development is made more difficult. Necessary services either are not available or are available only at high cost.

To sum up, regions which do not have large metropolitan centers will tend to be deficient in those business services found only in large places, consequently missing out both in respect to this critical type of employment expansion and to the associated secondary, amplifying effects. Inasmuch as these services are imported, the primary and secondary effects of increased purchases of such services will all be realized outside of the region in which the demand for the services originates.

Differences in the size distribution of MLM's by region are quite striking. While 33 percent of the employed labor force in New England resides in the Boston MLM, only 3 percent of the employed labor force in the Southeast reside in that region's largest MLM, Atlanta. Until recently, the Southeast has been dependent on the large metropolitan centers in other regions for many financial, advertising, engineering and professional services. One of the most interesting aspects of recent development is that certain types of the medium-size MLM's which have grown rapidly have moved toward the increased provision of such services.

Size-of-Place Differences in Composition
of Work Force: National

The above discussion raises the question of comparability of regions. To make valid comparisons, the size distribution of labor markets must be accounted for. Though employment mix in two regions may vary considerably, employment mix in MLM's in the same size group should be more comparable. Part of the regional variation in employment structure should be explainable in terms of variations in the proportions of employment in NMC's and MLM's of various size categories. The system of cities that binds the region together should reflect the type of activity that is taking place within the regional grid.

In the remainder of this chapter the investigation is restricted to an analysis of the employment composition of the labor force in different size groups of MLM's measured in terms of industry classifications. Such an analysis makes clear that the industrial composition of MLM's vary significantly with size of place, and that the differences found in the national size-of-place data tend also to be found within each region.

Perhaps of greater interest for subsequent discussion of the employment characteristics of MLM's is the manner in which the relative importance (i.e., the percentages of total employment) of business and consumer services changes with increasing size of place. The mainly business service category increases progressively, rising from 10.5 percent in the NMC category to 18.7 percent in the large MLM category (Table 4.3). The characteristic is found for every component of mainly business services (transportation, communications, wholesale, FIRE, and business/repair services.)

On the other hand, the mainly consumer services category is largest in the small MLM's. This characteristic is found in the two largest components of the consumer services—retail and medical/educational services—and in the recreation/entertainment category. It is not found in the private household services classification, however, where employment decreases in importance with size of place.

Manufacturing appears to comprise an increasingly large per-

TABLE 4.3

Industrial Structure of Employment in Each Size-of-Place-Category, National, 1960

| | Total Employment | | | |
| | NMC's | MLM's | | |
		Small	Medium	Large
Primary	20.7	7.1	3.4	1.0
Construction	6.3	6.0	6.1	4.8
Manufacturing	21.0	25.1	27.5	30.2
Utilities	1.3	1.4	1.4	1.3
Mainly business services	10.5	13.4	16.4	18.7
Transportation	3.4	3.9	4.4	4.6
Communications	0.9	1.2	1.3	1.5
Wholesale	2.3	3.0	3.8	3.9
FIRE	2.2	3.3	4.5	5.6
Business/repair	1.8	2.1	2.5	3.1
Mainly consumer services	31.5	34.8	32.8	31.7
Retail	14.3	15.0	14.8	13.9
Recreation/entertainment	3.2	4.0	3.8	3.9
Private household	3.5	3.4	2.8	2.2
Medical/education	10.4	12.4	11.5	11.7
Government	6.2	9.0	8.4	7.0
Administration	3.8	4.5	5.2	5.5
Armed forces	2.4	4.5	3.2	1.5
INR	2.6	3.1	4.1	5.3
Total	100.0	100.0	100.0	100.0

centage of total employment as we examine, successively, the NMC's and the larger size categories. We may not consider this pattern as representative, however, since the analysis in the following section fails to uncover well-established size-of-place tendencies at the regional level.

When we turn to the government-associated services the two components, administration and armed forces, are found to have quite different structure characteristics. In the former, the percentage of total employment increases in importance with size of place. In the latter classification, which relates largely to military bases, the largest percentage is found in the small MLM's. The percentage declines progressively in the medium- and large-size MLM's.

In examining these size-of-place differences in labor force composition, it is important to keep in mind the classic dictum of Adam Smith that "the division of labor (i.e., specialization) is dependent upon the extent of the market." Although the percentage of employment in a given industrial classification provides an indication of the importance of an economic function in a city, it does not provide a very clear indication of the level of specialization at which the function is carried out. For example, the extent of specialization in finance, insurance, and real estate in the very large cities is likely to be much greater than in the smaller cities, not simply because share of employment is larger but also because these large cities are large markets themselves and because they serve other markets. To a very important degree these activities are carried out in forms which offer a much greater expertise than is available in the smaller places. In a similar fashion, retail stores, recreation activities, and medical centers are likely to be more specialized in large-size MLM's than in small.

SIZE-OF-PLACE DIFFERENCES IN COMPOSITION OF WORK FORCE: REGIONAL[8]

The analysis of size-of-place differences in the composition of the employed work force *within* regions makes use of ranks to indicate for each industrial classification the importance of the classification (based on percentage of total employment accounted for by that classification) in one size of place relative to its importance in the others. Size-of-place categories were ranked within each region for each industrial classification.[9] For example, in the New England region the percentage of the labor force in mainly business services in the large-size category is highest; in the medium-size category, second highest;

---

[8] Hawaii and Alaska are not included in this regional analysis.

[9] In an effort to adjust for error due to overreporting of employment within the INR category, INR employment was redistributed pro rata among the remaining industrial classifications and the regional size-of-place categories were reranked. Revised rankings are shown in parenthesis. This adjustment altered none of the findings set forth herein. See Appendix B.

in the small-size category, next to lowest; in the NMC category, lowest.

The evidence for selected industrial classifications is presented for each region and for the nation in Table 4.4. The highest percentages are given the most favorable ranks.[10] Taken as a whole, the measures of rank indicate a marked tendency for regional size-of-place patterns of employment composition to be similar to those found at the national level. The prevalence of this tendency in spite of the differences among regions in the size distribution of MLM's and the dissimilarities in compositon of total regional employment is indicative of the pervasiveness of size-of-place tendencies in employment composition.

Mainly business services. The tendency for percentage of employment in the mainly business services category to increase with size of place which was so prominent in the national data is observed in every region with the single exception of the Plains. Here the percentage in the large-size MLM category is somewhat below that for the medium-size category, but this exception represents only the single MLM, St. Louis, which is characterized by a relatively heavy concentration of employment in manufacturing, and in some respects is more a part of the Great Lakes than the Plains region.

Within the mainly business services category this pattern is found

---

[10] To insure comparability between regions with large cities and those without, numbers have been used to rank the positions of NMC, small- and medium-size MLM categories in relation to each other; but letters have been used to rank the large city category relative to the other categories. The system employed is simple: the NMC, small-size MLM, and medium-size MLM are first ranked in relationship to one another. In the example of New England above, the medium-size MLM category would be given the rank of 1 (first), the small-size MLM category 2 (second), the NMC category 3 (third). The large-size MLM category would then be assigned an alphabetical designation of A, indicating that the percentage of employment in mainly business services was greater than any of the other three size categories. If the large-size MLM percentage had been second largest, however, it would have been assigned the alphabetical designation B (falling behind rank 1 but ahead of rank 2 in the remaining categories). If it had been the third largest, it would have been assigned the designation C (falling behind rank 2 but ahead of rank 3). If it had been smallest, it would have been assigned the designation D.

TABLE 4.4

Employment Structure as a Function of Size: Size-of-Place Categories Ranked According to Percentage of Employment in Selected Industrial Classifications, Regional and National, 1960

	All U.S.	New England	Mideast	Great Lakes	Plains	South-east	South-west	Rocky Mtns.	Far West
Mainly business services									
NMC's	3	3	3	3	3	3	3	3	3
Small-size	2	2	2	2	2	2	2	2	2
Medium-size	1	1	1	1	1	1	1	1	1
Large-size	A	A	A	A	B	—	—	—	A
Mainly consumer services									
NMC's	3	1	2	3	3	3	2-3(3)	3	2
Small-size	1	2	1	1	1	1	1(2)	1	1
Medium-size	2	3	3	2	2	2	2-3(1)	2	3
Large-size	D	A	A	D	D	—	—	—	C
Retail									
NMC's	3	2-3	2	1(1-2)	3	3	1	2(3)	1
Small-size	1	1	1	2-3(3)	1	2	2(3)	1	2
Medium-size	2	2-3	3	2-3(1-2)	2	1	3(2)	3(2)	3
Large-size	D	A	D[a](B)	D	D	—	—	—	D(C)
Medical/education									
NMC's	3	1-2	2	3	3	3	3	3	3
Small-size	1	1-2	1	1	1	1	1-2(2)	1-2(2)	1-2(1)
Medium-size	2	3	3	2	2	2	1-2(1)	1-2(1)	1-2(2)
Large-size	B	A	A[b]	D(C)	D	—	—	—	A[b]

Construction									
NMC's	1	1	1	1	2(3)	3	3	2(3)	1(1-2)
Small-size	2-3	2	2	3	1	3	1	1	2(1-2)
Medium-size	2-3	3	3	2	3(2)	2	2	3(2)	3
Large-size	D	C	D	D	D	—	—	—	D
Manufacturing									
NMC's	3	2(2-3)	3	3	3	3	2	3	2
Small-size	2	3(2-3)	2	2	2	2	3	2	3
Medium-size	1	1	1	1	1	1	1	1	1
Large-size	A	D	D	B(A)	A	—	—	—	A
Government Administration									
NMC's	3	2	3	2-3(2)	3	3	3	3	3
Small-size	2	1	2	2-3(3)	2	2	2	2	2
Medium-size	1	3	1	1	1	1	1	1	1
Large-size	A	A	B	B	B(A)	—	—	—	D
Armed Forces									
NMC's	3	2	1	3	2	3	3	3	3
Small-size	1	1	2	1	1	1	2	1	1
Medium-size	2	3	3	2	3	2	1	2	2
Large-size	D	C	B	A[b]	D	—	—	—	D

Note: Since some regions have no large-size MLM's, only the NMC's, the small-size, and the medium-size MLM's have been ranked by number—1, 2, or 3 (to indicate first, second, and third). Where there are large-size MLM's in a region, letters are used to rank them: the letter "A" ranks ahead of 1; the letter "B" ahead of 2; the letter "C" ahead of 3; and the letter "D" after 3.

Numbers or letters in parentheses show ranks which have been altered as a result of distributing INR employment *pro rata* among remaining classifications. See Appendix B for discussion. The national data were not adjusted.

[a] Same percentage as NMC.

[b] Same percentage as small-size MLM category.

in the FIRE and business repair services classifications, and, with one variation, in the wholesale classification.[11] In transportation we observe departures from the national pattern for several of the regions, but there is, nevertheless, a tendency for percentage share of employment to increase with size of place.

Mainly consumer services. In the mainly consumer services, although there are exceptions, the regional patterns tended in 1960 to conform to that of the nation: the share of employment accounted for by consumer services is typically highest in the small MLM's, second highest in the medium-size MLM's, followed by the NMC's and large-size MLM's.

From 1940 to 1960 the percentage of employment in the consumer services tended to rise sharply in the NMC's, to increase relatively less in the small-size MLM's and to decline in the medium-size and large-size MLM's.[12] The net effect of these changes was to alter the typical structure from one in which the percentage of employment in consumer services was larger the larger the size of place to one in which the pattern is as described above.

The two consumer services which contribute most to the observed size-of-place characteristics of the mainly consumer services category in 1960 are retailing and medical/educational services. Although in retailing a strong tendency for employment to increase with size of place had existed almost everywhere in 1940, this tendency is observed only in the Southeast two decades later. There is considerable variation in the 1960 regional patterns, but, clearly, the large metropolis is no longer characterized by relatively high percentages of employment in retailing. It is the small-size MLM's which most often ranks first, with the NMC category ranking second or better in more than half the regions.

In medical/educational services, the most typical pattern in 1960

[11] Rankings for the industrial classifications mentioned in this paragraph are not shown in Table 4.4.

[12] In the present section references to earlier periods are based on data not presented in Table 4.4.

was one in which percentage of employment in this classification was highest in the small MLM's and tended to lie in an intermediate position in the NMC's and medium-size MLM's. The position of the large-city categories varied. In New England, Mideast, and Far West the large-size MLM categories (influenced largely by the structures of Boston, New York, Philadelphia, San Francisco) ranked at the top among the size categories. In the Great Lakes and Plains (in a considerable measure because of the influence of Chicago and St. Louis) it ranked at the bottom.[13] Although the medical/educational services showed lower percentages of employment in the NMC's than in the small-size MLM's in 1960 just as had been the case in 1940, the differences were less than those observed at the earlier date.

Thus we see that employment concentration in both of these two important consumer services classifications had increased in the NMC's throughout the nation from 1940 to 1960. This development would appear to be the result of a combination of several fairly obvious factors. The first is simply the increase in size of markets everywhere with growth in population. Whereas, in 1940 it was not possible to establish large retail establishments in nonmetropolitan locations, in 1960 it was not only possible but necessary. Moreover, with increased urbanization of the NMC's there was a rapid development in the hospital and public school systems as well as in the colleges and universities. Everywhere, the growth in population was accompanied by increases in per capita income, with a resultant sharp increase not only in the effective demand for retail and medical/educational services but in the economic capability of the less-urbanized areas to provide such services locally.

Construction.   The apparent tendency for structure to decline as size of place increases, which is observed in the national data, is found in the Mideast, Great Lakes, New England, and Far West only. There does appear to be a general tendency for the percentage of employment in construction, however, to be smaller in the large city category. Per-

[13] Another factor was also the tendency of large state universities of the middle western states to be located in rural settings.

haps this is due in part to the use of much more elaborate equipment (i.e., higher capital to labor ratio) in metropolitan construction work. It is possible that it is due also to slower rates of total employment growth in the large city category or to a tendency for certain types of construction workers (e.g., highway construction) to be domiciled outside metropolitan areas.[14]

Manufacturing.   For the nation as a whole the 1960 data indicate a tendency for percentage of employment in manufacturing to increase with size of place. Among the regions the medium-size MLM's tend to rank higher than the small-size MLM's and the NMC's, but there is no well-developed tendency for the percentage to be largest in the large-size MLM category. The latter has higher percentages of employment in manufacturing than does the medium-size MLM category in only two regions, the Plains and the Far West. It is interesting that in the Southeast the percentage of employment in manufacturing is highest in the NMC's. In a large measure this reflects the importance of the textile and lumber/furniture industries.

Administration.   The size-of-place data for the nation as a whole indicates that the percentage of persons employed in administration tends to be progressively larger with increases in size of place. This pattern exists for only four of the eight national regions, however. It is inapplicable or only partially applicable in New England, Great Lakes, Plains, and the Far West.

Armed Forces.   In armed services there is considerable variation among regions in terms of patterns of structure in the size-of-place categories. In general, it is the small-size MLM category that ranks highest in percentage of persons employed in the armed forces. In three of the four regions for which the armed services is most important in terms of its percentage of total employment (i.e., the Southwest, Rocky Mountain, and Far West) the small-size MLM's rank first and the medium-size category ranks second in structure.

[14] For evidence based on regression analysis, see chapter 7.

REGIONAL DIFFERENCES IN COMPOSITION OF WORK FORCE
WITHIN SIZE-OF-PLACE CATEGORIES

In chapter 2 we saw that in 1960 there remained fundamental differences in the employment compositon of regions even after two decades of change had tended to result in increased similarity. In the present section we seek to determine whether or not consistent regional differences in employment composition appear *within* each of the size-of-place categories.

Our test is simply to rank the regions separately for each size-of-place category according to percentage of each region's employment in three major industrial categories: manufacturing, mainly business services, and mainly consumer services. These rankings are presented in Table 4.5. For convenience of analysis the regions are arranged in the table according to the percentage of the total (regional) employment accounted for by manufacturing, indicating thereby, at least from a manpower point of view, the extent of industrialization.

It will be seen that there are certain regional characteristics which are similar for most of the size-of-place categories. The evidence is found in the similarity of regional rankings among size-of-place categories when comparisons are made for a given industrial category.

We note first that there is a strong tendency for the regions which rank highest in overall industrialization (i.e., in total regional percentage of employment in manufacturing) to rank highest in percentage of employment in manufacturing in most of the size-of-place categories. In short, the tendency toward industrialization is found in both metropolitan and nonmetropolitan places.

We note further that the most industrialized regions tend to have the lowest ranks in business and consumer services and that this inverted ranking relationship is found in both metropolitan and nonmetropolitan places.

The extent of the tendency for regional differences in structure to be found in every size of place is indicated by measures of rank correlation. For each industrial classification the rankings of the various regions in each size-of-place category are correlated with similar

TABLE 4.5

Regional Comparisons of Employment in Manufacturing, Mainly Business Services (MBS), and Mainly Consumer Services (MCS) in Each Size-of-Place Category, 1960[a]

Region	NMC			Small-size			Medium-size			Large-size			Total region		
	Mfg.	MBS	MCS	Mfg.	MBS	MCS	Mfg.	MBS	MCS	Mfg.	MBS	MCS	Mfg.	MBS	MCS
New England	1	7	6	2	8	8	1	8	8	3	5	2	1	7	8
Great Lakes	3	6	7	1	7	6	3	7	6	1	4	5	2	6	7
Mideast	2	5	5	3	4	7	2	6	7	4	1	3	3	1	6
Far West	5	2	3	6	5	5	5	5	5	5	2	1	4	2	4
Southeast	4	8	8	4	6	3	6	4	2	—	—	4	5	8	5
Plains	6	3	4	5	2	1	4	1	4	2	3	—	6	5	3
Southwest	7	4	1	8	3	4	8	3	3	—	—	—	7	4	2
Rocky Mountains	8	1	2	7	1	2	7	2	1	—	—	—	8	3	1

TABLE 4.5a

Rank Correlation of Regional Rankings in Each Size-of-Place Category: Matrices of Coefficients

	NMC's	Small-size	Medium-size	Large-size
Manufacturing				
NMC's	X	.88	.88	−.1
Small-size	.88	X	.86	.7
Medium-size	.88	.86	X	.2
Large-size	−.1	.7	.2	X
Mainly business services				
NMC's	X	.79	.60	.7
Small-size	.79	X	.88	.7
Medium-size	.60	.88	X	.6
Large-size	.7	.7	.6	X
Mainly consumer services				
NMC's	X	.33	.36	.6
Small-size	.33	X	.86	−.2
Medium-size	.36	.86	X	−.2
Large-size	.6	−.2	−.2	X

[a] Regions are arranged according to the percentage of the total (regional) employment in *manufacturing*. Columns show rankings based on percentage in manufacturing, mainly business, and mainly consumer services.

regional rankings in every other size-of-place category and the coefficients of rank correlation are presented in matrix form.[15]

For the industry matrix as a whole the highest rank correlations are found in the case of the mainly business services. In this industrial category the rank correlation coefficients are .60 or better in every case. In short, regional rankings based on percentage of employment in mainly business services are very similar in each of the size-of-place categories.

In the manufacturing matrix the coefficients are even higher, except in cases where large-size MLM rankings are compared to those of other size categories. Here coefficients range from −.1 to .7. This indicates that regions that are heavily industrialized tend to rank high in percentage of employment in manufacturing in the NMC, in the small- and medium-size MLM category but that the tendency toward relatively large percentages of employment in manufacturing in the large-size MLM category is not well established. Examples of this lack of consistency are found in the fact that in New England, which ranks first in regional concentration of manufacturing employment, the large-size MLM category ranks third (among the five regions with large

[15] As an example of the procedure followed the rankings of percentages of employment in *manufacturing* and the coefficient of rank correlation are shown for comparison between the NMC and small-size MLM categories (regions are arranged in order of percentage of total manufacturing employment):

Region	Rank	
	NMC	Small-Size MLM
New England	1	2
Great Lakes	3	1
Mideast	2	3
Far West	5	6
Southeast	4	4
Plains	6	5
Southwest	7	8
Rocky Mountains	8	7
Coefficient of rank correlation .88		

cities); and in the Plains, which ranks fifth, the large-size MLM category ranks second.

It is in the mainly consumer services matrix that the correlations are poorest. The rankings of the small- and medium-size MLM's are rather closely correlated, but the other coefficients are smaller than most of those found in the business services and manufacturing matrixes. We must conclude that the regional size characteristics relating to structure of consumer services are not so clearly established as they are for business services and manufacturing.

These findings should be interpreted in the light of the evidence presented in the previous section. What we are observing now is that where a region as a whole ranks high (or low) relative to other regions in say, mainly business services, it tends to rank high (or low) in most of the size-of-place categories *within* that region. For example, each of the regions showed a strong tendency for percentage of employment in mainly business service to increase with size of place (Table 4.4). Yet the heavily industrialized regions show a well-developed tendency in *each* size-of-place category (except the large-size MLM) for percentage of employment in mainly business services to be relatively low when compared with the same size-of-place category in the other regions.

This suggests that the importance of employment in the services is strongly influenced by whether or not manufacturing is an important basic industry. The evidence would seem to indicate that manufacturing requires fewer business services from outside the firm than do primary or other basic activities. This may be in part due to the fact that manufacturing firms *internalize* the production of services (i.e., produce them within the firm either locally or at distant headquarters offices), that manufacturing firms require fewer services, or both.

Moreover, in the less-industrialized areas, where primary activities dominate, firms are more likely to make use of external suppliers of services. It is not unlikely also that under conditions of wide dispersal of both population and firms in these areas, the provision of both consumer and producer services may be less efficient and less subject to economies of scale, resulting in the need for relatively greater employment in service activities.

SUMMARY

We have examined the system of NMC's and various-size MLM's which exists in the nation and regions. We note that the importance of NMC's varies among regions, and that where they are important agricultural employment is relatively large, MLM's tend to be small and scattered, and there are no large cities. On the other hand, where the NMC's are relatively unimportant, employment tends to be concentrated in industrial activities. It is in these latter regions that large metropolitan economies have developed.

In the latter part of the chapter, 1960 employment composition is analyzed by size-of-place category. This analysis yields two general findings. The first is that there are well-defined tendencies for industrial composition of employment to vary according to size of place. The tendency is best established for the business services classification where, with only minor exceptions, percentages increase with size of place. For consumer services the tendency is for the share of total employment to be highest in small-size MLM's, second highest in medium-size MLM's, followed by NMC's and large-size MLM's in that order.

For the most part the tendencies noted for mainly consumer services apply for the two largest consumer classifications, retailing and medical/educational services, but are less applicable for recreation services and private household services. In manufacturing the regional size-of-place data reveal a strong tendency for medium-size MLM's to rank higher than small-size MLM's and NMC's, but there is no well-developed tendency for the large-size MLM category.

The second general finding is that there is a very strong tendency toward consistency in regional rankings *within* the NMC, the small-, and the medium-size MLM categories (e.g., when comparisons are made on the basis of percentage of employment in a specific classification a given region tends to show about the same rank among regions in the small-size MLM as in the medium-size MLM category). Regional structural characteristics are less well defined in the large-size MLM's.

The significance of this second general finding is that it indicates that there are variables *in addition to size* which influence the employment structure of the NMC's and the MLM's. It seems reasonable to suppose that they are associated with differences in functions performed within the regional economies. In general, we find that in those regions in which manufacturing is important the proportion of employment in the services tends to be smaller in all of the size categories than in those regions where agriculture is important. We suggest that this may be due to the fact that in less-industrialized areas, where primary activities are important, firms are more likely to make use of external sources for their business services. Moreover, both individuals and businesses are more widely dispersed, and the provision of both consumer and producer services may be less efficient and less subject to economies of scale.

5 VARIATIONS IN EMPLOYMENT CHANGE
AMONG SIZE-OF-PLACE CATEGORIES

IN CHAPTER 4 we examined variations in employment structure among the size-of-place categories in 1960 and found fundamental differences. This leads us to expect that growth characteristics will also vary by size of place. In this chapter we examine the variations in employment change for the years preceding 1960, focusing attention largely on the 1950-60 decade.

We make use of two principal types of measures. The first is a measure of decadal rates of job increases, job decreases, and net employment change. The second, of shares of job increases and of job decreases accounted for by each industrial classification. Both types are employed for each size-of-place category within the nation and within each region.

RATES OF EMPLOYMENT CHANGE,
NATIONAL AND REGIONAL, 1950-1960

The bare outlines of the processes of employment change may be discerned in the chart. Rates of job increases tend to rise as we move progressively from the NMC's to the small- and medium-size MLM's, but are lower for the large-size MLM's than for the medium- or small-size MLM's. There are exceptions, however. In New England, the Mideast, and the Plains, rates of job increases were higher in the small-than in the medium-size MLM's. Nevertheless, taking the nation as a whole, the pattern was quite well established.

In the Southeast and Southwest, rates of job decreases are high in the NMC's and rates of job increases are high in the MLM's, indi-

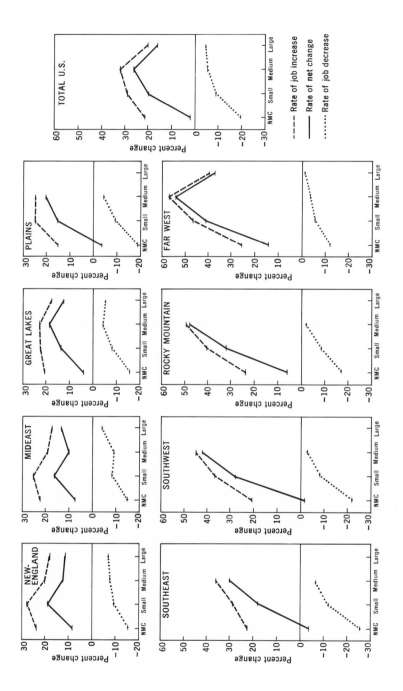

Regional and National Employment Change: Rates of Job Increases and Job Decreases, and Net Employment Change, by Size of MLM, 1950-1960

cating rural to urban migration. The Plains, another highly agricultural region, appears to be undergoing much less of an urbanization
movement. Here, the rates of job decreases in the NMC's are slightly
less than in the Southeast and Southwest, and rates of job increases in
the small- and medium-size MLM's are well below. Further west, in
the Rocky Mountains and Far West Regions, the rates of job increases
were relatively high in all size places reflecting the general tendency
toward an east-to-west migration in the United States. In the manufacturing regions of Great Lakes, New England, and the Mideast, the
pattern was mixed.

Employment changes occurring in the NMC's reveal much about
the kind of factors at play in a region (Table 5.1). The rate of job
decrease in agriculture, the key NMC industry, varied widely. It was
highest in the Southeast and Southwest (50 percent and 44 percent),
regions in transition, and lowest in the Far West (21 percent), a
region where large-scale, capital-intensive agricultural methods are
common. Decadal rates of job decreases in agriculture in the other
regions varied between 30 percent and 37 percent. There was little
correlation between the importance of agriculture in a region and the
rate of job decrease in agriculture, however. For example, the rate of
job decrease was relatively low in the Plains, the region with the
highest share of employment in agriculture.

The transition within the NMC's is also reflected in the measures
of job increases and decreases for manufacturing (Table 5.1). In all
but the Far West region, manufacturing's share of job increases in the
NMC's was larger than the share of total employment accounted for
by that classification at the beginning of the decade. Only in New
England was the share of job decreases due to manufacturing larger
than the percent of employment in that category at the beginning of
the decade. The net result was a shift toward an increased share of
NMC employment in manufacturing. The percentage of total NMC
employment accounted for by manufacturing was larger in 1960 than
in 1950 in all but two of the eight regions.

The transition of the NMC's from agricultural to manufacturing
activities was most prominent in the Southeast region, which had the
highest regional share of job decreases in agriculture and next to the

TABLE 5.1

Measures of Industrial Transition in NMC's: Employment Structure and Rates of Job Increases/Job Decreases for Agriculture and Manufacturing, 1950-1960

	Agriculture[a]				Manufacturing					
	% Employment		Decreases, 1950-60		% Employment		Increases, 1950-60		Decreases, 1950-60	
	1950	1960	rate	share	1950	1960	rate	share	rate	share
New England	13.0	7.5	37.0	31.6	34.1	33.8	26.6	37.5	18.7	42.1
Mideast	13.6	8.2	35.3	31.7	26.2	29.2	29.5	34.6	10.1	17.4
Great Lakes	26.0	15.6	37.5	59.0	22.5	28.0	38.6	42.1	9.0	12.2
Plains	41.7	29.8	32.2	67.3	7.5	11.1	52.3	26.0	11.5	4.3
Southeast	35.6	18.2	50.0	70.9	17.7	23.9	45.7	35.1	13.5	9.6
Southwest	31.0	18.0	43.8	62.6	8.1	10.6	50.7	19.8	21.6	8.1
Rocky Mtns.	29.4	19.4	30.3	50.1	7.0	9.8	61.7	18.2	12.9	5.1
Far West	20.2	14.8	20.5	34.9	19.3	19.0	23.3	17.5	11.6	18.8
All U.S.	12.0	6.4	38.9	46.9	25.4	26.4	27.8	27.7	7.8	20.0

[a] Rates and shares of job increases in agriculture are not shown since for every region and for the nation the rate of increase is negligible.

highest share of job increases in manufacturing. In New England, a transition was taking place within the manufacturing sector, which accounted for 38 percent of the job increases and 42 percent of the job decreases. In general, the rates of increases in manufacturing were highest in those regions where the share of employment in the sector had been lowest at the beginning of the decade: e.g., 62 percent in the Rocky Mountains, where manufacturing structure was 7.0 percent in 1950; 52.3 percent in the Plains, where the structure had been 7.5 percent; and 50.7 percent in the Southwest, where the structure had been 8.1 percent. The rate of job increases in manufacturing was considerably lower in regions where the sector had played a greater role in 1950, e.g., 26.6 percent in New England, 29.5 percent in the Mideast, and 38.6 percent in the Great Lakes, which had respectively, 34.1 percent, 26.2 percent, and 22.5 percent of employment in manufacturing at the start of the decade.

Variations in Number of Job Increases and Job Decreases: National

We must keep in mind that the rate of change statistics fail to show the importance of the size-of-place categories as sources of job increases and decreases. When actual numbers of job increases and decreases within the national economy (1950-60) are examined, we find that relative positions of certain of the size-of-place categories are changed significantly:

Size-of-place category	Job increases* (in 000's)	Job decreases* (in 000's)	Net change (in 000's)
NMC	3,489.7 (2)	3,367.9 (1)	121.8
Small-size MLM's	2,133.5 (4)	676.6 (4)	1,456.9
Medium-size MLM's	5,526.7 (1)	965.6 (2)	4,561.1
Large-size MLM's	3,490.1 (3)	732.9 (3)	2,757.2

* Numbers in parentheses are ranks.

For job increases the NMC and large-size MLM's categories are no longer found to have ranked behind the small-size MLM category as they did when measured in terms of rate of change. Now they rank second and third respectively among all size-of-place categories with the medium-size MLM continuing to hold the first position. For job decreases the data for numbers of employees serves to emphasize the importance of the NMC's as the major source of employment contraction within the economy.

SHARES OF JOB INCREASES AND JOB DECREASES: NATIONAL AND REGIONAL
HIGHLIGHTS FOR THE NATION

For the nation as a whole the various size-of-place categories tend to show significant differences in shares of job increases and job decreases accounted for by the various industrial classifications, particularly the business and consumer services. These shares are shown for the period 1950-60 in Table 5.2.

Business and consumer services. The fast-growing medium-size MLM category is found to have a relatively large share of job increases in the business services and the same is true for the important but slower growing large MLM category. On the other hand, the small-size MLM's and, to an even greater degree, the NMC's have relatively small shares of job increases accounted for by the business services.

For the mainly consumer services category the pattern is quite different: percentages tend to be lower in the large-size MLM's than in the small. The patterns vary to some extent among the component industrial classifications, however. For example, the same pattern is observed in the retail services classification as was noted for the entire mainly consumer services category. But such is not the case for the important medical/educational services classification. Here the share is largest in the large-size MLM's and smallest in the NMC's.

The share of job decrease data must be interpreted with care. Job decreases have been much smaller than job increases except in the NMC category, where the rate of job decrease (20.2 percent) was

TABLE 5.2

*Evidence of Changes in Functional Specialization: Distribution of
Job Increases/Job Decreases among Selected Industrial
Classifications by Size of MLM and for
the U.S., 1950-1960*

	NMC's	Small-size	Medium-size	Large-size	All U.S.
Net Change	1.3	20.0	26.5	16.6	15.5
Rate of Job increases	21.6	29.3	32.1	21.1	25.5
Rate of Job decreases	20.2	9.3	5.6	4.4	10.0
Distribution of Job INCREASES					
Primary	2.4	1.0	0.7	0.1	1.0
Construction	4.5	3.9	4.0	0.7	3.3
Manufacturing	31.4	25.9	25.9	27.6	27.7
Utilities	1.4	1.1	1.0	0.3	0.9
Mainly Business Services	9.6	11.0	15.0	15.2	13.1
Transportation	2.5	2.0	2.5	1.9	2.3
Communications	0.9	1.0	1.1	0.7	0.9
Wholesale	1.9	1.7	2.6	1.3	2.0
FIRE	3.5	4.8	6.1	6.2	5.3
Business/repair	0.9	1.5	2.6	5.1	2.6
Mainly Consumer Services	34.8	34.2	31.0	26.3	31.3
Retail	11.6	9.5	8.9	3.7	8.4
Recreation/hotel	2.1	2.3	1.7	0.4	1.6
Private household	4.4	2.8	1.9	0.5	2.3
Medical/education	16.7	19.6	18.4	21.8	19.0
Government	11.1	14.8	10.3	6.7	10.2
Administration	4.3	5.3	5.3	4.4	4.9
Armed forces	6.7	9.5	5.0	2.2	5.3
INR	4.9	8.1	12.2	23.1	12.4
Distribution of Job DECREASES					
Primary	71.3	47.4	33.7	10.6	54.4
Manufacturing	8.8	15.7	18.9	18.8	12.6
Mainly Business Services	10.1	25.1	35.0	40.4	20.0
Transportation	5.0	12.3	17.6	17.1	9.6
Mainly consumer services	4.4	6.5	8.0	24.8	7.9
Retail	2.4	3.5	4.5	14.0	4.4
Private household	0.4	0.6	0.7	4.4	1.0
All other	5.4	5.3	4.4	5.4	5.1

approximately as large as the rate of job increase (21.6 percent) during the 1950-60 decade. The job decrease data do, however, permit us to observe the relative importance of the various industry categories as sources of employment decline.

For the NMC's and small MLM's, the primary sector is the major source of job decrease. For the medium- and large-size MLM's, manufacturing has been the major source. Business services comprised 15.7 percent or more of the job decreases in each of the MLM categories, but these job decreases were accounted for almost entirely by the transportation industry category (principally, the railroad/railway express classification). As regards the consumer services, except in the large-size MLM's where retailing accounted for 14 percent, job decreases in consumer services were relatively unimportant.

These observations tell us much of the developmental processes which are taking place in the American economy. As the nation develops, those functions which were once performed centrally for the nation are passed down to regional centers and may, to some extent, be passed down even further. Currently we are witnessing the emergence of regional stock exchanges and the opening up of regional offices by national advertising and accounting firms that previously operated primarily out of New York. As the regional demand for these specialized services grows, it becomes more and more feasible to produce them at the regional level. As these activities are spun off from New York or some other large metropolitan economy, some of that economy's resources can be redirected to activities that are of even greater strategic importance within the system.

The higher order cities, those at the top of the national system of cities, must be continually tooling up new services which can then be sold to lower order cities. Should the largest cities fail to provide this form of leadership, then gradually other cities will increase their relative position in the system as they prove that they can provide the leadership required. Competition between cities can be quite intense at all levels. No city has a permanent monopoly on its position, except perhaps Washington D.C. Moreover, since the attributes of a successful city change with changing technology and changing tastes, comparative advantages are continuously being altered.

The changing role of the medium- and large-size MLM's is readily seen in the share of job increases and job decreases for the business services. The FIRE classification accounts for a significantly larger share of job increases in both large- and medium-size MLM's than in the small-size MLM's and NMC's. In the case of medium-size MLM's such as Atlanta and Houston, this larger percentage of employment represents the assumption of new roles as these cities provide to an increasing degree the banking, insurance, and brokerage needs of rapidly growing hinterlands. In the case of the large-size MLM's, especially New York, this represents a refinement of these categories of business services to a more specialized level as these great metropolises serve, in turn, the rapidly growing regional centers and as they increasingly orient themselves to an expanding world economy.

It is especially interesting to note that the share of job increases in business/repair services in the large-size MLM's is more than three times as large as in the small-size MLM's. This category includes the strategically important business services such as advertising and electronic data-processing services which are contracted-out.[1] These are examples, *par excellence*, of the external economy types of activities discussed in chapter 3. As the large metropolises become increasingly specialized in financial, commercial, and headquarters activities, there is greater and greater need and justification for the development of such external economies.[2]

---

[1] The role of electronic data processing as a service industry has been studied for the New York metropolitan economy by Boris Yavitz and Thomas M. Stanback, Jr. See their *Electronic Data Processing in New York City* (Columbia University Press, New York, 1967).

[2] Industry classifications do not reveal the extent of headquarter activity specialization. A disproportionately large share of employment classified as manufacturing in New York is in administration rather than production. These activities have very different manpower requirements; more white-collar workers, higher female participation, higher proportion of high salaried executives, etc. Space requirements also vary and tend to be met by building vertically rather than horizontally. Thus corporate headquarters activity resembles an industry and should be treated as such. Unfortunately, data classified by type of activity, i.e., administrative vs. production, are not available.

The increasing emphasis on certain economic functions in the larger metropolises is not necessarily limited to the business services. Almost 22 percent of job increases in the large-size MLM's was accounted for by medical/educational services compared to 18.4 percent in the medium-size MLM's. If our data were more detailed it is not unlikely that additional examples could be found of increasing concentration of large-size MLM employment in certain consumer services.

Expanding industries in any city must compete with existing or prospective local industries for the factors of production, land, labor and capital. This competition tends to increase with an increase in the size of place, at least for land and labor. Trends in employment changes reflect such economic forces at work, especially in the private households classification, and the three retail classifications—food/dairy stores, eating and drinking places, and other retail services. In all these industries, the share of job increases declines and the share of job decreases rises, as the size of MLM increases (Table 5.3).

In New York City, the largest MLM, private households and retailing accounted for almost 40 percent of all job decreases but none of the job increases. At the other end of the size spectrum, these same sectors accounted for only 3 percent of job decreases in the NMC's, but 16 percent of job increases. While employment in these industries is eroding in the largest cities, it is increasing in the smaller places.

Many factors are at play here, the most important of which would seem to be the upgrading of employment by industries in the larger cities in an attempt to remain competitive. Moreover, the wages will tend to be higher since they must be commensurate with the cost of living which tends to be higher than in the smaller places, and may also be higher due to a tighter supply of labor in the large MLM's.[3]

Accordingly, in the large places, there is a greater incentive to substitute capital for labor and increasingly, suburban land for downtown land. These are the very real constraints that a large-size MLM

[3] For evidence of the increase in wages with size of place, see Victor Fuchs, *Differentials in Hourly Earnings by Region and City Size, 1959,* Occasional Paper 101 (New York, National Bureau of Economic Research, 1967).

TABLE 5.3
Share of Job Increases/Decreases

	Private household		Retail total		Food/dairy		Eating/drinking		Other retail	
	Incr.	Decr.	Incr.	Decr.	Incr.	Decr.	Incr.	Decr.	Incr.	Decr.
NMC's	4.35	0.37	11.57	2.39	1.31	1.27	2.03	0.67	8.42	0.45
Small-size MLM's	2.82	0.57	9.51	3.52	0.81	2.18	1.34	0.92	7.36	0.42
Medium-size MLM's	1.87	0.69	8.93	4.54	0.85	2.41	1.11	1.29	6.97	0.84
Large-size MLM's	0.50	4.38	3.67	14.04	0.11	8.31	0.43	3.55	3.12	2.18

confronts. The smaller MLM will usually be characterized by a greater abundance of cheap land for expansion and by lower wage costs. It will tend to economize less on both of these factors of production and more on capital.

The Census of Population employment data used in this study do not reveal differences in wages or productivity. Final interpretation of the trends described above must wait the examination of city wage and productivity data, which is beyond the limits of this study.

Manufacturing. The manufacturing category is comprised of a large number of industrial subclassifications which have very different locational requirements. Some must locate close to basic raw materials, some close to markets. Others are relatively footloose and may respond to the attractions of labor supply or amenities such as climate or a metropolitan environment. For these and other reasons employment expansion in certain manufacturing industries will tend to occur in metropolitan areas while in others it will tend to occur in NMC's.

Generalizations regarding job increases and decreases in the total manufacturing category must be made with caution. In terms of shares of job increases accounted for by manufacturing during the 1950-60 decade, this major industrial category appears to have been most important in the NMC's, second most important in the large MLM's (Table 5.2). Where actual numbers of job increases and decreases are examined for each size-of-place category, however, we note that it was the medium-size MLM category which provided the largest number of increases in manufacturing and the NMC's which provided the second largest number. The small-size MLM's were least important, and the large-size MLM's occupied an intermediate position.

Manufacturing 1950-60

Size-of-place category	Job increases (in 000's)	Job decreases (in 000's)	Net change (in 000's)
NMC	1,128.3 (2)	340.4 (1)	787.9 (2)
Small-size MLM	552.8 (4)	169.7 (4)	383.1 (4)
Medium-size MLM	1,429.7 (1)	337.8 (2)	1,091.9 (1)
Large-size MLM	964.7 (3)	296.1 (3)	668.6 (3)

Ranks are shown in parenthesis.

The measures of shares of job decreases fail to convey the relative importance of different size-of-place categories. When actual number of job decreases in manufacturing are compared by size-of-place category we find that the NMC's rank first, whereas in terms of shares of job decreases accounted for by manufacturing (Table 5.2) the large-size MLM's were found to rank first.

The actual number of job increases in manufacturing in 1950-60 does not vary greatly from the decade 1940-50. Only in large cities did the number of job increases decline. But job decreases rose significantly in all size classes, from 28,000 to 296,000 in large places and from 126,000 to 360,000 in the NMC's. As a result, the net change in manufacturing jobs declined in all size categories during the second decade. In large places it declined by half—from 1,309,000 jobs in the 1940s to 669,000 jobs in the 1950s.

SIZE-OF-PLACE DIFFERENCES IN SHARES OF JOB INCREASES: REGIONAL

To make possible regional comparisons, we have computed separately for each industrial classification within each region and the nation a ranking of the size-of-place categories based on shares of job increases and decreases. Rankings are presented in Table 5.4 for selected industrial classifications.[4]

Mainly business services. An initial observation is that in most of the regions, shares of job increases in mainly business services becomes larger as one compares first the NMC's and small-size MLM's and then the medium- and large-size MLM's. Typically, the shares are much larger for the medium-size MLM's than for the small, indicating that these more rapidly growing MLM's have tended to develop their facilities for rendering business services significantly more than have the smaller places.[5] The shares of job increases are not always

---

[4] The system of ranking NMC's, small- and medium-size categories by numerical ranks and large categories by alphabetical ranks is the same as employed in chapter 4.

larger in the large-size MLM's than in the medium-size, however. For this latter category the share of job increases accounted for by mainly business services is either largest or second largest in every comparison. We conclude that both the large- and medium-size MLM's were increasing their relative concentration of employment in business services throughout the various regions during the 1950s.

Among the individual business service classifications there is also a very strong tendency for share of job increases to rank higher in the medium- and large-size MLM's than in the small city and NMC categories. This is true for wholesale, FIRE, business-repair services and, to a lesser extent, communications.[6] In the FIRE classification the large-size MLM ranks first or second in every region (in which there are large MLM's). In business-repair services the large-size MLM's category ranks first in every such region. Small though this classification may be in terms of both numbers of persons employed and shares of total job creation, it appears to play a strategic role in the economic development of our major metropolitan economies.

Mainly consumer services.   The regional data for mainly consumer services are also generally consistent with the national size-of-place share of job increases. For most regions shares of job increases in consumer services are highest in the NMC's and tend to decrease with size of place.

To a large extent the above patterns for mainly consumer services reflect the influence of retailing. Here the tendency for share of job increases to be progressively smaller with increasing size of place is well established.

The important medical/educational services classification does not show such a pattern in shares of job increases, however. Shares tend to be smaller in the NMC's than in the MLM's. Shares are relatively high in the large-size MLM category, especially in the cases of New England and the Mideast regions. Beyond this there is no clear-cut tendency among the MLM size categories.

[5] The rank measures fail to make clear the extent of these differences.

[6] Rank measures are not shown for these classifications in Table 5.4.

TABLE 5.4

Employment Change (Job Increases) as a Function of Size, by Region and U.S., 1950-1960[a]

	All U.S.	New England	Mideast	Great Lakes	Plains	South-east	South-west	Rocky Mtns.	Far West
Mainly business services									
NMC's	3	3	3	3	3	3	3	3	3
Small-size	2	2	2	2	2	2	2	2	2
Medium-size	1	1	1	1	1	1	1	1	1
Large-size	A	B	A	A	B	—	—	—	A
Mainly consumer services									
NMC's	1	1	1	2(3)	1	2(3)	1(3)	1	1
Small-size	2	3	2(3)	1	2	1	2(2)	2	2
Medium-size	3	2	3(2)	3(2)	3	3(2)	3(1)	3	3
Large-size	D	C(A[b])	D(A)	D(C)	D(C)	—	—	—	D
Retail									
NMC's	1	1	1	1	1	1	1	1	1
Small-size	2	2	2	2-3(2)	2	3	2(3)	2(3)	2
Medium-size	3	3	3	2-3(2)	3	2	3(2)	3(2)	3
Large-size	D	D	D	D	D	—	—	—	D
Medical/education									
NMC's	3	2	3	3	2(3)	3	3	2	1
Small-size	1	3	2	1	1	1	2	1	2
Medium-size	2	1	1	2	3(2)	2	1	3	3
Large-size	A	A	A	B[b](A)	B	—	—	—	C[b](B)

	8	7	6	5	4	3	2	1
Construction								
NMC's	1	1	3	2	1	1	2	2
Small-size	2	2	2	1	2(2-3)	2	1	3
Medium-size	3	3	1	3	3(2-3)	3	3	1
Large-size	D	D	D	D	—	—	—	D
Manufacturing								
NMC's	1	2	1	2	1	2	2-3	2-3
Small-size	3	1	2	3	2	3	2-3	2-3
Medium-size	2	3	3	1	3	1	1	1
Large-size	D	D	D	A	—	—	—	A
Administration								
NMC's	3	1	3	3	2	2-3	3	1-2
Small-size	2	2-3	2	1-2	1	1	2	1-2
Medium-size	1	2-3	1	1-2	3	2-3	1	3
Large-size	C[b]	A	C	D	—	—	—	D
Armed forces								
NMC's	2	1	1	2	3	2	2	3
Small-size	1	3	3	1	1	1	1	1
Medium-size	3	2	2	3	2	3	3	2
Large-size	D	B	C	D	—	—	—	D

[a] Rankings are for share of job increases. For explanation of ranking system and numbers in parentheses, see note to Table 4.4.

[b] Same percentage as NMC category.

Construction.   In construction for the nation as a whole there is a
very strong tendency for percentages to be inversely ranked according
to size of place. For the regions, shares of job creation are smallest in
the large MLM's in every case and are largest or second largest in the
NMC's, except in the Great Lakes.

Manufacturing.   In the national data (Table 5.2) it appeared that
the share of job increases accounted for by manufacturing was highest
in the NMC's, second highest in the large cities, and the same in the
small- and medium-size places. Among the regions the same general
tendency can be discerned but there are variations. In the New England, Great Lakes, and Southeast, shares of job increases in manufacturing are higher in the NMC's than in other size-of-place categories. In the Mideast the NMC's rank second to the small cities; in
the Plains, Rocky Mountains, and West Coast they rank second to the
medium-size cities.

   Rankings of the large MLM's show the greatest variation among
regions. In the rapidly growing West Coast and in the Plains the share
is largest in the large-size MLM group. In New England, the Mideast,
and the Great Lakes, however, it is smallest. Taken as a whole we
find here evidence that the manufacturing category contains diverse
components, and does not lend itself to strong generalization.

Administration.   In administration the national pattern provides a
very rough indication of patterns which exist within regions. The
small- and medium-size categories rank high; NMC's rank low except
in the Mideast and the Far West. The large-size MLM category ranks
high except in the Mideast (Washington D.C.).

Armed Forces.   In armed forces, the national pattern again provides
a rough approximation of regional shares of job increases in the various size-of-place categories except in the cases of the Mideast and
Great Lakes regions. In most regions the small-size MLM category
is the one within which the shares of job increases due to armed forces
is largest. The NMC's category ranks next; the medium- and large-size
SMSA's tend to show lower shares.

VARIATIONS IN SHARES OF JOB DECREASES

The observations made previously regarding shares of job decreases within the national size-of-place categories apply for the most part at the regional level. Where exceptions to the national patterns exist they tend to occur in the Western and Southwestern areas where rates of job decrease are quite low. Certain observations are of interest. Manufacturing accounted for about a third or more of job decreases (1950-60) in the various MLM size categories of the three most heavily industrialized regions (Great Lakes, Northeast, and Mideast); it accounted for 23 percent of job decreases in the small- and 20 percent in the medium-size MLM categories of the Southeast in the same decade, but elsewhere was not an important source of job decrease. Only transportation comprised a significant source of job decrease among the business services and only retailing within the consumer services during the 1950s. The private household classification was, of course, a major source of job decreases through the nation during the first decade.

SUMMARY AND CONCLUSIONS

The data presented in this chapter permit us to observe the size-of-place categories in which employment growth has been most rapid and the industrial classifications which have contributed most to job increases and decreases within each size-of-place category.

Once again, as in the previous chapter, we find fairly systematic differences among size-of-place categories, which serve to underline the importance for manpower policy, of recognizing the basic differences in employment structure and dynamics which exist among MLM's. The medium-size MLM's have shown the fastest rate of employment increase with the small-size MLM's in second place. There have been exceptions at the regional level, but taking the nation as a whole the pattern is well established.

In the case of the NMC category, the low rates of net employment change, used in conventional analysis, fail to reveal the lively transition which has been occurring in several regions. Relatively high overall rates of job decreases, due mainly to declines in primary employment in the Southeast and Southwest but also to declines in certain manufacturing classifications in New England, have taken place at the same time that job increases have occurred in expanding sectors of manufacturing and consumer services. In short, the data for net employment changes fail to reveal the extent of industrialization and employment expansion which is taking place.

When we examine national and regional rankings of shares of job increases among the size-of-place categories we note that for the mainly business services category shares tend to increase with size of place whereas for the mainly consumer services category shares tend to decrease with size of place. In the business services category, shares are much larger for the medium-size MLM's than for the small, indicating that these more rapidly growing MLM's have tended to develop aggressively the role of business service centers. In some regions, though not in all, the share of job increases is still larger in the large-size MLM's. Among the individual business service classifications, in wholesale, FIRE, and business/repair services, the share of job increases tends to rank higher in the medium-size than in the small-size MLMs or the NMCs. It is only in business/repair services, however, that there is a well-established tendency among the regions for share of job increases to be largest in the large-size MLM.

To an important extent the pattern for mainly consumer services, in which share of job increases declines with size of place, reflects the influence of retailing and private households. The important medical/educational services classification does not show such a pattern. Shares of job increases accounted for by this classification tend to be smaller in the NMC's than in the MLM's, and there is a tendency in some regions for shares to be largest in the large-size MLM category. Beyond this, however, we cannot generalize.

The remaining major industrial category is manufacturing. Within this category the share of jobs created tends to decline with size of place indicating a tendency of industrialization to play a larger role in the growth of smaller places. There is considerable variation among regions for this category, however.

The principal implication of the analysis in this and the preceding chapter is that there tend to be similar size-of-place characteristics in rates of growth, in sources of job creation and in industrial structure. Such a degree of similarity strongly supports our earlier contention that any study of labor market behavior must recognize at the outset the existence of a highly significant size-of-place variable.

The evidence presented in the preceding two chapters also supports the general thesis that there exists a national hierarchy of metropolises and further, that size is an important variable in determining the position of an MLM in the hierarchy and the functions performed there. Much of the variance in regional hierarchies can be explained by the importance of primary activity in the NMC's. The dynamics of growth suggest that the functions performed by MLM's change as the national economy grows. However, employment expansion will vary by MLM depending on the type of employment change occurring in the surrounding region, the functions the city performs, its position in the hierarchy, and changes occurring in the other MLM's in the regional system of cities.

An issue of great importance remains: Do MLM's vary significantly within size category? In chapter 6 we turn to this question analyzing variations in employment structure among MLM's and classifying metropolitan places according to a twofold scheme based on size and major functions. In chapters 7 and 8 we proceed to examine the characteristics of employment expansion and contraction for these groups of MLM's.

6 AN APPROACH TO THE CLASSIFICATION OF METROPOLITAN LABOR MARKETS

THE DISCUSSION in chapter 3 leads us to expect that cities which have different functions will have different employment structures: nodal cities are expected to have relatively heavy concentrations of employment in a number of services; manufacturing cities, in the manufacturing classifications; and so on. Moreover, both the analysis in chapter 3 and the empirical evidence of chapter 4 indicate that employment structure varies according to size, probably as a result of both special economic characteristics of larger cities (e.g., the greater prevalence of external economies, economies of scale) and their assumption of a different set of functions from those of smaller cities.

A more complete understanding of metropolitan economies requires that employment structure be studied in detail. Such knowledge is important not only for the light it may shed on the way cities function, but also because it provides guidelines for manpower policy. If labor markets differ widely in composition from place to place, such differences must be recognized and understood in arranging, through training and guidance, for the most effective adjustment of the labor supply to the needs which lie at hand and which are projected.

In the present chapter the industrial composition of the MLM's is analyzed, and each MLM is classified along functional lines.[1] Fol-

[1] There have been several classification systems proposed and applied in large cities in the recent past. Most of these studies were done with less detailed information. For example, see: Gunnar Alexanderson, *The Industrial Structure of American Cities* (Lincoln, University of Nebraska Press, 1956); Otis D. Duncan et al., *Metropolis and Region* (Baltimore, Johns Hopkins University Press,

lowing this we classify MLM's further, using a dual system based on both function and size, and proceed to make certain observations regarding rate of growth and labor force characteristics for each type–size group of MLM's.

THE QUARTILE ANALYSIS OF AGGLOMERATION

We begin our analysis of structural characteristics of employment by determining the extent to which a high (or low) percentage of employment in a given industrial classification tends to be associated with a high or low percentage of employment in another industrial classification. To carry out this investigation, a nonparametric test was devised, which is designated the quartile analysis of agglomeration. For each industrial classification we arranged the 368 MLM's according to percentage of total employment within that classification. Following this we divided each array of MLM's into quartiles. We then asked the question, "How many of the (92) MLM's which fall in the top quartile of the industry A array are MLM's which fall in the top quartile of the industry B array? The question was repeated for the second, third, and fourth quartiles (e.g., how many MLM's in the second quartile for industry A are in the second quartile for industry B?)

On the basis of pure chance (i.e., if the percentage of employment in one classification were independent of the percentage of employment in another classification) we would expect 25 percent of the 92 MLM's (23 MLM's) in a given quartile in industry A to fall in the same quartile for industry B. There is only a 5 percent probability that more than 34 percent (31 MLM's) might fall in the same quartile as a result of chance alone. Accordingly, we accept values in excess of 34 percent as indicating that the relationship

1960); Chauncy D. Harris, "A Functional Classification of Cities in the U.S.," *Geographical Review* (1963), pp. 86-99; Victor Jones and R. L. Forstall, "Economic and Social Classification of Metropolitan Areas," *Municipal Yearbook 1963* (Chicago, City Managers' Association, 1964).

observed for a given quartile is statistically significant, i.e., the percentages are related.

An initial and striking finding was that in those cases in which the relationships between the pairs of industry classifications are significant for the upper and for the lower quartiles they are generally much weaker in the middle quartiles. For example, the quartile test indicated that as regards the relationship between FIRE and wholesaling there is a tendency for those MLM's which specialize in FIRE to specialize also in wholesaling and for those MLM's which are relatively understructured in FIRE to be relatively understructured in wholesaling. For the remaining MLM's, however, the relationship is much less close. Such relationships indicate that there tends to be an agglomeration of these services in those places which fall within the top quartiles of the arrays for these two service classifications.[2]

In view of this initial finding the test was applied with special attention given to the top quartiles. In addition, the test was used to determine whether negative relationships exist. In the latter case we asked the question, "How many of the MLM's which fall in the *top* quartile for industry A fall in the *bottom* quartile for industry B?" Again, a finding of more than 34 percent was judged to indicate the percentages were, in fact, related. The answers to this question are of interest principally in examining the manufacturing category.

The results of the test are shown in matrix form for the top quartiles of all industrial classifications except the primary and manu-

[2] It was this finding which caused us to adopt the quartile test in preference to an analysis of coefficients of (simple) correlation among percentages of employment in the industrial classifications. The correlation analysis (which was employed experimentally) provides an indication of the extent to which two variables are related throughout the *entire range* of observations. Accordingly, a high coefficient would be found only where the relationship between the variables is close over the entire range. If the relationship were close for only those values observed for two variables in certain portions of the arrays and were random for the remainder, the measured correlation would be relatively low and would not indicate the strength of the relationship which did, in fact, exist. The quartile test permits us to focus attention upon the upper and lower portion of the arrays, which are of interest, in the analysis.

facturing activities (Table 6.1). The table presents for each cell of the matrix the percentage of top quartile MLM's which are "shared" among the two industrial classifications represented.[3] The general finding is that there is a relatively high degree of agglomeration (clustering) among a number of service classifications.

Mainly business services. There is a tendency for MLM's which show a relatively high concentration of employment in one of the business services to show a relatively high concentration in the other business services. Among six of the seven business services (i.e., trucking/warehousing, other transportation, communication, wholesale, FIRE, and business/repair services), there is only one of the fifteen comparisons in which the percentage of top quartile MLM's which are "shared" is not statistically significant. The relationships are, in general, stronger among the latter four classifications. Among these classifications there is not one comparison in which the percentage of shared MLM's is less than 48 percent.

Mainly consumer services. There also exists among the three retailing classifications, the hotels/personal services, and the entertainment/recreation classifications, a tendency for MLM's in the top quartiles to be shared. For the ten possible comparisons among those five classifications there are only two in which the percentage of shared MLM's is not statistically significant.

The medical/educational classification is much less closely related to the other consumer services, however. The only significant tendency for MLM's in the top quartile in this classification to be found in the top quartile of any of the other consumer services is noted in comparisons with hotels/personal services. For these two classifications, 40 percent of the top quartile MLM's are shared.

---

[3] We shall henceforth use the term "shared" to describe the situation in which an MLM lying in the top quartile of an array of one industrial classification also lies in the top quartile of an array of another classification. Such an MLM is said to be shared by both classifications.

TABLE 6.1

Agglomeration in Selected Industries: Matrix of Percentages of "Shared" MLM'.
in Top Quartiles, 368 MLM's, 1960[a]

	Construction	Utilities	Railroad/railway express	Trucking/warehousing	Other transportation	Communications	Wholesale
Construction	X	36.9			38.0	40.2	
Utilities	36.9	X	34.8				40.2
Railroad/railway express		34.8	X				
Trucking/warehousing				X		36.9	51.1
Other transportation	38.0				X	38.0	36.5
Communications	40.2			36.9	38.0	X	52.2
Wholesale		40.2		51.1	36.9	52.2	X
FIRE	34.8			36.9	46.7	57.7	50.0
Business/repair services	42.4			38.0	45.6	48.9	54.
Food/dairy stores	34.8	42.4					34.8
Eating/drinking places	40.2	41.3				36.9	34.8
Other retail	41.3	44.6		45.6		42.4	57.1
Hotel/personal services	54.3	40.2			39.1	36.9	36.9
Entertainment/recreation	45.6	35.9			41.3	48.9	40.2
Private household	43.5						
Medical/education	34.8					35.9	
Administration						38.0	
Armed forces							

Consumer and business services relationships. When we examine the relationships among consumer and business services we find that there is a tendency for MLM's in the top quartile in the other retail services classification to fall to a significant extent in the top quartile of most of the business service classifications.

Also of interest is the observation that MLM's which fall in the top quartile of two services, hotels/personal services and entertainment/recreation, which together comprise the recreation category, fre-

FIRE	Business/repair services	Food/dairy stores	Eating/drinking places	Other retail	Hotel/personal services	Entertainment/recreation	Private household	Medical/education	Administration	Armed forces
34.8	42.4	34.8	40.2	41.3	54.3	45.6	43.5	34.8		
		42.4	41.3	44.6	40.2	35.9				
36.9	38.0			45.6						
46.7	45.6				39.1	41.3				
57.7	48.9		36.9	41.3	36.9	48.9		35.9	38.0	
50.0	56.5	34.8	34.8	57.7	36.9	40.2				
X	60.0			38.0	35.9	51.1		34.8	36.9	
60.0	X		33.7	51.1	38.0	47.8				
		X			34.8	36.9				
			X		51.1	41.3	54.3			
38.0	51.1	34.8	51.1	X	50.0	41.3				
35.9	38.0	36.9	41.3	50.0	X	41.3	50.0	40.2		34.8
51.1	47.8		54.3	41.3	41.3	X				
					50.0		X			
34.8					40.2			X	35.9	
36.9								35.9	X	60.9
					34.8				60.9	X

[a] An MLM is considered to be "shared" by two industrial classifications if it lies in the same quartile of the array in each of the two industrial classifications. Arrays are based on percentage of employment within the given industrial classification. For example, 36.9 percent of the 92 MLM's which comprise the top quartile of an array of MLM's based on the proportion of total employment in utilities are also found in the top quartile of an array based on proportion of employment in construction. Where no numbers are shown percentages are less than 34.8 percent.

quently fall in the top quartiles of other service classifications, especially consumer services. In terms of direct employment the hotels/ personal services and entertainment/recreation classifications are not

of great importance.[4] But in conjunction with the relatively high proportions of employment in the various services with which they appear
to be significantly associated, the total percentage of service employment (excluding government) for these top quartile MLM's is relatively high. This may be seen in the cases of the following cities falling
within the top 10 percent of the MLM's arrayed on the basis of percent of total employment in recreation. If we examine the percentages
of total employment accounted for by all consumer services in these
MLM's we find them far above the average:

Top-Ranking MLM's in Recreation

Percentiles[a]	Name of MLM and percentage employment in recreation		Percentage employment in all consumer services
(1)	(2)		(3)
100th (largest)	Las Vegas	26.9	49.9
95th	Lexington	5.6	46.1
90th	Temple (Tex.)	4.9	54.3
Average, all MLM's in U.S.		3.8	32.7

[a] From array of MLM's based on percentage of employment in recreation.
(See Table 3.1)

On the other hand, MLM's in the top quartile of the medical/
educational classification are found to a significant extent in the top
quartile of only two business service classifications, communications
and FIRE.

Government. The most solid finding regarding the administration
classification is that it is closely associated with armed forces: 60.9
percent of the MLM's in the top quartile of each is shared. This is a
reflection of the fact that military installations typically require a large

---

[4] A glance back at Table 3.1 will show that for those MLM's lying below
the 95th percentile of the array for recreation category, the combined employment in these two recreation-type service classifications comprised less than 6
percent of employment.

civilian contingent, classified within the administration category.[5]

There is a tendency for MLM's in the top quartile of administration to fall in the top quartiles of communications, FIRE, and medical/education. These relationships are not particularly strong, however (the highest percentage of shared cities in any of these three comparisons is 38). Moreover, MLM's in the top quartile of armed forces are not significantly linked to any of the business services and are found within the top quartile of only one consumer service, hotels/personal services.

Construction.   MLM's in the top quartile of this classification are significantly related to all of the consumer service classifications, except private households. These MLM's are also found in the top quartiles of other transportation, communication, FIRE, business/repair services, and utilities in a significantly large number of comparisons. The strongest relationship is found, however, between construction and the entertainment/recreation classifications. In these comparisons the percentages of shared MLM's are relatively high, 54.3 and 45.6 percent, respectively. Since the hotels/personal services and entertainment/recreation classifications tend to be characterized by relatively high growth rates, we find here evidence to support the acceleration principle hypothesis which was advanced in chapter 3 and is examined further in chapter 7.

Manufacturing and the service categories.   The manufacturing category presents a very different picture. The relationships between the percentage of employment in manufacturing and services is essentially negative. If we ask the question, "Of the MLM's which lie in the *top* quartile for the manufacturing category what percentage lies in the

[5] From such evidence as can be gleaned from the 113-MLM sample (which provides detailed classifications) these MLM's which fall in the top quartile of both public administration and armed forces are in most instances specialized in federal rather than state or local public administration.

bottom quartile for each of the other industrial classifications?", we find the following:[6]

Construction	54.3	Retail	44.6
		Mainly Consumer Services	
Utilities	34.8	Food/dairy products	17.4*
		Eating/drinking places	41.3
Mainly Business Services	50.0	Other retail	45.7
Transportation	41.3	Recreation	63.0
Railroad/railway express	40.2	Hotels/personal	64.1
Trucking/warehousing	19.5*	Entertainment/recreation	47.8
Other transportation	45.7	Private household	51.1
Communications	50.0	Medical/education	38.0
Wholesale	37.0	*Government*	
FIRE	40.2	Administration	57.6
Business/repair	45.7	Armed forces	50.0

N.B.: The percentages accompanied by asterisks were not statistically significant.

These measures suggest much about the essential nature of these MLM's. Their specialization in manufacturing has resulted in an employment structure which tends to be lacking in the external economies provided by business service firms. It also appears to have resulted in a lack of the amenities provided in the form of consumer services.

In part the low percentage of employment in business services is simply the result of the fact that these MLM's do not serve the needs of a hinterland. But general observation tells us that it is also, at least in part, a reflection of the fact that manufacturing firms tend to provide for their own service needs within their organizational structures (i.e., they "internalize" their services) or provide for such needs in some distant headquarters city. In any event the fact that these places have failed to develop to a significant extent facilities for making services available to new firms creates a situation in which the location of newly developing industry may be expected to be discouraged.

One possible criticism of the above line of reasoning runs as follows: If the MLM has a relatively large percentage of employment in manu-

---

[6] There were no significant relationships when top quartile manufacturing MLM's were compared with top quartile MLM's for the remaining industrial classifications.

facturing it must of necessity have a relatively small percentage of employment in the remaining classifications since the total percentages must add to 100. Therefore, the findings are only what one would expect and do not provide new or significant insights.

We cannot subscribe to this argument. In the first place, the analysis reveals that a high percentage of employment in manufacturing in an MLM need not result in the percentages of employment within *each* of the other classifications being relatively low. An example of this may be seen in the fact that although almost 46 percent of the MLM's falling in the manufacturing top quartile fall in the bottom quartile of the other transportation classification, less than 20 percent fall in the bottom quartile of the trucking/warehousing classification.

In the second place, to question the significance of the findings on the basis of the observation that the arithmetic of the computations alone creates a bias toward MLM's from the top quartile of manufacturing falling in the lower quartile of the remaining classifications appears to us to beg the question. The employment data are descriptive of the employment composition of the MLM's. They tell us that certain metropolises exist in which there is a heavy concentration of employment in manufacturing and in which the economy functions with a relatively small share of its workers in construction, utilities, the services, or government. Such a finding is significant because it illuminates the nature of the labor market of these metropolitan places and implies certain things about their capability to attract new firms and to engage in transition. The significance of the finding is by no means invalidated by the arithmetic of the computations.

THE CLASSIFICATION OF MLM'S

CRITERIA FOR CLASSIFICATION

An approach to a scheme for classification is clearly indicated by the quartile analysis above. We find that a significant number of the same MLM's fall within the top quartiles of the various business services and of the other retail services classification. This evidence of agglomeration of services suggests that metropolises possessing the characteristics which were attributed to a nodal city (see chapter 3) do, in fact, exist, and that they may be identified by observing the tendency for relatively large proportions of employment to be found concurrently in several of the business service classifications and (for certain MLM's) in the other retail classification. Accordingly, our criterion for designating an MLM as a nodal center is that its employment be relatively concentrated in all or in a relatively large number of these classifications.

On the other hand, we have seen that MLM's which specialize heavily in manufacturing tend to be understructured in both business and consumer services. Such being the case, a high percentage of employment in manufacturing provides a basis for identifying this type of MLM.

Similarly, relatively high percentages of employment in the medical/education, armed forces, administration, or recreation/entertainment categories may be used to identify MLM's specializing in these services.

There is, of course, no definitive method of classifying metropolitan places. Each is in some sense unique since its structure is the result of its resources, its markets, and its history. Our objective is to break out a relatively small number of major categories so that we may better observe the processes of employment expansion. These categories cannot be completely homogeneous in terms of structure and function, but, if our scheme is reasonably satisfactory, there will be a significant improvement in homogeneity.

It will be apparent that if classification is carried out using the above scheme there is likely to remain a sizable number of MLM's which do not fall in any of the categories. These MLM's we designate as "mixed." Since all MLM's except the most specialized tend to provide business and consumer services to the area surrounding them to some extent, and since MLM's with high concentrations of employment in manufacturing and in certain service activities such as government and recreation will have already been classified, these residual, mixed MLM's may be expected to be somewhat "service oriented" in their employment structure. This does not mean, however, that some of them will not be specialized in one or more individual manufacturing or service classifications (e.g., an MLM in the residual mixed category might fall in the top quartile of apparel manufacturing or FIRE).

PROBLEMS OF CLASSIFICATION

There were several practical difficulties which were encountered in classifying the MLM's. The first was to decide how many types of specialized non-nodal MLM's would be included within the classification scheme. Clearly manufacturing was a major category, but a question arose as to whether or not medical/education, FIRE, transportation, recreation, and government should not also be recognized separately.[7] The second difficulty was to determine the cut-off point beyond which an MLM would not be classified in a given MLM group. The third difficulty was to make a satisfactory designation in those cases in which an MLM qualifies for more than one category of specialization (e.g., to determine how an MLM is to be classified if it is both a resort center and a nodal service center for a hinterland).

Types of specialized non-nodal MLM's. In classifying the specialized non-nodal MLM's only four types were recognized: manufacturing, government, medical/education, and resort. In the top ranges of the arrays for these classifications the percentages of total employment were large enough to indicate that the production of these goods or services were major export-type activities. For example, the MLM representing the 95th percentile classifications in manufacturing, government, and medical/educational services had percentages of total employment in these classifications of 46.3, 29.8, and 20.0 percent, respectively (Table 3.1). The recreation category (resort centers) showed little concentration (less than 6 percent) in employment at the 95th percentile, but there was a high degree of employment con-

---

[7] No attempt was made to study employment concentration within the industrial classifications which comprise the manufacturing category. These classifications are not sufficiently detailed to permit such an investigation.

centration at the upper extremity of the array (the most specialized MLM showed 26.9 percent of employment in recreation). Moreover, as already noted, for MLM's with relatively high percentages of employment in recreation the quartile analysis afforded strong evidence of an associated concentration in certain other service activities. Thus there was a cluster of closely related services in which the combined percentage of employment was greater than would seem to be indicated by examination of the data for the single category, recreation.

Several possible specialty classifications (e.g., transportation, wholesaling, insurance, mining) were omitted because there were so few cities in which these classifications accounted for a substantial proportion of total employment. For example, even the MLM's with the greatest concentration of employment in wholesaling, FIRE, or business/repair services do not have proportions of employment in these classifications in excess of 10 percent.

Nodal MLM's (66).   To qualify as a nodal center it was required that an MLM be in the top quartile in four of the following six business or consumer services categories: transportation, wholesale, communications, FIRE, business/repair services, and other retail. The four-out-of-six rule was established after it was noted that further relaxing of the criterion (to say, three out of six) resulted in a marked tendency for MLM's classified as nodal to be classified in other categories as well.

A special difficulty arose in determining under what conditions an MLM should be considered as falling within the top quartile of the transportation category. This difficulty arose out of the fact that different MLM's require a different mix of transportation services. In some instances rail transportation is important; in others, trucking; in still others (especially ports), the other transportation classification. Moreover, the employment requirements for these classifications vary: the top quartiles in railroad/railway express, trucking/warehousing, and other transportation range from 2.2 to 18.5 percent, 1.7 to 3.8 percent, 1.1 to 6.2 percent, respectively. Our rule was to consider that an MLM was in the top quartile in transportation if it fell in the top quartile of any one of the three transportation categories.

Manufacturing MLM's (114). MLM's were placed in the manufacturing category if they fell within the top third of the entire array (based on percentage of employment in manufacturing).[8] This cut-off level was selected because MLM's falling below this point tended to show considerably more concentration of employment in the business service categories and to appear as more logical candidates for the mixed MLM category. Moreover, in a region-by-region study of arrays of percentages of employment in manufacturing in the various MLM's it was found that there was a strong clustering of percentages in the New England and Mideast regions and a somewhat looser clustering in the Great Lakes region. The cut-off point which we have used includes the clustered portions of the arrays in the New England and Mideast and a major portion of the cluster of the Great Lakes region. This cut-off level, 32 percent of MLM employment in manufacturing, lies well above the average of 26 percent for the nation, but only slightly below the percentage shown for the 75th percentile in Table 3.1 (which bounds the top quartile) of 35.8 percent. We recognize that the cut-off point excludes some MLM's which are important exporters of specific manufactures. The evidence indicates that such excluded MLM's do not tend to show the well-established structural patterns which are characteristic of cities with heavy concentrations of total manufacturing employment. For this reason they are better classified within the more general, mixed category.

Resort-type MLM's (8). MLM's were judged to be specialized in resort-type activities if the percentage of employment in this category was 6.6 or above. The cut-off point here was made after the analysis revealed that below this point in the array there were a number of MLM's with stronger claims for classification under other headings.

---

[8] There was one exception to this rule, Philadelphia (classified as mixed) qualified as a manufacturing MLM, but also showed certain distinct nodal characteristics.

Ten MLM's fell within the range indicated but two were excluded
from the list. One, Miami, is a well-developed nodal center. The other,
Key West, is an important government base.

Government-associated MLM's (45).   The government category includes 45 MLM's with a minimum share of employment of 18 percent
in this industrial classification. We did not attempt to distinguish between MLM's with employment concentrations in administration and
in armed forces because the quartile analysis had revealed previously
that there was a close association between the two (civilian employees
or armed forces bases are classified as administration). A number
of MLM's with important military bases fell below the cut-off point
and were not included. These MLM's tended, however, to show
employment concentrations also in manufacturing or the services
classifications.

Medical/education MLM's (21). The remaining specialized classification, medical/education, includes 21 MLM's. The minimum proportion of employment in medical/education services for MLM's in
this category is 15 percent. Below this cut-off point, MLM's tended
to show specialization in various other services.

Mixed-type MLM's (114).   Using the criteria outlined above there
were relatively few problems of cross-classification. Of course, we were
left with a sizable group of "mixed" MLM's (114 in number), but
this was our intention. In view of the fact that we wished to break out
nodal and specialized non-nodal MLM's as unambiguously as possible,
it was reasonable to expect that there would be a sizable group remaining whose functions would be less well articulated. To have reduced
the size of this group by using more relaxed standards in selecting
nodal and non-nodal MLM's would have resulted in a less clear-cut
distinction between the functional groups. One possible way to further
classify these mixed MLM's is to determine whether there are common structural tendencies among a significantly large number of these
places.

Specifically, we sought to determine how many of the mixed-type MLM's gave evidence of concentrations of service employment which were sufficiently heavy to indicate that the metropolis was functioning to some extent as a nodal place but had failed to meet the criteria of a nodal type place.

On inspection, we found that mixed-type MLM's with relatively heavy concentrations of employment in service classifications tended to fall into two groups. The first group was made up of those that resembled nodal places but failed to pass the qualifying test. In these cases there were three (but not the necessary four) of the required classifications in which percentage of 1960 employment fell within the top quartile. In the second group, however, there was a somewhat different pattern of concentration of employment in service classifications. In this latter group there tended to be a concentration of employment in at least one of the following, recreation/entertainment, medical/educational services, or administration, and, in addition, a concentration in at least one of the six classifications used to identify nodal places. Accordingly we established two sets of criteria. If an MLM qualified under either set it was designated as mixed with nodal characteristics. Those mixed-type MLM's with nodal characteristics are designated by an asterisk in the list of MLM's presented in Table 6.2.

Roughly half, 54, of the 114 mixed-type places were classified as having nodal characteristics. With the exception of a few mining centers, the mixed-type places have no distinguishing industrial features. In general, mixed-type places with nodal characteristics are small-size MLM's, half of them are located in the Southeast.

Summary of classification procedure. To summarize the above, we have distinguished those MLM's in which employment concentration is well developed in terms of rendering general nodal-type services or of exporting manufactures, resort activities, government, or medical/education services. Cut-off points were determined after analysis revealed that below these points the distinctions between groups became less clear.

TABLE 6.2
Classification of MLM's, 1960[a]

NODAL

	Size		Size
New England		Little Rock (Ark.)	8
Boston	12	Orlando (Fla.)	8
Portland (Me.)	7	Charlotte (N.C.)	8
Mideast		Lexington (Ky.)	7
New York	13	Roanoke (Va.)	7
Newark	11	Lafayette (La.)	6
Paterson	10	Paducah (Ky.)	5
Great Lakes		Fort Pierce (Fla.)	5
Chicago	12	Southwest	
Fort Wayne (Ind.)	8	Houston	10
Bloomington (Ill.)	6	Dallas	10
Plains		Phoenix (Ariz.)	9
Kansas City (Kan.–Mo.)	10	Fort Worth (Tex.)	9
Minneapolis	10	Tulsa (Okla.)	9
Omaha (Neb.)	9	Oklahoma City (Okla.)	9
Des Moines (Iowa)	8	Corpus Christi (Tex.)	8
Lincoln (Neb.)	7	Lubbock (Tex.)	7
Springfield (Mo.)	7	Tyler (Tex.)	6
Sioux City (Iowa)	7	San Angelo (Tex.)	6
Fargo (N.D.)	7	Odessa (Tex.)	6
Sioux Falls (S.D.)	6	Midland (Tex.)	6
Hutchinson (Kan.)	5	Enid (Okla.)	5
Joplin (Mo.)	5		
Grand Island (Neb.)	5	Rocky Mountains	
Burlington (Iowa)	5	Denver	10
Grand Forks (N.D.)	5	Salt Lake City (Utah)	9
Mason City (Iowa)	5	Boise (Idaho)	6
Bismarck (N.D.)	5	Billings (Mont.)	6
		Casper (Wyo.)	5
Southeast		Idaho Falls (Idaho)	5
New Orleans	10	Pocatello (Idaho)	5
Miami	10		
Atlanta	10	Far West	
Nashville (Tenn.)	9	Los Angeles	12
Memphis (Tenn.)	9	San Francisco	11
Tampa (Fla.)	9	Portland (Ore.)	10
Jacksonville (Fla.)	9	Seattle	10
Richmond (Va.)	9	Fresno (Cal.)	8
		Spokane (Wash.)	8

TABLE 6.2 (*continued*)

MANUFACTURING

	Size		Size
New England		New Brunswick (N.J.)	5
New Haven (Conn.)	9	Elmira (N.Y.)	5
Bridgeport (Conn.)	9	Jamestown (N.Y.)	5
Hartford (Conn.)	9	Vineland (N.J.)	5
Providence (R.I.)	9	Auburn (N.Y.)	5
Worcester (Mass.)	9	Cumberland (Md.)	5
Springfield (Mass.)	9	Great Lakes	
Fall River (Mass.)	8	Detroit	12
Pittsfield (Mass.)	7	Cleveland	11
Manchester (N.H.)	7	Milwaukee	10
Auburn (Me.)	6	Cincinnati	10
Middleton (Conn.)	5	Grand Rapids (Mich.)	9
Torrington (Conn.)	5	Flint (Mich.)	9
Mideast		Gary (Ind.)	9
Pittsburgh	11	Youngstown (Ohio)	9
Buffalo	10	Toledo (Ohio)	9
Wilmington (Del.)	9	Dayton (Ohio)	9
Allentown (Pa.)	9	Akron (Ohio)	9
Jersey City (N.J.)	9	Rockford (Ill.)	8
Syracuse (N.Y.)	9	Peoria (Ill.)	8
Rochester (N.Y.)	9	Davenport (Iowa)	8
York (Pa.)	8	South Bend (Ind.)	8
Wilkes-Barre (Pa.)	8	Lorrain (Ohio)	8
Scranton (Pa.)	8	Canton (Ohio)	8
Reading (Pa.)	8	Racine (Wis.)	7
Lancaster (Pa.)	8	Kenosha (Wis.)	7
Johnstown (Pa.)	8	Saginaw (Mich.)	7
Erie (Pa.)	8	Muskegon (Mich.)	7
Utica (N.Y.)	8	Kalamazoo (Mich.)	7
Binghamton (N.Y.)	8	Jackson (Mich.)	7
Kingston (N.Y.)	5	Bay City (Mich.)	7
Sharon (Pa.)	5	Muncie (Ind.)	7
Williamsport (Pa.)	5	Anderson (Ind.)	7
Lebanon (Pa.)	5	Steubenville (Ohio)	7
New Castle (Pa.)	5	Springfield (Ohio)	7
Amsterdam (N.Y.)	5	Lima (Ohio)	7
Poughkeepsie (N.Y.)	5	Hamilton (Ohio)	7

TABLE 6.2 (*continued*)

	Size		Size
Wayne City (Ind.)	5	Southeast	
Port Huron (Mich.)	5	Chattanooga (Tenn.)	8
Portsmouth (Ohio)	5	Greenville (S.C.)	8
Oshkosh (Wis.)	5	Greensboro (N.C.)	8
Mansfield (Ohio)	5	Gadsden (Ala.)	6
Zanesville (Ohio)	5	Winston-Salem (N.C.)	5
Sheboygan (Wis.)	5	Lynchburg (Va.)	5
Midland (Mich.)	5	Danville (Va.)	5
Beloit (Wis.)	5	Kingsport (Tenn.)	5
Kankakee (Ill.)	5	Rome (Ga.)	5
Michigan City (Ind.)	5	Parkersburg (W.Va.)	5
Appleton (Wis.)	5	Rock Hill (S.C.)	5
Manitowoc (Wis.)	5	Spartanburg (S.C.)	5
Kokomo (Ind.)	5	Gastonia (N.C.)	5
Findlay (Ohio)	5	Kannapolis (N.C.)	5
Marion (Ind.)	5	Anderson (S.C.)	5
Lancaster (Ohio)	5	Burlington (N.C.)	5
Sandusky (Ohio)	5	Southwest	
Elkhart (Ind.)	5	None	
Battle Creek (Mich.)	5		
Plains		Rocky Mountains	
St. Louis	12	Pueblo (Colo.)	7
Waterloo (Iowa)	7	Far West	
Cedar Rapids (Iowa)	7	Bremerton (Wash.)	5
Austin (Minn.)	5	Eureka (Cal.)	5

MIXED

	Size		Size
New England		Watertown (N.Y.)	5
Bangor (Me.)	5	Hagerstown (Md.)	5
*Concord (N.H.)	5	*Long Branch (N.J.)	5
*Burlington (Vt.)	5	Great Lakes	
Mideast		*Indianapolis	10
*Philadelphia	12	*Columbus (Ohio)	9
Baltimore	11	Lansing (Mich.)	8
*Albany (N.Y.)	9	*Evansville (Ind.)	8
Harrisburg (Pa.)	8	*Green Bay (Wis.)	7
*Trenton (N.J.)	8	*Springfield (Ill.)	7
Altoona (Pa.)	7	Decatur (Ill.)	7
Newburgh (N.Y.)	5	Terre Haute (Ind.)	7

TABLE 6-2 (*continued*)

	Size		Size
Danville (Ill.)	5	*Wilmington (N.C.)	6
Freeport (Ill.)	5	*Petersburg (Va.)	5
*Marion (Ohio)	5	Bowling Green (Ky.)	5
*Galesburg (Ill.)	5	Wilson (N.C.)	5
Newark (Ohio)	5	Johnson City (Tenn.)	5
Wausau (Wis.)	5	Greenville (Miss.)	5
*LaCrosse (Wis.)	5	*Vicksburg (Miss.)	5
Fond du Lac (Wis.)	5	El Dorado (Ark.)	5
*Eau Claire (Wis.)	5	Rocky Mount (N.C.)	5
Plains		Jackson (Tenn.)	5
Wichita (Kan.)	8	Lakeland (Fla.)	5
Duluth (Minn.)	8	Decatur (Ala.)	5
*Topeka (Kan.)	7	*Alexandria (La.)	5
*St. Joseph (Mo.)	6	Florence (Ala.)	5
Dubuque (Iowa)	6	*Meridian (Miss.)	5
Fort Dodge (Iowa)	5	*Dothan (Ala.)	5
Ottumwa (Iowa)	5	Laurel (Miss.)	5
St. Cloud (Minn.)	5	Owensboro (Ky.)	5
*Minot (N.D.)	5	Fairmont (W.Va.)	5
*Clinton (Iowa)	5	Selma (Ala.)	5
		Clarksburg (W. Va.)	5
Southeast		*North Iberia (La.)	5
*Birmingham (Ala.)	9	*Hattiesburg (Miss.)	5
Louisville (Ky.)	9		
*Shreveport (La.)	8	**Southwest**	
*Baton Rouge (La.)	8	*Tucson (Ariz.)	8
*Jackson (Miss.)	8	*Albuquerque (N.Mex.)	8
Mobile (Ala.)	8	Beaumont (Tex.)	8
Knoxville (Tenn.)	8	Waco (Tex.)	7
Huntington (W.Va.)	8	*Galveston (Tex.)	7
*Charleston (W.Va.)	8	Brownsville (Tex.)	7
*Monroe (La.)	7	*Abilene (Tex.)	7
Lake Charles (La.)	7	*Texarkana (Tex.)	6
*Fort Smith (Ark.)	7	Victoria (Tex.)	5
Huntsville (Ala.)	7	McAllen (Tex.)	5
Savannah (Ga.)	7	Longview (Tex.)	5
*Raleigh (N.C.)	7	Bartlesville (Okla.)	5
*Asheville (N.C.)	7	*Muskogee (Okla.)	5
Wheeling (W. Va.)	7	*Hobbs (N.Mex.)	5
Pine Bluff (Ark.)	6	Carlsbad (N.Mex.)	5

TABLE 6.2 (*continued*)

	Size		Size
Rocky Mountains		Stockton (Cal.)	8
Greeley (Colo.)	5	Bakersfield (Cal.)	8
*Butte (Mont.)	5	*Santa Barbara (Cal.)	7
*Missoula (Mont.)	5	*Salem (Ore.)	7
*Cheyenne (Wyo.)	5	*Eugene (Ore.)	5
		*Modesto (Cal.)	5
Far West		*Santa Rosa (Cal.)	5
*San Bernardino	10	*Santa Cruz (Cal.)	5
*San Jose (Cal.)	9	Yakima (Wash.)	5
Anaheim (Cal.)	9	*Bellingham (Wash.)	5

OTHER

GOVERNMENT

	Size		Size
New England		Biloxi (Miss.)	5
New London (Conn.)	7	Anniston (Ala.)	5
Portsmouth (N.H.)	5	Panama City (Fla.)	5
Newport (R.I.)	5	Southwest	
Mideast		San Antonio (Tex.)	9
Washington D.C.	11	El Paso (Tex.)	8
Plains		Wichita Falls (Tex.)	7
Salina (Kan.)	5	Amarillo (Tex.)	7
Rapid City (S.D.)	5	Lawton (Okla.)	6
Jefferson City (Mo.)	5	Laredo (Tex.)	6
		Big Springs (Tex.)	5
Southeast		Bryant (Tex.)	5
Norfolk (Va.)	9	Las Cruces (N.M.)	5
Pensacola (Fla.)	8	Roswell (N.M.)	5
Columbus (Ga.)	8	Rocky Mountains	
Charleston (S.C.)	8	Ogden (Utah)	7
Newport News (Va.)	8	Colorado Springs	7
Columbia (S.C.)	8	Great Falls (Mont.)	6
Augusta (Ga.)	8		
Montgomery (Ala.)	7	Far West	
Macon (Ga.)	7	San Diego (Cal.)	9
Fayetteville (N.C.)	7	Sacramento (Cal.)	8
Albany (Ga.)	6	Vallejo (Cal.)	6
Goldsboro (N.C.)	5	Tacoma (Wash.)	7
Valdosta (Ga.)	5	Oxnard (Cal.)	7
Key West (Fla.)	5	Salinas (Cal.)	5

TABLE 6.2 (*continued*)

	Size		*Size*
Alaska		Hawaii	
Anchorage	5	Honolulu	9

MEDICAL/EDUCATION

	Size		*Size*
Mideast		Columbia (Mo.)	5
Ithaca (N.Y.)	5	Southeast	
Great Lakes		Tuscaloosa (Ala.)	7
Madison (Wis.)	8	Durham (N.C.)	7
Ann Arbor (Mich.)	7	Tallahassee (Fla.)	6
Champaign (Ill.)	7	Charlottesville (Va.)	5
Lafayette (Ind.)	5	Athens (Ga.)	5
Bloomington (Ind.)	5	Gainesville (Fla.)	5
		Southwest	
Plains		Austin (Tex.)	8
Ames (Iowa)	5	Temple (Tex.)	5
Rochester (Minn.)	5	Rocky Mountains	
Iowa City (Iowa)	5	Provo–Orem (Utah)	7
Lawrence (Kan.)	5	Fort Collins (Col.)	5

RESORT

	Size		*Size*
Mideast		Sarasota (Fla.)	5
Atlantic City (N.J.)	7	Hot Springs (Ark.)	5
Southeast		Far West	
West Palm Beach (Fla.)	8	Las Vegas (Nev.)	7
Fort Lauderdale (Fla.)	8	Reno (Nev.)	6
Daytona Beach (Fla.)	5		

[a] The figures are keys to the size (population) of the MLM.

Size 5	25,001 to	50,000	⎫
6	50,001 to	100,000	⎬ Small
7	100,001 to	200,000	⎭
8	200,001 to	400,000	⎫
9	400,001 to	800,000	⎬ Medium
10	800,001 to	1,600,000	⎭
11	1,600,001 to	3,200,000	⎫
12	3,200,001 to	6,400,000	⎬ Large
13	6,400,001 and over		⎭

* Denotes MLM's with nodal characteristics.

CLASSIFICATION RESULTS

CROSS CLASSIFICATION

Choices between alternative classification possibilities were necessary, however, in the case of the following 11 MLM's:

Name	Actual classification	Possible alternative classification
Paterson	nodal	manufacturing
Newark	nodal	manufacturing
Fort Wayne	nodal	manufacturing
Chicago	nodal	manufacturing
Miami	nodal	resort
Key West	nodal	government
Champaign	medical/education	government
Portsmouth (N.H.)	government	manufacturing
New London	government	manufacturing
Philadelphia	mixed (with nodal characteristics)	manufacturing
Topeka	mixed (with nodal characteristics)	government

The first two, Paterson and Newark posed special problems of classification in that they were contiguous to New York City and in many ways integrated into the Greater New York economy. For example, the Newark airport and many of its shipping facilities are operated by the Port Authority of New York. This raises the question of how interdependent these places are and whether we are justified in considering them as separate MLM's. We have followed the practice, however, of treating each SMSA as an individual labor market, relying upon the research already done by the Bureau of the Budget in delimiting geographical boundaries.[9]

[9] There remains for further research the important question as to how metropolitan labor markets are clustered and how such clusters affect the functioning of labor markets. For example, we may ask whether or not the megalopolis as discussed by Jean Gottmann is a useful concept for labor market analysis. See Jean Gottmann, *Megalopolis* (New York, Twentieth Century Fund, 1961).

In every instance the classification which was chosen appeared to have a better claim to selection than the one that was passed over. In the case of the first six MLM's each was a highly eligible candidate for classification as a nodal center, whereas percentages of employment in manufacturing, recreation, or government were not particularly high although they meet the test. In the case of Champaign, Portsmouth (N.H.), and New London the choice was more difficult but the evidence afforded by the employment data indicates that the claim of the medical/educational or government classifications were stronger than those of the rival classifications. Philadelphia represents a special case. This MLM was unable to meet all the requirements for classification as a nodal center, but it did fall within the top quartile of three business services (transportation, FIRE, business/repair). On the other hand its share of employment in manufacturing was not especially high (it ranked 105th). In view of this evidence it was deemed advisable to classify this MLM as mixed with nodal characteristics.

THE DISTRIBUTION OF MLM'S AMONG TYPES, SIZE CATEGORIES, AND REGIONS

Not unexpectedly the relative importance of the type of MLM varies widely among regions. This may be observed both in the map and in the summary (Table 6.3). In the industrialized regions of New England, Mideast, and Great Lakes 60 percent or more of the MLM's are in the manufacturing category. In the Southeast the proportion is 16 percent, and in the remaining regions, 10 percent or less.

On the other hand, no more than 10 percent of the MLM's in each of the three heavily industrialized regions is classified as nodal, in contrast to 33 percent or more in the Plains, Southwest, and Rocky Mountain regions. The remaining regions, the Southeast and the Far West, fall in between these two groups with 16 and 21 percent, respectively. The medical/education classification is of greatest relative importance in the Plains regions where it comprises 13 percent of all MLM's. Elsewhere the proportion of MLM's in this class is 5 percent or less. The resort classification which is even smaller than the

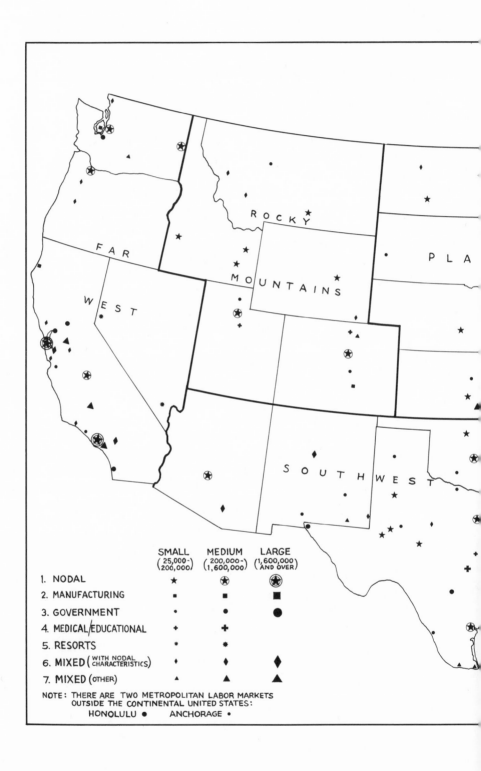

R O C K Y

F A R

W E S T

M O U N T A I N S

P L A

S O U T H W E S T

	SMALL (25,000-200,000)	MEDIUM (200,000-1,600,000)	LARGE (1,600,000 AND OVER)
1. NODAL	★	✪	✪
2. MANUFACTURING	▪	■	■
3. GOVERNMENT	•	●	●
4. MEDICAL/EDUCATIONAL	+	✚	
5. RESORTS	✳	✱	
6. MIXED (WITH NODAL CHARACTERISTICS)	♦	♦	◆
7. MIXED (OTHER)	▲	▲	▲

NOTE: THERE ARE TWO METROPOLITAN LABOR MARKETS
    OUTSIDE THE CONTINENTAL UNITED STATES:
        HONOLULU ●   ANCHORAGE •

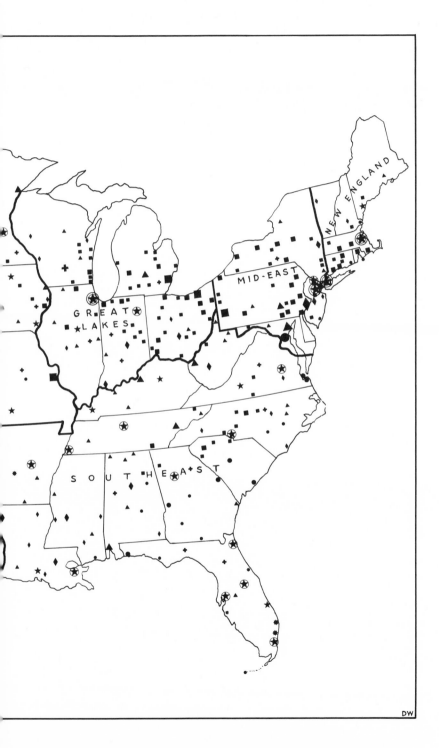

Metropolitan Labor Markets by Major Function and Size, 1960

TABLE 6.3

Number of MLM's within Each Size and Type Category and Percentage of Employment by Size, 1960: A Regional Summary

	Nodal	Manu-facturing	Mixed[a]	Other[b]	Total	Percent employment
New England (4137.9)[c]						
Large	1				1	32.4
Medium		7			7	41.5
Small	1	5	3(2)	3	12	13.6
NMC's						12.5
Total	2	12	3(2)	3	20	100.0
Mideast (14892.1)						
Large	2	1	2(1)	1	6	60.3
Medium	1	15	3(2)		19	23.3
Small		13	5(1)	2	20	6.8
NMC's						9.7
Total	3	29	10(4)	3	45	100.0
Great Lakes (13403.4)						
Large	1	2			3	34.6
Medium	1	15	4(3)	1	21	30.2
Small	1	33	13(5)	4	51	14.6
NMC's						20.6
Total	3	52	15(8)	5	75	100.0
Plains (5683.3)						
Large		1			1	13.5
Medium	4		2		6	26.3
Small	12	3	8(4)	8	31	14.5
NMC's						45.6
Total	16	4	10(4)	8	38	100.0
Southeast (13414.1)						
Large						
Medium	11	3	9(5)	9	32	37.1
Small	5	13	33(12)	19	70	17.7
NMC's						45.2
Total	16	16	42(17)	28	102	100.0
Southwest (5045.6)						
Large						
Medium	7		3(2)	3	13	51.8
Small	6		12(5)	9	27	17.6
NMC's						30.6
Total	13		15(7)	12	40	100.0

TABLE 6.3 (*continued*)

	Nodal	Manu-facturing	Mixed[a]	Other[b]	Total	Percent employment
Rocky Mtns. (1588.3)						
Large						
Medium	2				2	33.1
Small	5	1	4(3)	5	15	26.2
NMC's						38.9
Total	7	1	4(3)	5	17	100.0
Far West (7880.3)						
Large	2				2	44.2
Medium	4		5(2)	4	13	35.3
Small		2	8(7)	4	14	8.8
NMC's						11.7
Total	6	2	13(9)	8	29	100.0
Alaska, Hawaii (347.6)						
Large						
Medium				1	1	
Small				1	1	
NMC's						
Total				2	2	
Total U.S. (66372.6)						
Large	6	4	2(1)	1	13	
Medium	30	40	26(14)	18	114	
Small	30	70	86(39)	55	241	
Total	66	114	114(54)	74	368	

[a] Numbers in parentheses indicate places with nodal characteristics but which do not meet criteria for nodal classification.

[b] Government, medical/education, or resort.

[c] Regional employment in thousands.

medical/education in terms of numbers of MLM's is of greatest relative importance in the Far West (two MLM's, or 7 percent of all MLM's in the region) and Southeast (five MLM's, or 5 percent).

Evidence relating to regional systems of MLM's. The size–type classification of MLM's sheds additional light on a subject which was discussed in chapter 4: the concept of regional systems of metropolitan places. By separating the nodal places, which play the most important role as service centers, from the manufacturing and other non-nodal places, the classification makes it possible to view each region in terms of the functional composition of the size hierarchy of metropolitan economies.

In interpreting the classification results, however, we must keep in mind that the regional boundaries are arbitrary and that the MLM's are metropolitan areas, not cities. The latter characteristic reults in the regional size hierarchies of metropolitan places being somewhat different from what they would have been had the city been the unit of study. This is particularly true in the case of the smaller cities, which are often clustered around the large city and are sometimes included within the large MLM.

Nevertheless, the classification of MLM's permits us to make a very interesting observation regarding the organization of metropolitan places within regions (Table 6.3) in those regions in which there are large nodal MLM's there are very few medium- and small-size nodal MLM's, whereas in those regions in which there are no large-size nodal MLM's, the medium- and small-size nodal places are relatively numerous. In the combined industrialized regions of New England, Mideast, and Great Lakes, (49 percent of U.S. employment) where the large nodal MLM's of Boston, New York, Newark, and Chicago are located there are only two medium- and two small-size nodal MLM's. In the Far West (12 percent) where we find the large-size nodal MLM's, Los Angeles and San Francisco, there are four medium- and no small-size nodal MLM's.

On the other hand in the combined regions of the Plains, Southeast, Southwest, and Rocky Mountains, which contain a much smaller proportion of total U.S. employment (39 percent), there are no large-size MLM's and there are a total of 24 medium- and 28 small-size nodal MLM's.

How are such differences in regional systems of MLM's to be explained? The answer appears to be mainly in terms of the way in which businesses provide themselves with services. As we have seen, where there is heavy concentration of employment in manufacturing, there seems to be a tendency for business services to be provided within the firm's own organization or by firms located in headquarters cities. The evidence for this statement is found both in common observation and in the analysis of employment structure of metropolitan places in the industrialized regions. For these regions the overall share of employment in business services is small and the large nodal places account for a large share of total employment in the business service classifications. Under such conditions smaller nodal centers have failed to develop and there is little reason to think that such development is forthcoming.

In the Far West there is less manufacturing, but primary activities are frequently organized on the basis of large corporate entities. Here again the large nodal centers appear to have taken over a large share of the service functions of the regions, although there are four well-developed medium-size nodal MLM's and a number of other MLM's which may be evolving toward a full-fledged service role.

In the Plains, Southeast, Southwest, and Rocky Mountains there is more primary activity and greater geographic dispersion. Firms (largely farms) tend to be smaller and are also geographically dispersed. In general, they must make extensive use of the services provided by supplying organizations such as truckers, warehousing firms, auction markets, insurance agencies, banks, and wholesalers. It is necessary that nodal centers must be located closer to the goods-producing firms. Accordingly, these centers tend to be smaller and more numerous. No single great nodal city has as yet developed in these regions.[10] Instead we find a sizable number of vigorous medium-size nodal places such as Atlanta, Memphis, Dallas, Phoenix, and Denver, which play major roles in the business and cultural life of the hinterland they serve, and a number of small nodal MLM's as well. When we examine the evidence relating to the growth process we shall find that these places have grown more rapidly than their regions and that relatively large shares of job increases have tended to

[10] The fact that St. Louis is located within the Plains region does not contradict this observation. St. Louis is located in the extreme southeast corner of the Plains adjacent to the Great Lakes region. Moreover, it does not have well-developed nodal characteristics, and it has been classified as a manufacturing MLM.

be within the business service sector, indicating their rapid development into more complete and highly specialized service centers.

It is clear from this evidence that there is no one problem relating
to manpower in metropolitan areas, and there can be no one solution.
Training, guidance, and placement programs must vary according to
type of place and according to the kind and rate of development taking
place.

This is a theme to which we shall return in later chapters. It
arises out of the very nature of the analysis. Our strategy has been
to adopt the metropolitan labor market as a unit of study. By so doing
we have thus far been able to observe among MLM's certain fundamental differences in employment structure. In the chapters which
follow we shall also observe fundamental differences among MLM's
in the processes of employment change.

SOME CHARACTERISTICS OF STATE CAPITALS

It is interesting to note the distribution of state capitals among the
MLM type–size categories:

Type of MLM	Total			Number of MLM's		
	Number	Percent	NMC's	Small	Medium	Large
Nodal	14	28	. .	3	10	1
Manufacturing	3	6	. .	. .	3	. .
Medical/educational	3	6	. .	1	2	. .
Recreation	. .	. .	. .	. .	. .	. .
Government	6	12	. .	3	3	. .
Mixed	15	30	. .	5	10	. .
Unclassified (NMC's)	9	18	9	. .	. .	. .
All capitals	50	100	9	12	28	1

Forty-one of the fifty capitals are large enough to be classified as
MLM's. Among these twenty-nine (almost 60 percent) are nodal or
mixed places. Only six are classified as government centers, and five
of these have military bases that account for important shares of total
employment (i.e., they fall within armed forces top quartile).

The data do not indicate that public administration's direct con- tribution to employment is large for most of these capitals. Although all of the forty-one capitals which are MLM's lie in the top quartile of the array for administration, in only nine of these capitals is the percentage of total employment accounted for by public adminis- tration as much as 10 percent. In twelve other capitals it lies between 7 and 10 percent, and in the remaining twenty it is less.

A brief analysis of growth characteristics indicates a tendency for employment in the state capitals to grow somewhat more rapidly than for the typical MLM. From 1950 to 1960 the median rate of employment change for the forty-one capitals classified as MLM's was 25.0 percent compared to a median rate of 21.3 percent for all MLM's. When the state capitals are analyzed by size we find that the median for the small MLM's was 25.2 percent, for the medium-size MLM's, 26.3 percent.[11] These rates were well above medians for all small- and all medium-size MLM's. When comparisons of median employ- ment changes were made with the relatively fast-growing nodal places for the small- and medium-size categories we found, once again, that the capitals showed higher rates. The difference is probably not signifi- cant for the medium-size places, however:

	State capitals (MLM's)	All nodal MLM's
Small-size	25.2	18.2
Medium-size	26.3	26.0

STRUCTURAL VARIATIONS BY TYPE AND SIZE OF MLM

We are now in a position to examine variations in employment struc- ture among types of MLM's and among size categories within types. We observe for each type of MLM the number and percentage of places in each size-of-place category which show relatively high pro- portions of employment in selected industrial classifications (Table 6.4). The criterion employed in determining "relatively high propor- tions of employment" is that the MLM fall within the top quartile of a given classification.

[11] Since there was only one large MLM (Boston) among the state capitals no comparison was made for this size category.

TABLE 6.4
Some Key Structural Characteristics of Different Types and Sizes of MLM's

(Percentage of MLM's in the indicated type and size categories falling in the top quartile of selected industrial classifications, 1960)[a]

Type and number of MLM's		Business services	Whole-saling	FIRE	Consumer services	Retail	Recrea-tion	Medical/education	Adminis-tration
Nodal		%	%	%	%	%	%	%	%
	66	83.3	86.4	72.7	40.9	65.5	47.0	34.9	24.2
Small	30	76.7	83.3	50.0	66.7	86.7	46.5	43.3	16.7
Medium	30	90.0	96.7	90.0	23.3	33.3	50.0	26.7	30.0
Large	6	83.3	50.0	100.0	0.0	0.0	33.3	33.3	33.3
Manufacturing	114	4.5	2.7	6.3	3.6	4.5	3.3	7.1	4.5
Small	70	2.9	2.9	0.0	5.8	7.2	5.8	10.1	2.9
Medium	40	5.1	2.6	15.4	0.0	0.0	0.0	2.6	7.7
Large	4	25.0	0.0	25.0	0.0	0.0	0.0	0.0	0.0
Mixed	114	20.3	22.9	16.1	28.0	33.1	15.6	33.1	23.7
Small	86	18.0	22.5	7.9	30.3	40.4	25.0	32.6	15.7
Medium	26	29.6	25.9	37.0	22.2	11.1	22.1	37.0	48.1
Large	2	0.0	0.0	100.0	0.0	0.0	—	0.0	50.0
Resort	8	37.5	0.0	87.5	100.0	75.0	100.0	0.0	37.5
Small	6	16.7	0.0	83.3	100.0	66.7	100.0	0.0	50.0
Medium	2	100.0	0.0	100.0	100.0	100.0	100.0	0.0	0.0
Large	0								
Medical/education	21	0.0	0.0	19.4	90.5	4.8	44.6	100.0	19.1
Small	19	0.0	0.0	10.3	79.0	5.3	47.4	100.0	5.3
Medium	2	0.0	0.0	100.0	100.0	0.0	50.0	100.0	100.0
Large	0								
Government	45	10.9	10.9	15.2	6.5	10.9	24.0	10.9	78.3
Small	30	12.9	12.9	9.7	9.7	16.1	35.4	12.9	74.2
Medium	14	7.1	7.1	21.4	0.0	0.0	—	0.0	85.7
Large	1	0.0	0.0	100.0	0.0	0.0	—	100.0	100.0

[a] Top quartile represents the upper fourth of arrays of cities based on percentages of MLM employment in indicated industrial classifications. The important manufacturing industrial classification is not shown. MLM's in top quartile of this classification were classified as manufacturing-type MLM's with the single exception of Paterson, N.J., classified as nodal.

Nodal MLM's. There are basic differences among the three size groups of nodal MLM's. The medium-size nodal places tend to be characterized by the heaviest employment concentrations in the business services (90 percent of these places fall within the mainly business services top quartile). The large-size nodal MLM's show somewhat less tendency toward high concentration (83.3 percent) and the small-size nodal MLM's the least (76.7 percent). Among the detailed business service classifications, however, somewhat different tendencies may be observed. All of the large-size and 90 percent of the medium-size MLM's lie in the top FIRE quartile, but only 50 percent of the small nodal places may be so classified. On the other hand, 83.3 percent of the small- and 96.7 percent of the medium-size MLM's fall in the top wholesaling quartile, compared to only 50 percent of the large-size nodal places.

These data demonstrate how either size or type of place classifications taken *alone* fail to make clear the full extent of differences in employment composition among MLM's. It will be recalled from chapter 4 that there was a very strong tendency for the percentage of employment in each of the business services to increase with size. We now find, however, that for the nodal MLM's there is a tendency for the percentage to be largest in the medium-size MLM's. The reason for the discrepancy is, of course, that among certain other types of MLM's (especially the manufacturing, see below) the medium-size MLM does not have a high percentage of employment in the business services. When we average the various types of MLM's together we get the size of place characteristics previously noted.

For the consumer services, however, the employment composition of nodal MLM's by size category is essentially the same as was observed in chapter 5 for all types of MLM's combined. Among the nodal places it is the small-size MLM's which tend to fall most frequently in the top quartile of the mainly consumer services array (66.7 per cent as compared to only 23.3 percent of the medium-size MLM's and none of the large-size MLM's). This tendency is largely due to concentrations of employment in retailing employment. In this industrial classification, 86.7 of the small nodal MLM's lie in the top quartile as compared to 43.3 percent in the top medical/educational quartile, and 46.5 percent in the top recreation services quartile.

Manufacturing MLM's.   Among manufacturing MLM's there is virtually no representation in the top quartiles of any of the service classifications. The lone exception is the large-size MLM St. Louis, which has been classified within the manufacturing category but which falls in the top quartile of mainly business services.[12]

Resort-, medical/education-, and government-type MLM's.   The resort-type MLM's stand in sharp contrast to the medical/education and government-type MLM's in that they fall to a significant extent in the top quartiles of certain of the business and retail services, whereas the medical/educational and government-type MLM's do not. This, of course, merely bears out what was noted earlier in examining the results of the quartile analysis for MLM's with relatively heavy concentrations of employment (i.e., falling in the top quartiles) in the three service classifications, recreation, medical/educational services, and government services.

Mixed-type MLM's.   Turning to the mixed MLM classification we observe the relatively unspecialized nature of these MLM's (in so far as specialization may be judged by employment concentration). Less than a third (30.3 percent) of those places which are classified within the small-size mixed MLM's category fall in the top quartile of the mainly consumer service classification, and only 18 percent are in the top quartile of mainly business services. Among those places classified as medium-size mixed MLM's, 22.2 percent fall in the top quartile of mainly consumer services and 29.6 percent in the top quartile of the mainly business service category. Here again, as in cases of small- and medium-size nodal MLM's, we observe a tendency for the small-size MLM to show smaller employment concentration in the business services. As regards the two large-size mixed-type MLM's, Philadelphia and Baltimore, neither falls in the top quartile of mainly business

[12] It does not, however, meet the tests which were supplied in classifying MLM's as nodal.

TABLE 6.5

Growth Characteristics of Different Types and Sizes of MLM's, 1950-1960

(Medians of percentage increases in employment, regional growth indexes, and job decrease/job increase)

	Net employment increase, 1950-60		Ratio of job decreases to job increases (urban-type employment)[b]
	Percentage increase	Regional growth index[a]	
Nodal	23.5	1.73	.11
Small	18.2	1.81	.14
Medium	26.1	1.76	.07
Large	12.3	1.02	.24
Manufacturing	13.0	1.36	.20
Small	13.0	1.49	.18
Medium	15.3	1.27	.20
Large	10.6	1.09	.34
Medical/educational	31.8	2.60	.08
Resort	76.6	4.24	.04
Government	41.6	2.14	.04
Small	42.2	2.36	.06
Medium	44.8	1.40	.04
Large	27.1	2.08	.02
Mixed	13.3	.84	.18
Small	11.7	.69	.27
Medium	21.2	1.16	.09
Large	15.8	1.38	.20
368 MLM's	21.3	not computed	not computed

[a] Regional growth indexes are computed for each city by computing the ratio of the city's percentage net employment increase to that of the region in which it is located.

[b] Job decreases are total decreases in employment in those nonagricultural industrial classifications which showed declines from 1950 to 1960. Job increases are total increases in employment in nonagricultural industrial classifications which showed increases.

services or mainly consumer services. Both have rather heavy concentrations of employment in manufacturing (34.8 and 29.3 percent, respectively) but do not fall within the top quartile of this industrial classification.

Growth Characteristics of MLM's by Type and Size

Analysis of growth for each major size category of the nodal manufacturing, government and mixed-type places revealed significant differences within the type-of-place groupings (Table 6.5). The medical/ educational and resort types were too few for division according to size. In every grouping growth rates are highest for the medium-size MLM's. The decadal rate of increase from 1950-60 for the medium-size nodal cities was 26.1 percent in contrast to 18.2 percent for the small- and 12.3 percent for the large-size nodal places. Among the mixed-type MLM's the decadal rate for the medium-size was 21.2 percent in contrast to 11.7 percent for the small- and 15.8 percent for the large-size MLM's.

In general, the growth rates of the small-size MLM's tend to be above those of the large, a characteristic already noted in chapter 5. The exception, as noted above, is found in the case of the mixed-type category where the two large cities, Baltimore and Philadelphia, show an average growth rate of 15.8 percent, somewhat above the median rate of 11.7 for the 86 small-size MLM's in the group.

Net rates of employment change present a very inadequate picture of employment expansion and contraction, however. Behind these net changes lie significant variations in job increases and decreases. These measures will be examined in detail in chapters 7 and 8, but we can present highlights of the analysis through the use of job-decrease to job-increase ratios.

These ratios tell an interesting story.[13] The low net growth rates

[13] These ratios are computed on the basis of employment changes exclusive of agricultural employment. The justification of this technique is that the use of county building blocks in constructing MLM's results in the inclusion of agricultural employment which has no place in the analysis of urban struc-

of the large MLM's are found to be due in a considerable measure to the effect of job decreases. In the large nodal MLM's roughly one non-agricultural job was destroyed for every four created; in the large manufacturing MLM's, one for three; in the large mixed MLM's, one for five. These measures suggest that larger metropolitan economies facing constraints upon space and, frequently, higher-than-average wage rates are involved in a continuous process of losing firms at the same time that new firms and new jobs are being created.

When types of MLM's are compared the medical/educational, resort, and government-associated MLM's show the highest rates of net employment increase, highest relative growth indexes, and lowest ratios of job decrease to job increase of all the types of metropolitan labor markets. We observe, however, that there are considerable differences among these three classifications. The resort-type MLM's show much the highest rate of employment increase, the medical/educational MLM's the least.

The manufacturing MLM's are the slowest-growing MLM's and are characterized by the highest ratios of job decreases to job increases. This is true for every size classification except the small-size MLM's and even within this size classification the manufacturing MLM's show the slowest rate of net employment change and the highest ratio of job decrease to job increase of any but the mixed-type MLM's.

Among the nodal places fairly large differences are noted when size classifications are compared, but in each size classification rates of employment increase are found to be higher, ratios of job decreases to job increases, lower, than for manufacturing MLM's. Higher rates of employment increase and lower ratios of job decreases to job increases are also found in comparisons with the mixed-type MLM's, except in the case of the large-size mixed-type MLM's.

---

ture. Specifically, this decrease in agricultural jobs within the MLM counties has no more reason to be included in an analysis of their job destruction than do job decreases in outlying (non-NMC) counties. Use of nonagricultural data permits us to make meaningful comparisons between large MLM's where there was virtually no agricultural employment and thus no opportunity for agricultural jobs to be destroyed, and small- and medium-size MLM's, where, in many instances, very sizable numbers of agricultural jobs were destroyed.

Taken as a whole, the mixed-type MLM's experienced the slowest employment growth of any but the manufacturing MLM's. Among size classifications, however, there were very considerable differences in the employment growth measures and ratios of job decreases to job increases. The mixed-type small-size MLM's experienced a median rate of net employment increase of only 11.7 percent, lower than even the small manufacturing MLM's (13 percent). The median relative growth index for the small-size mixed-type places was only .69 (the only index less than 1 among all of the MLM's size–type groups), and the median ratio of job decrease to job increase ratio was also very high—well over 1 to 4. On the other hand, the medium- and large-size mixed-type MLM's rates of employment increase and ratio measures indicate employment growth which was more vigorous than that of the manufacturing MLM's and roughly comparable to that of nodal MLM's of similar size.

SUMMARY

A first step in analyzing employment structure was to measure for the 368 MLM's the extent to which a high or low percentage of employment in a given classification tends to be associated with a high or low percentage of employment in each of the remaining industrial classifications (INR excluded). This led to the observation that the percentages of employment accounted for by most of the business services and certain of the consumer services were significantly associated. On the basis of this knowledge we developed criteria for classifying 66 MLM's with relatively high concentrations of employment in the service industries as nodal places whose principal function was to act as service centers for surrounding hinterlands.

The remaining 302 MLM's were classified within five categories: manufacturing (114), recreation/resort (8), government-associated (45), medical/educational (21), and mixed (114). MLM's were placed within the first four of the above categories when it was observed that employment was relatively heavily concentrated in the related industrial classifications. There remained 114 MLM's which appeared to be mixed in terms of economic function, since they failed to qualify as full-fledged nodal centers and at the same time did not show sufficiently high concentrations of employment to quality as specialized non-nodal places. However, 54 of these places did display distinct nodal characteristics.

The relative importance of the type and size categories of MLM's varies widely among regions. Manufacturing MLM's are, of course, found principally in the industrialized regions, but there are relatively few nodal- or mixed-type places with nodal characteristics in these regions. In the nonindustrialized regions there are a relatively large number of nodal places.

Analysis of the size distribution of nodal MLM's makes possible a further observation: in those regions in which there are large nodal MLM's (principally, the industrialized regions) there are very few medium- or small-size nodal MLM's, whereas in those regions in which there are no large-size nodal MLM's the medium- and small-size nodal places are relatively numerous. We suggest that these basic differences in the structure of regional systems of metropolitan places may arise out of the fact that manufacturing firms require fewer services from outside the business organization and, accordingly, do not demand the development of nodal places near at hand. Primary activities, however, must be serviced from outside the organization by firms located within a relatively short distance. This need has probably favored the development of a relatively large number of small- and medium-size nodal MLM's.

Analysis of structural characteristics of the several types of MLM's serves to lay bare the very considerable differences in employment composition. Manufacturing MLM's are found to have relatively little employment in either the business or consumer services, a characteristic which augurs ill for the ability of these places to attract new firms and to develop in the years ahead. The resort-type MLM's have relatively heavy concentrations of service employment whereas the medical/educational, government-associated, and most of the mixed-type MLM's have relatively low concentrations.

Growth characteristics of MLM's were examined for each type–size classification. In every case growth rates were highest for medium-size MLM's. In general, growth rates for the small-size MLM's tended to be above those for the large. In the latter size category, rates of net employment change reflect not only low rates of job increases but also relatively high rates of nonagricultural job decreases, indicating that large metropolitan economies face significant constraints of space and are in a continuous process of transition. Among the types of MLM's the recreation/resort, government-associated, and medical/ education had the highest rate of employment increase. The rate of increase for the nodal cities, though somewhat less, was above the national average for MLM's. Rates for the manufacturing and mixed MLM's lay below the average.

7 ANALYSIS OF EMPLOYMENT-CHANGE RELATIONSHIPS IN METROPOLITAN LABOR MARKETS

GROWTH IN AN INDUSTRY is often responsive to the overall growth of the metropolitan economy. This is most likely to be true of the residentiary industries, which are largely service activities. In the first half of this chapter we treat the question, "How closely is the rate of change in each of a number of service industries associated with the rate of change in overall MLM employment."

Following this we ask a related question, "To what extent is the rate of employment change in a given service industry associated with the rate of employment change in each of the other service industries?" In other words, "How closely does employment in the various service industries tend to move together as growth or decline takes place in the metropolitan economy?" Finally, we examine the relationship between the level of employment in the construction industry and the change which occurred in total MLM employment.

It should be noted that the relationships which are being studied represent changes occurring over an entire decade, not the sort of adjustments that are usually considered in short-run multiplier analysis.

EMPLOYMENT CHANGE IN CERTAIN SERVICE CLASSIFICATIONS AND TOTAL EMPLOYMENT CHANGE IN THE MLM ECONOMY

In chapter 3 it was noted that the service activities tended to be more "ubiquitous" than nonservice activities (i.e., more widely dispersed

throughout the economy with less variation in percentages of employment from place to place). This evidence suggests that it is a reasonable hypothesis to look upon most of the services as being responsive
to growth in the metropolitan economy even though they may both
contribute and respond to the economy's growth. Accordingly we have
analyzed twelve of the service-type industries (six business services,
and six consumer services) making use of regression analyses in which
employment change in the given service industry is related to total
employment change in the MLM.[1]

We must recognize that regression analysis can do no more than
make it possible to estimate the most typical relationship between
employment increase in a given industrial classification and that in
total employment (or some other variable). There is no way to disentangle the web of cause and effect suggested by the earlier theoretical discussion in chapter 3. Although the most typical relationship
would seem to be one in which change in the level of service activity
is responsive to change in overall economic activity within the MLM,
the expansion of services may also act as a catalyst for further growth
in the MLM or surrounding region. It is also conceivable that growth
in some places may be dependent upon growth of services rather than
vice versa. Growth in FIRE, for example, may be merely responsive
to growth in income within the city, but it may be due to some extent
to an exporting of FIRE services as well. Furthermore, growth in
FIRE may stimulate growth in other industrial activities within the
city via the income multiplier, by the attractiveness it contributes to
the city as a place to locate, or by its contribution simply in adding
to the size of the market.

[1] The six business services are as follows: trucking/warehousing, other
transportation, communications, wholesaling, FIRE, business/repair services.
The consumer services were: food/dairy product stores, eating/drinking places,
other retail stores, entertainment/recreation, hotel/other personal services,
medical/educational services. Excluded were railroad/railway express services,
and also private households. The railroad/railway express services classification
was excluded because of the very strong negative trend characteristics which
were apparent during the 1950s. Private household services was excluded because
there was evidence that employment in this classification varied on a regional
basis due to differences in labor supply conditions.

Regression analysis is much more appropriate for examining the service than the basic industries. For example, manufacturing is frequently the principal if not the only sector which exports to the outside world. Growth in the city is sparked by growth in this (export base) sector. In other instances, however, growth in an individual manufacturing industrial classification may be largely responsive to growth in the city (example, manufacturers of bricks or bakery products). Our decision has been to confine the investigation of changes in employment in manufacturing to the analysis of shares of jobs increases and decreases, which is presented in the following chapter.

Analysis of change in employment in the primary industries and in the armed forces category is also postponed to the following chapter. These industry classifications may contribute to the forces of growth or decline within a metropolitan economy, and in the cases of the armed forces and certain of the extractive industries, may in some instances even comprise the export base of a city. But there is little reason to expect changes in employment in these classifications to be directly responsive to total employment change within the economy of the city. Growth in these industries is related to regional or national market demand which is exogenous to the city. For this reason, regression analysis does not suggest itself as a useful analytical tool, and has not been employed.

EVIDENCE BASED ON REGRESSION ANALYSIS

In this analysis the dependent variable is percentage change in employment in the individual industry and the independent variable is percentage change in total MLM employment. The relationship between dependent and independent variables, which is estimated by the regression analysis, is stated in the form: $X_1 = a + b X_2$ where X_1 is the estimated percentage change in employment in the service-type industry, X_2 is the percentage change in total MLM employment, and b is the coefficient which indicates the (linear) relationship between X_1 and X_2. The b coefficient we shall refer to as the "rate multiple," since it indicates the amount by which the percentage change in total MLM employment must be multiplied to estimate the associated rate of change in employment in the given service-type classification.[2] The *a* term is a constant which indicates the estimated change in the service-type industry unassociated with employment change in the MLM as a whole (i.e., the rate of employment change in the given industry which would occur if there were zero growth in the MLM as a whole). Very often, in statistical analysis, the *a* term is difficult to interpret. In this analysis we shall view the term as a measure of unassociated employment change which may reflect to a marked extent the influence of a nationwide change in demand for labor arising out of change in final demand for the goods or services produced, changes in labor productivity, factor substitution, or some combination of the above.

The degree of (statistical) confidence with which we may accept these findings is indicated by estimates of possible error in the value of *a* and *b* and by the estimates of degree of correlation between the dependent and independent variables. The former are shown by "standard error," measures given in parentheses along with the estimating equations. They indicate that the true values of *a* and *b* may vary from those indicated by as much as the value of the standard error in about one case out of three on the basis of chance alone, by as much as two times the value of the standard error in 5 cases out of 100 on the basis of chance. The degree of correlation is expressed by coefficient of correlation measures, which indicate the extent to which the estimating equation "explains" the changes in X_1 in terms of changes in X_2.

Two estimating equations for the group of 30 medium-size nodal MLM's for the decade 1950-60 are shown below.[3] The numbers in parentheses are the standard errors of *a* and *b*, respectively. The coefficients of correlation for the two estimating equations are .93 and .96, respectively.

Percentage change,　　=　　8.89 + 1.48 × percentage change, MLM employment
　FIRE employment　　　(5.32)　(.11)

Percentage change,　　= −5.87 + .89 × percentage change, MLM employment
　other retail　　　　　(2.47)　(.05)
　employment

---

[2] In formal statistical terminology the *b* value is known as the regression coefficient.

[3] The coefficients and average percentages of MLM change for FIRE and other retail presented in the following paragraphs are shown in Table 7.3.

Using the median percentage change (1950-60) in employment among medium-size nodal MLM's, the estimates of percentage change for these MLM's, taken as a group, would be as follows:

Percentage change, FIRE employment $= \ \ 8.89 + 1.48 \ (26.05) = 47.4$
Percentage change, other retail employment $= -5.87 + \ \ .89 \ (26.05) = 17.3$

In the case of FIRE the estimated percentage change in employment for the individual classification is much greater than for the total MLM. The estimated rate multiple indicates that the MLM employment growth *rate* is amplified in FIRE by almost one and a half times.[4]

On the other hand, the estimated percentage change in other retail employment is much less than the rate of change in MLM employment. Here the rate multiple is less than one, indicating that estimated other retail employment does not increase in proportion to total MLM employment. Moreover, the unassociated employment change rate is negative, reflecting apparently a decreased demand for workers in the other retail classification (under no-growth conditions) because of a reduced demand for other retail services in medium-size nodal places, to an increased output per worker in this classification, or to a combination of the two types of causes.

THE TWO DECADES COMPARED

Examining the results of the regression analysis for all 368 MLM's without classification by size or type (Table 7.1) we find that for the second decade, the estimates of unassociated employment rates of change (*a* values) are typically lower than for the first decade (ten cases out of twelve) and the rate multiples typically higher (ten cases out of twelve). The implication is that during the first decade, a considerable amount of the employment expansion in the services was associated not with growth in the metropolitan economies, but with the effects of trend (i.e., new and more important roles for these services everywhere).

[4] We observe that the value of the *a* term (8.89) in the FIRE equation is less than twice as large as its standard error (5.32). This indicates that the *a* term is not statistically significant at the .95 level of probability. In other words, we cannot be 95 percent certain that the *a* term varies from zero. In this case, however, the results of the estimate are not appreciably altered if *a* is assumed to have a value of zero.

TABLE 7.1

Employment Growth in Selected Service Industries as a Function of Metropolitan Growth, 368 MLM's

(Values of estimating equations and associated measures for regression of rates of employment change in selected industrial classifications with rates of total MLM employment changes, 1940-1950, 1950-1960)

	1940 to 1950		1950 to 1960		Change 1940-50 to 1950-60		Standard error of coefficients				Coefficient of correlation		Coefficient of variation
	Unassociated multiple change *a*	Rate multiple change *b*	Unassociated multiple change *a*	Rate multiple change *b*	*a*	*b*	1940 to 1950 *a*	*b*	1950 to 1960 *a*	*b*	1940-50	1950-60	1960
Selected business services													
Trucking/warehousing	28.21	.56	17.58	1.08	–	+	3.22	.06	2.42	.06	.43	.67	.41
Other transportation	66.82	.77	25.61	.97	–	+	5.92	.11	1.97	.05	.34	.70	.80
Communications	70.82	1.04	.47	1.19	–	+	4.89	.09	2.47*	.06	.51	.70	.32
Wholesale	36.01	.97	–.30	.74	–	–	4.08	.08	2.00*	.05	.55	.61	.38
FIRE	7.07	1.20	29.43	1.33	+	+	2.75	.05	1.83	.05	.77	.83	.35
Business/repair services	32.87	.81	–5.24	1.27	–	+	2.20	.04	2.73*	.07	.71	.69	.36
Median	34.44	.89	.09	1.14									
Selected consumer services													
Food/dairy stores	7.46	.52	14.84	.79	–	+	1.73	.03	.99	.03	.64	.85	.16
Eating/drinking places	44.09	.76	–3.47	.64	–	–	2.36	.04	1.00	.03	.66	.79	.24
Other retail	27.78	.65	3.86	.88	–	+	1.54	.03	.96	.02	.76	.88	.15
Entertainment/recreation	17.57	.77	17.29	1.01	–	+	4.01	.08	2.05	.05	.47	.71	.89
Hotel/other personal services	2.77	.61	–9.14	.84	–	+	1.59	.03	1.43	.04	.73	.77	.45
Medical/education	32.66	.72	41.39	1.16	+	+	2.17	.04	1.27	.03	.68	.88	.37
Median	17.57	.68	–3.47	.86									

Note: The letters *a* and *b* represent the *a* and *b* terms of the estimating equation which is of the form $x_1 = a + bx_2$. x_1 represents percentage change in employment in indicated industrial classification (i.e., the dependent variable); x_2 represents percentage change in total MLM employment; *a* represents percentage of employment change unassociated with change in the total MLM employment; *b* represents the coefficient which indicates the relationship between x_1 and x_2.

Coefficients of variation are taken from Table 3.1.

* The asterisk indicates that the value is not statistically significant at the .95 level of probability.

We observe also that in most cases the standard error measures were larger for both the *a* and *b* values and correlation coefficients smaller for the first decade than for the second. Here again the implication is that the employment increases which occurred in the service classifications over the first decade were more haphazard—less closely related to overall employment growth—than over the ten-year period which followed. It is possible that local differences in tastes and income levels were diminished to a greater extent during the first decade than during the second. We would expect growth patterns to be irregular while these differentials are being reduced, whereas after such changes have taken place (or when their importance is minimized), growth patterns are likely to be more uniform. We find this pattern above: The relationship between growth in these industries and overall MLM growth appears to have become more stable during the second decade.

THE SECOND DECADE EXAMINED

Although the estimates of unassociated employment change during the second decade were quite low in most instances, there were two business services, trucking/warehousing and FIRE, and one consumer service, medical/educational services, in which this was not the case. For these three classifications the estimated values indicated that there were important positive trends.

In contrast, negative unassociated change values suggest that substantial negative trends occurred in other transportation services, food/dairy product stores, and entertainment/recreation services. The negative unassociated change value in other transportation services reflects, presumably, a combination of decreased demand for employment in bus, streetcar, and taxi services (with increased use of private automobiles) and relatively high productivity increases in water transportation and air transport which offset the increased demand for these services.[5] As regards the negative unassociated employment change estimates for food/dairy product stores and entertainment/recreation

[5] The detailed data from the 113-MLM sample (1950, 1960) lend support to this thesis. For the entire sample, employment in the bus and streetcar transportation classification decreased by 17.3 percent whereas employment for the remaining classifications listed under the other transportation heading increased by 13.7 percent.

services, the first would seem to reflect the tendency for employment demand to decline due to the increased importance of self-service and the rise of the supermarkets. The second is consistent with the general observation that employment in movie theaters and other places of amusement has been affected by the tremendous increase in television viewing as a source of entertainment and by other technological changes such as automatic pin setters and golf carts.

When the rate multiple measures for the business and consumer services are compared, it is observed that the employment expansion in the individual classification associated with overall employment expansion in the MLM tends to be greater for the business services than for the consumer services: the median value for the former group is 1.14, for the latter group .86. Thus in terms of rates of growth employment expansion in the business services appears to have been more dynamic than in the consumer services, resulting in greater amplification (relative to the size of the industry category) of any employment change which occurs elsewhere within the metropolitan economy.

But this finding must be tempered by the reminder that the business services represent a smaller proportion of total MLM employment than the consumer services. For example, Table 7.1 shows that the business/repair services classification has a rate multiple of 1.27 compared with .88 for other retail. Yet other retail services is a much larger classification. In 1950 (the base year from which percentage change is measured) this classification comprised 9.0 percent of total MLM employment whereas business repair services comprised only 2.3 percent. Thus, in an MLM with a 1950 employment of 1,000,000 and a 1950-60 rate of employment increase of 26 percent, the employment increase for business/repair services and other retail would be estimated as follows:

	1950 Employment	Unassociated change	Rate of MLM increase × rate multiple	Estimated employment increase	
				number	rate
Business/repair services	23,000	− 5.24%	+ (26% × 1.27) =	+6,394	27.8
Other retail services	90,000	+ 3.86%	+ (26% × .88) =	+24,030	26.7

REGRESSION ANALYSIS, BY SIZE OF MLM

During the entire twenty-year period, there was a very strong tendency for both unassociated change values and rate multiples to be lowest for the large cities. This may be seen by observing the averages of these two values for each of the three MLM size categories, based on regression analysis of twelve of the service classifications. In every comparison, the average is lowest for the large-size MLM's.

TABLE 7.2

Employment Growth in an Industry as a Function of
Metropolitan Growth, Size-of-Place Summary
(Averages of unassociated change values and rate multiples—
twelve business and consumer service classifications,
1940-50, 1950-60)[a]

	Average of:	
MLM size category	*Unassociated change*	*rate multiple values*
	1940-50	
Small	32.15 (1)	.92
Medium	19.03 (2)	1.02
Large	15.18 (4)	.69
	1950-60	
Small	4.28 (3)	.95
Medium	.56 (4)	.96
Large	.54 (6)	.69 (1)

[a] Numbers in parentheses indicate number of service classifications with values that are not statistically significant at .95.

In interpreting this finding we must keep in mind not only that, for the large-size MLM, the rates of growth in most of the services tend to be low relative to the overall growth rate, but also that the large-size MLM's growth rate itself tends to be low in comparison to that of the medium- and small-size places (Table 6.5). We have noted in chapter 3 that growth in the large city is probably inhibited by restrictions of space, high costs of labor, congestion, taxes, and other factors. It now appears that it is also inhibited by the tendency of a number of service-type activities to fail to grow in step with total employment. Just why this tendency exists we cannot state conclu-

TABLE 7.3

*Employment Growth in Selected Service Industries as a Function of
Metropolitan Growth, by Size and Type of MLM, 1950-1960*

(Rate multiple and coefficients of correlation measures for FIRE, Other Retail, Six Business
Services [Median], and Six Consumer Services [Median]. Measures based on regressions between rates of employment change in industrial classification and rates of total MLM employment change.)

	FIRE				*Six business services*	
	Unassociated change	*Rate multiple*	*Estimated % MLM empl't change, median*	*Estimated % employment change, FIRE*	*Median rate multiple*	*Median coeff. of correl'n*
	a	*b*			*b*	*r*
All MLM's	29.43	1.33	21.33	57.80	1.14	.70
Small, total	32.43	1.39	19.98	60.20	.93	.53
Nodal	27.84	1.56	18.18	56.20	1.41(1)	.77
Manufacturing	33.88	1.13	12.97	48.54	1.03(1)	.47
Government	41.34	1.19	42.15	91.50	.66(3)	.35
Mixed	35.28	1.16	11.74	48.90	.95	.46
Medium, total	23.73	1.31	26.48	58.42	1.25	.87
Nodal	8.89*	1.48	26.05	47.44	.92	.88
Manufacturing	29.70	1.00	15.26	44.96	.96	.58
Government	42.17	.94	44.85	84.33	.73(2)	.56
Mixed	25.94	1.34	21.17	54.31	1.14	.86
Large, total	14.49	.77	16.64	27.30	.82(1)	.70
All nodal	19.29	1.41	23.46	52.37	1.01	.66
All manufacturing	31.24	1.15	12.95	46.13	1.02	.49
All resort	37.16	1.33	76.58	139.01	1.33	.92
All medical/education	32.16	1.41	31.79	76.98	1.10(3)	.38
All government	39.92	1.23	41.62	91.11	.76(1)	.37
All mixed	32.79	1.26	13.32	49.57	1.11	.68

Other retail				Six consumer services	
Unassociated change	Rate multiple	Estimated % MLM empl't change,	Estimated % employment change,	Median rate multiple	Median coeff. of correl'n
a	b	median	other retail	b	r
3.86	.88	21.33	22.63	.86	.82
5.58	.91	19.98	23.76	.90	.76
—1.72	1.10	18.18	18.28	1.13(1)	.90
7.90	.74	12.97	17.50	.67	.57
15.45	.63	42.15	42.00	.58(1)	.42
8.21	.84	11.74	18.07	.80	.68
— .31*	.88	26.48	22.99	.81	.95
—5.87	.89	26.05	17.31	.76	.92
.40*	.99	15.26	15.50	.81	.66
14.14	.60	44.85	41.05	4.59	.79
3.22	.82	21.17	20.58	.78	.97
— .77*	.49	16.64	7.38	.47(1)	.68
—3.58*	.94	23.46	18.47	.85	.84
4.54	.83	12.95	15.29	.71	.59
5.94	.99	76.58	81.75	.97	.93
—5.44	1.11	31.79	29.85	.85(4)	.42
15.66	.64	41.62	42.30	.59(1)	.44
7.63	.80	13.32	18.29	.75	.84

Note: The six business services are: trucking/warehousing, other transportation, communications, wholesale, FIRE, business/repair services. The six consumer services are: food/dairy product stores, eating/drinking places, other retail, entertainment/recreation, hotel/personal services, medical/education services.

The letters a and b represent the terms of the estimating equation which is of the form $x_1 = a + bx_2$. For explanation, see note to Table 7.1.

* The asterisk indicates unassociated change value is not significant at .95 level of probability.

Numbers in parenthesis indicates number of services classifications whose rate multiple values are not statistically significant at .95 level of probability.

sively, but it seems reasonable to suppose that there is little chance for further import substitution and that economies of scale and the increasingly intensive use of resources play a role. When the metropolis is very large, further growth in employment in the nonservice sectors need not require proportionate increases in employment in service activities. Moreover, there is less "catching up" and less import substitution. It is probable that there is a spinning off of some export-type service functions to lower order centers that are developing rapidly. This observation does not imply that income does not grow in large metropolitan places. Development may occur through the use of more capital intensive methods, higher rates of utilization of infrastructure, and higher labor productivity. Under such conditions total income would be expected to rise more rapidly than would be implied by employment growth.

Comparisons between the small- and medium-size MLM's indicate a tendency for the estimates of unassociated employment change to be larger for the former. This would seem to indicate the existence of conditions favoring the development of some service activities in small-size MLM's. There is no well-defined tendency as regards the rate multiples, however.

REGRESSION ANALYSIS, BY TYPE AND SIZE OF MLM

When the results of the regression analysis are examined for more detailed type–size classifications of MLM's additional light is shed on the responsiveness of employment expansion in the service-type industrial classification to overall employment growth in metropolitan labor markets.

Table 7.3 presents for most of the size-type groups of MLM's the unassociated change and rate multiple values for one business service, FIRE, and one consumer service, other-retail services.[6] In addition, for the same size–type groups of MLM's, median rate multiple values

[6] The large-size MLM's were not broken down by type because there would have been too few in each subclass to secure significant results from the analysis. Moreover, the resort-type MLM's and the medical/education MLM's were not broken down by size category for the same reason.

and median coefficients of correlation are shown for the six business services and the six consumer services.[7]

Coefficients of correlation.   It is immediately apparent that the relationship between rate of employment increase in the individual services and in the MLM as a whole is much better established for certain sizes and types of MLM's than for others. Median coefficients are largest for the medium-sized MLM's taken as a group, smallest for the small-sized MLM's. Within each size category, coefficients vary widely. The coefficients tend to be high for the nodal, resort-type, and government-associated MLM's.

It is for the above reason that it is particularly unfortunate that the number of places in the important large-size MLM group was too small to permit statistically reliable regression analysis of the subgroups (i.e., nodal, mixed, manufacturing, government-associated). In these large MLM's where data collection is more detailed and frequent it would be desirable to run time series analyses of these relationships. Analysis of these types of large MLM's must await the examination of shares of job increases and decreases in chapter 8.

Rate multiples.   Turning to the rate multiples we observe very different values among the different size–type groups. This is true for the FIRE and other-retail estimating equations and for the medians of rate multiples for business services and for consumer services. The rate multiple values vary both among size categories and among types of MLM's. We observe that for both business and consumer services the rate multiples tend to be lowest in the large-size MLM's when comparisons are made among size categories, but we cannot tell the extent to which these rate multiples vary by types of large-size MLM's.

When comparisons are made among types of small- and medium-

---

[7] Values of the standard error measures are not shown. However, where the *a* value or rate multiple value is less than two times the standard error in the FIRE and other retail estimating equations, this fact is indicated by an asterisk. Moreover, for the six business and six consumer services the number of rate multiple values which are less than twice the respective standard errors is indicated in parenthesis. It will be observed that there are relatively few such cases.

size MLM's, the rate multiples tend to be relatively low for the government-associated places. Apparently, in this type of MLM a given rate of overall employment growth does not tend to spark much expansion in service employment. Perhaps this is due to the fact that government establishments require few business services and that government employees do not purchase as wide a range of consumer goods and services in the local market as do persons in private employ. Most military supplies are procured directly from the manufacturer through the Pentagon.

It may appear to be a paradox that the medium-size nodal places do not show large rate multiples for the business and consumer services. But once again we must keep in mind that the rate multiples measure only one aspect of the employment change in a given industrial classification: the extent to which its rate of change is associated with the overall rate of change in employment. If the rate multiple is of only average size, but the percentage of total employment found within the industrial classification at the beginning of the period is quite large, the contribution to employment growth is made by the industrial classification will be substantial. The initial structure of employment must be considered as well as the size of the rate multiple.

To demonstrate the significance of this point it is only necessary to show that the relative importance of employment in business- and consumer-type services varies among type–size categories of MLM's. This is done by presenting, for each category, averages of the normalized employment structure in 1950 for the six business and six consumer services (Table 7.4).[8]

These measures put into perspective our findings based on the rate multiples. Although for medium-size nodal places the median rate multiple for six business services is slightly less than for medium-size manufacturing MLM's, we see that it must be applied to 1950 base structures which are very much larger. Thus the amplifying effect

[8] Averages are based on "normalized" percentages of employment (see chapter 2 for explanations of procedure used) in each of the twelve service classifications. The year 1950 was selected rather than 1960 since 1950 was the base year for the regression analysis.

TABLE 7.4

Normalized Structure of Employment, Averages for Six Business and Six Consumer Services, by Type and Size of MLM, 1950[a]

	Six business services,[b] average	Six consumer services,[c] average
Nodal		
Small	1.28	1.19
Medium	1.40	1.24
Manufacturing		
Small	.76	.92
Medium	.88	.95
Government		
Small	.88	1.07
Medium	.87	1.00
Resort	1.02	2.24
Medical/educational	.82	1.36
Mixed		
Small	.94	1.07
Medium	1.00	1.11
All small	.90	1.10
All medium	1.04	1.08
All large	1.24	1.12
368 MLM's	.96	1.09

[a] For each group of MLM's the normalized structure for a given industrial classification is the ratio of that classification's percentage of employment to the mean percentage of employment in 368 MLM's.

[b] Trucking/warehousing, other transportation, communications, wholesale, FIRE, and business/repair services.

[c] Food/dairy product stores, eating/drinking places, other retail, entertainment/recreation, hotel/personal services, medical/education services.

of overall employment growth upon employment growth in the business services is much greater for the nodal places.

We see also that the government-associated MLM's and the medical/education MLM's were characterized by relatively small percentages of employment in the business services in 1950. These places give no evidence of significant evolution toward increasing emphasis on the performances of business services since the small rate multiples apply to a sector of these metropolitan economies which were relatively unimportant in the base year.

When we look once again at the small nodal, resort-type, and medium-size mixed MLM's, we find that these places tended to have average or larger percentages of employment in both business and consumer-type services employment in 1950. The combination of relatively heavy initial structuring in the services, generally higher-than-average median rate multiples in the services (Table 7.3), or higher average overall growth rates (Table 6.5) provides evidence of a significant evolution of these places toward development of nodal-type functions.

An additional observation is that the median coefficients of correlations for the business services shown in Table 7.3 are lower than those for consumer services in every instance but one (the combined large MLM's). This would appear to reflect the fact evidenced by the coefficient of variation measures presented in Table 7.1 that the percentages of employment accounted for by the various consumer services tend to vary less from place to place than do the percentages accounted for by the business services. Accordingly, it is to be expected that changes in employment in the consumer services will tend to be more closely associated with changes in total employment than will changes in employment in the business services.

RELATIONSHIP OF EMPLOYMENT EXPANSION
IN ONE SERVICE-TYPE CLASSIFICATION
TO EMPLOYMENT EXPANSION IN ANOTHER

We must now inquire regarding a somèwhat different matter—the extent to which employment expansion in one classification is related to employment in each of the others. Clearly, this is of importance in assessing the extent to which the growth process feeds upon itself. If the rate multiples for a number of service-type industrial classifications are relatively large there is still the possibility that the relationship between the change which occurs in one classification and that which occurs in another may be haphazard: in a given MLM, growth in one classification will not necessarily be tied to growth in another. In such a case, the network of relationships among the various industrial classifications is disturbed, and the amplification of the original growth stimulus is diminished. Tendencies for growth to feed upon itself are diminished.

In this analysis we have included two classifications, utilities and administration, in addition to the six business services and six consumer services examined above, to be able to observe a larger number of industry interrelationships. Utilities has been included because it is viewed as an industry which is largely dependent upon the metropolitan economy's size and level of economic activity, and because it includes employment in certain public service activities. Administration is included because general observation indicates that in most cities employment in administration is likely to be responsive to change elsewhere within the urban economy. It has been shown earlier, however, that in certain cities employment in this classification is also associated with employment in the armed forces.

Our approach in studying the relationship between employment expansion in one classification and in another is to prepare regressions between decadal rates of employment change among each pair of industrial classifications discussed thus far in the present chapter and to compute the correlation coefficients for the regressions. A separate matrix of coefficients was prepared for each group of MLM's setting forth the coefficients of correlation between each pair of industrial classifications. Averages of correlation coefficients were prepared for each industrial classification as well as an average for all coefficients in the entire matrix presented.

An example of this procedure is shown in Table 7.5, where a matrix for medium-size nodal MLM's is shown. For this size–type group of MLM's, the relationships among the service-type classifica-

TABLE 7.5

Inter-Industry Growth Patterns, Thirty Medium-Size Nodal MLM's

(Matrix of coefficients of correlation based on regression of percentage employment changes (1950-1960) between pairs of selected industrial classifications)[a]

	Other retail	Medical/ educational	Hotel/ personal	FIRE	Business/ repair	Food/ dairy	Trucking/ warehouse	Communi- cations	Entertainment/ recreation	Eating/ drinking	Adminis- tration	Utilities	Other transportation	Wholesale
Other retail	X	.96	.93	.94	.91	.88	.88	.91	.83	.82	.81	.78	.70	.46
Medical/educational	.96	X	.91	.89	.89	.93	.84	.84	.81	.74	.75	.75	.72	.49
Hotel/other personal	.93	.91	X	.88	.85	.87	.83	.83	.81	.80	.80	.70	.75	.50
FIRE	.94	.89	.88	X	.91	.87	.84	.87	.80	.81	.72	.72	.64	.44
Business/repair services	.91	.89	.85	.91	X	.85	.90	.81	.73	.70	.75	.78	.76	.45
Food/dairy products	.88	.93	.87	.87	.85	X	.79	.74	.84	.75	.73	.62	.67	.52
Trucking/warehousing	.88	.84	.83	.84	.90	.79	X	.77	.69	.74	.76	.75	.72	.40
Communications	.91	.84	.83	.87	.81	.74	.77	X	.76	.80	.82	.73	.55	.18
Entertainment/rec.	.83	.81	.81	.80	.73	.84	.69	.76	X	.71	.70	.63	.52	.45
Eating/drinking	.82	.74	.80	.81	.70	.75	.74	.80	.71	X	.70	.52	.56	.30
Administration	.81	.75	.80	.72	.75	.73	.76	.82	.70	.70	X	.67	.56	.18
Utilities	.78	.75	.70	.72	.78	.62	.75	.73	.63	.52	.67	X	.42	.33
Other transport.	.70	.72	.73	.64	.76	.67	.72	.55	.52	.56	.56	.42	X	.59
Wholesale	.46	.49	.50	.44	.45	.52	.40	.18	.45	.30	.18	.33	.59	X
Average	.83	.81	.80	.79	.79	.77	.76	.74	.71	.69	.69	.65	.63	.41
Average (excluding wholesale)	.86	.84	.83	.83	.82	.80	.79	.79	.74	.72	.73	.67	.63	X

Average of entire matrix = .72
Average of entire matrix excluding wholesale = .77

[a] Industrial classifications have been arranged according to size of average coefficients of correlation.

tions are generally quite close.[9] In the portion of the matrix which shows the degree of correlation among the eight most closely associated industrial classifications (28 relationships in industries 1 through 8) there is only one correlation coefficient as low as .74.

Here again is evidence of the value of classifying MLM's on a dual type–size basis. We find that the medium-size nodal MLM's in Table 7.5 not only have demonstrated a tendency for relatively rapid growth but that their growth is of a certain sort: increases in employment in the various services tend to occur together in a process of agglomeration and, very likely, to interact. Apparently, these places are increasingly taking on an important role as service centers. Such knowledge should be of considerable importance for planning and for dealing with the sort of manpower problems which confront such MLM's.

The averages computed for each group (including medium-size nodal MLM's) have been brought together in Table 7.6.[10] We are immediately struck by the very substantial differences in the averages

[9] It is interesting that employment change in wholesaling is not closely related to employment change in any of the other classifications in this MLM type-size group. A check into the detailed regression findings from the earlier analysis in which rate of change in the individual classification was regressed with rate of changes in total employment is informative: we find that the rate multiple for wholesaling is only .28 whereas the rate multiples for the other classifications are .60 or above. Moreover, the correlation coefficient for the regression of employment change in wholesaling with overall MLM employment change is only .42 whereas the correlation coefficients for the remaining classifications range from .69 to .93. From this evidence we conclude that there has been little tendency for wholesaling employment to grow, taking these MLM's as a group, and that employment growth in this classification relative to overall MLM employment growth has been quite erratic.

[10] Since the result of these analysis, 13 matrices (13 MLM size–type categories, see Table 7.6) each with a 14 by 14 grid of correlation coefficients, provided far too many data for ready presentation and analysis, we consolidated the data in the following manner. For each matrix we recorded the average of the correlation coefficients for each industrial classification. For example, in the medium-size nodal city matrix the mean coefficient of correlation for FIRE related to each of the other classifications is .79 but the mean coefficient for wholesale and the other classifications is .41. We interpret these measures as indicating that among the medium-size nodal cities the linkages between employment expansion in FIRE and the various other industrial classifications examined

of correlation coefficients for the various type–size categories of MLM's. If we examine the MLM's simply on the basis of size, we find that the average correlation coefficients for the small- and large-size matrixes are .50 and .52 but for the medium-size matrixes the average coefficient is .82. Turning to the type–size categories we observe that whereas the average correlation coefficients for the small- and medium-size nodal places are .64 and .72, the averages for the small- and medium-size manufacturing MLM's are only .27 and .42. Still another interesting contrast is found in the fact that the average for resort-type MLM's is .82 but for medical/education MLM's it is only .24.

These measures of correlation provide additional information which may be summarized as follows:

1. The medium-size nodal MLM's showed the highest average correlation coefficients, indicating that growth in these places is a process of agglomeration, growth which is shared by most service categories. The linkages among the services are strong for this type–size MLM group, although we noted earlier that rate multiples (based upon the relationships between growth in the individual industrial classification and overall MLM growth) were not unusually large.

The small-size nodal places show a similar tendency. The chief difference between the small- and medium-size nodal MLM's is that in the former the average of coefficients for relationships between wholesale and the other classifications is relatively high (average .75) and for business/repair services, relatively low (average .56), whereas in the latter the situation is reversed (the wholesale average is .41 and the business/repair services average .79). It would appear that the growth in the smaller nodal places was more closely related to the development of the wholesaling functions, that growth in the medium-size nodal places was more closely related to the increased provision of nonwholesale-type business services.

---

are typically much stronger than those which exist between employment expansion in wholesale and the other classifications.

A further step toward summarization was to compute the average of all coefficients of correlation for each type of MLM matrix. In the case of the medium-size nodal MLM the overall average was .72.

TABLE 7.6

Inter-Industry Growth Patterns: Type and Size of Place Summary

(Average coefficients of correlation of types indicated in Table 7.5)

	Trucking/ warehouse	Other transportation	Communi- cations	Utilities	Wholesale	FIRE	Business/ repair	Food/ dairy	Eating/ drinking	Other retail	Hotel/ personal	Entertainment/ recreation	Medical/ educational	Administration	Average
All MLM's															
Small	.38	.42	.42	.42	.48	.61	.51	.59	.49	.66	.54	.42	.63	.38	.50
Medium	.82	.81	.83	.75	.77	.86	.67	.86	.84	.89	.88	.85	.88	.77	.82
Large	.51	.37	.46	.59	.52	.64	.49	.60	.55	.66	.64	.28	.61	.33	.52
Nodal															
Small	.62	.61	.22	.47	.75	.74	.56	.71	.71	.78	.64	.67	.78	.74	.64
Medium	.76	.63	.74	.65	.41	.79	.79	.77	.69	.83	.80	.71	.81	.69	.72
Manufacturing															
Small	.30	.31	.20	.17	.30	.31	.27	.33	.19	.44	.27	.12	.34	.18	.27
Medium	.37	.36	.35	.38	.44	.45	.34	.49	.48	.61	.52	.36	.55	.23	.42
Government															
Small	.32	.42	.49	.43	.47	.63	.59	.52	.35	.65	.60	.41	.63	.01	.46
Medium	.29	.24	.27	.52	.38	.62	.64	.53	.53	.61	.58	.46	.59	.12	.47
Resort	.83	.85	.88	.87	.85	.85	.67	.86	.81	.84	.65	.72	.88	.87	.82
Medical/ educational	.27	.13	.27	.35	.32	.18	0.0	.23	.29	.42	.17	.25	.34	.19	.24
Mixed															
Small	.25	.37	.33	.35	.36	.50	.39	.48	.45	.58	.49	.29	.50	.40	.41
Medium	.82	.77	.80	.70	.73	.88	.59	.87	.86	.88	.87	.86	.88	.80	.81

2. The very low averages of correlation coefficients in manu-facturing MLM's support earlier observations regarding these places. Not only is the percentage of persons employed in the service classi-fications small but employment expansion in the services is extremely haphazard. Any stimulus to growth in the major export base activity (i.e., manufacturing) which is experienced in these economies does not tend to be transmitted broadly through the service categories.

3. The same general observation may be made for the govern-ment and medical/education-type MLM's, but the sources of growth in these types of MLM's (i.e., the growth trends in the export base industries, government services, and medical/education services) are very much stronger than is the case for manufacturing, the export base in the manufacturing-type MLM's.

4. Quite in contrast, the average of correlation coefficients for the resort-type MLM's was very high. We have observed previously that in these cities the rate multiples also tended to be high. Appar-ently, we are observing here the amplifying processes from growth in the services at work to a remarkable degree.

5. Finally, we must observe, once again, characteristics of large-size MLM's which serve to explain why growth rates tend to be low in these places.[11] Correlations between the growth rates of the various service categories are generally weak. This may be interpreted as a reflection of the economies of scale which already obtain. Once a service industry is established on a certain scale further expansion of services rendered may become largely a matter of capacity utilization. Because of its great size, growth in one segment of the large metro-politan economy need not spark significant growth in another. For example, retail employment will not necessarily respond to an increase in FIRE. This does not mean that rate multiples for certain of the services are not large (e.g., business/repair services) but there is little evidence of significant (employment) growth linkages among a ma-jority of the services.

Of course, a low average of the correlation coefficients is found also for the overall small-size MLM category. But here the most likely

[11] Separate correlation matrices were not prepared for the large cities within any of the type of MLM classifications.

explanation would seem to be a different sort: the small-size MLM's may be presumed to be more heterogeneous than the large-size MLM's. Some of these MLM's have nodal characteristics, and for them we observe that the linkages among certain of the services are fairly strong (i.e., the correlations are relatively high). Another quite sizable group is composed of manufacturing places in which the relationship between growth in one service activity and another is very low, indeed. Finally, there is a large group of unspecialized (i.e., mixed) MLM's in which the correlations in growth rates among the services are quite low. Many of these latter places are not in a position to grow in a balanced fashion because business and consumer services are being provided by some nearby nodal center. These places may be regarded as satellites of the larger centers. Their problems and their outlook are likely to be quite different from the other small places.

EMPLOYMENT IN THE CONSTRUCTION INDUSTRY AND THE ACCELERATION PRINCIPLE

We now turn to a consideration of the factors influencing employment in the construction industry. What makes employment in construction of special interest is the fact that the goods produced by this industry are to a very large extent highly durable goods such as houses, industrial plants, institutional and commercial buildings, and roads. These "products" for the most part go to enlarge the stock of durable capital goods, although some, of course, go to replace units that are worn out or for some other reason considered to be uneconomic. Once produced, these durable goods provide a stream of services over very long periods of time. Unlike short-lived products, they do not require immediate replacement. The level of current demand for the construction industry rests, principally, therefore, upon the need to *enlarge* the stock of housing and other physical facilities. This demand relationship, as we have noted in chapter 3, is an example of the so-called "acceleration principle."

The implication of the above is that the level of construction employment should be closely related to the *increase* in total employment. This hypothesis rests on the assumption that an increase in total employment will stand as a proxy for the increments in the stock of new housing, plants, buildings, and roads during each time period or, put differently, as a proxy for the demand for new construction.

There are a number of difficulties in testing the acceleration hypothesis by Census employment data. Change in total employment may not be a satisfactory proxy for the demand for new structures because the amount of labor inputs required per unit of plant or building varies widely by type of construction. It is also likely that in a new and expanding urban area where no demolition is necessary, less construction employment will be associated with a given increment of employment than in an area which is more fully developed. Implicit in the acceleration hypothesis is the assumption that there is an equilibrium level of capital goods, which each MLM tries to attain.

Further, where demolition is important, the relationship will be different from that which obtains where it is not. It is probable that demolition costs increase with size of place and degree of previous site development. Moreover, the need for maintenance acts to weaken further the acceleration relationship.

Another problem is that the construction industry is relatively flexible in terms of the output it can produce. Persons employed in the industry can work part time, full time, or over-time. This would make for a "loose" relationship between the demand for construction and the number of persons classified as construction workers in the employed work force. Moreover, employment change does not necessarily reflect the industrial transition which takes place within a metropolitan economy. If there is a shift from manufacturing to the services or from production to administration within the manufacturing classification there may be a demand for new structures even though there is no change in overall MLM employment.

Finally, the time period over which such an hypothesized relationship holds is unclear. Frequently, construction of housing anticipates growth, but on other occasions there is a lag. Should the existing level of construction employment be related to change during the current period? Over the most recent one-year period? Two-year period? Five-year period? Ten-year period?

Since we are limited to decadal census data, we have no choice but to test the relationship between the level of employment in construction in a given MLM to the change in total employment in the MLM during the preceding ten-year period. While there is no evidence that a period of such duration in any way approximates the "ideal," it can be argued that it has the virtue of being a sufficiently long period to permit adjustment of the work force to the demand arising from the forces of growth. On the other hand, there is no way of knowing whether the observed decadal change is representative of growth occurring during the most recent years of the period or is due largely to change occurring during the earlier years.

As we turn to the empirical investigation of the relevance of the acceleration principle hypothesis as an explanation of the level of employment in construction, we are immediately struck by the observation that the percentage of employment accounted for by fast-growing places is higher than the percentage for the slow-growing. For the 184 fastest-growing MLM's (top half) the mean share of employment in construction (1960) was 6.67 percent. For the 184 slowest-growing MLM's (bottom half) it was 5.47 percent.

A second observation, however, is that the extent of variation among shares of total employment accounted for by construction is not especially large relatively to those in many other industrial classifications. We note in Table 3.1 that the coefficient of variation (which expresses the standard deviation as a percentage of the mean) for shares of employment in construction is only .27, well below the coefficient for medical/educational services, .37, though higher than that for retail, .13.

These two observations imply that the relative level of employment in construction is to a significant degree influenced by growth but that there is an important element of stability as well. It would seem that, in effect, there are two major components to construction demand. One arises out of growth; the other, which tends to be a function of scale, arises out of requirements occasioned by the need for maintenance, renovation, and changes arising out of new technology, industrial transition, and changing residential patterns within the community, and out of shifting demographic characteristics (e.g., the demand for schools increases with an increase in the percentage of young people) as well.

To investigate the accelerator hypothesis more thoroughly, we employed regression analysis in which the dependent variable is percentage employment in construction and the independent variable is percentage change in total MLM employment. The relationship between dependent and independent variables is stated, as in the first section of this chapter, in the form: $X_1 = a + bX_2$. Here X_1 is the estimated percentage of employment in construction in a given census year, X_2 is the percentage change in total MLM employment, a is the estimated percentage of MLM employment in construction in the census year in question which is unassociated with employment change in the MLM as a whole, and b (the rate multiple) is the coefficient which indicates the (linear) relationship between X_1 and X_2.[12]

In carrying out these analyses two measures of employment change were used experimentally. The first was percentage net change in total employment; the second was percent change in total job increase. Regressions were computed for all 368 MLM's, for the 184 fastest-growing MLM's, and for the 184 slowest-growing MLM's. For each group of MLM's, especially in the case of the slowest-growing MLM's it was found that the relationship was improved by using the rate of job increase as a measure of employment change rather than rate of net employment change:

[12] Typically the acceleration hypothesis is stated in the form: investment demand (here, MLM employment in construction) is a function of change in final demand (here, change in total MLM employment during a preceding period). Experiment indicated, however that it was not feasible to test the relationship in this form because of a high correlation due to size alone: a large-size MLM would show a large employment in construction even though rate of growth was low; a small MLM-size would have a small absolute employment in construction even though rate of growth was high. For this reason we made use of an equation in which the dependent and independent variables were expressed as a percentage of total MLM employment in a given year. Thus,

$$\frac{\text{MLM employment in construction 1960}}{\text{total MLM employment 1960}} =$$
$$a + b \left(\frac{\text{change in MLM employment 1950-60}}{\text{total MLM employment 1960}} \right)$$

	Rate of net change in employment (1950-60)	Rate of total job increase (1950-60)
368 MLM's	51.7	53.4
184 fastest-growing MLM's	48.6	50.5
184 slowest-growing MLM's	12.2	21.8

This finding is easily rationalized: the demand for construction employment is related to the opening up of new employment, not to the closing out of employment. In a measure of employment change in which job decreases have been subtracted from job increases, the amount of change giving rise to the need for new facilities will tend to be underestimated.

Making use of job increases as a measure of change the estimating equations for the three groups of MLM's are shown below (X_1 = estimated percentage of employment in construction, 1960; X_2 = 1950-60 percentage MLM job increase):

$$X_1 \text{ 368 MLM's} = 5.02 + 0.32\, X_2$$
$$(.0026)$$

$$X_1 \text{ 184 fastest-growing MLM's} = 5.32 + 0.28\, X_2$$
$$(.0036)$$

$$X_1 \text{ 184 slowest-growing MLM's} = 4.47 + .057\, X_2$$
$$(.019)$$

Substituting the average percentage job increase (1950-60) for X_2 the estimates of percentage of employment in these groups of MLM's would be as follows:

$$X_1 \text{ 368 MLM's} = 5.02 + .032\,(32.8) = 5.02 + 1.05 = 6.07$$
$$X_1 \text{ 184 fastest-growing MLM's} = 5.32 + .028\,(48.0) = 5.32 + 1.34 = 6.66$$
$$X_1 \text{ 184 slowest-growing MLM's} = 4.47 + .057\,(17.6) = 4.47 + 1.00 = 5.47$$

From these estimating equations we learn that by far the largest share of employment in construction may not be associated with employment change. For each group of MLM's the unassociated share is roughly four-fifths of the estimated percentage of construction employment.[13] Thus the regression analysis supports the earlier observation: that the accelerator mechanism should be regarded as a significant but secondary influence—only one of the factors acting to determine the level of construction employment.

A further finding is that the relationship is much stronger in those MLM's in which growth is rapid than in those in which it is not. The correlation measures shown previously indicate that the correlation is much closer for the upper half of the 368 MLM's ranked according to 1950-60 growth rates than for the lower. For the former group the coefficient of correlation is 50.5 as compared to 21.8 for those MLM's lying in the bottom half.

Finally, we must take note of the fact that the correlation coefficients for the regressions are not high, even though for the 368 MLM's and the 184 fastest-growing MLM's they are statistically significant (the coefficients of correlation are 53.4 and 50.5, respectively). Apparently, the relationship described by the estimating equation is marred by the inadequacy of the data in the decadal form used and by the influence of other variables mentioned but not tested.

SUMMARY

In this chapter three analyses of employment change or structure were performed.

The *first* focuses attention on twelve of the service industry classifications—six business services and six consumer services. We test the relationship between percentage employment change in the specific service industry, the dependent variable, and percentage change in total MLM employment, the independent variable. The regression analysis permits us to estimate the rate of decadal change in the service-type employment which is associated with change in total MLM employment. The value of this estimate is shown in the form of a regression coefficient which is called the "rate multiple."

[13] For the 368 MLM's it is 83 percent (5.02 ÷ 6.07), for the 184 fastest-growing, 80 percent, for the 184 slowest-growing, 82 percent.

We observe also an estimate of rate of change in service employment which is unassociated with overall MLM employment change (which it is estimated would have occurred under zero growth conditions).

Comparison of the regression analysis for two decades reveals that values for the unassociated change measures for the first period were typically larger and the rate multiples typically smaller than for the second. Thus it appears that expansion of the service sector in individual MLM's during the 1940s was due more to general trends of expansion than to overall growth of employment in MLM's. In the second decade, overall MLM expansion played a greater role and general trends a lesser role in the expansion of the service sector.

Analysis for the second decade reveals that employment change in the business services was more responsive to change in overall MLM employment than was employment change in the consumer services. The latter, however, represented a large proportion of total employment at the beginning of the decade and, in spite of smaller rate multiples, accounted for a larger share of total job increases during the period.

Among the size categories of MLM's the larger places had the smaller unassociated change and rate multiple values. This finding indicates that for these metropolitan economies, taken as a whole, there was relatively little amplification of existing growth tendencies as a result of employment expansion in the services measured in terms of rates of change. We see here an indication that, when the city is very large, further growth originating in the nonservice sectors does not tend to set off substantial increases in service employment. Unfortunately the group of large-size MLM's is too small to be analyzed by type-of-place subgroups using regression analysis. Analysis of shares of job increase by size–type groups is presented in the following chapter.

The relationship between rate of employment change in individual services and in total MLM employment varied widely among types of place and also among type–size subgroups. This was true for measures of correlation and for the rate multiple values. Excluding the large-size places, where correlation coefficients were generally low, correlation was highest for resort-type and nodal MLM's and for medium-size mixed MLM's; lowest for medical/educational, government-associated, and manufacturing MLM's. Rate multiples tended to be relatively small for the government-associated places and, in consumer services, for manufacturing MLM's. Highest rate multiples were found in the resort-type (medium- and small-size) and small-size nodal MLM's.

The *second* analysis measures the relationship between employment change in one service-type classification and employment change in each of the other service-type classifications. This analysis permitted us to observe the extent to which any employment expansion which occurs is diffused through the service sector of a given type–size group of MLM's. Where high average correlation coefficients are found they indicate that growth is a process of agglomeration, i.e., that growth is shared by most service categories and that linkages are strong. Results of these regression analysis lent strong support to the findings in the preceding section. Resort-type (medium- and small-size), nodal MLM's, and medium-size mixed type MLM's showed the highest levels of correlation; manufacturing, government-associated, medical/educational MLM's, both medium-size and small, along with small-size mixed MLM's showed the lowest correlations.

We conclude that the nodal and resort-type MLM's demonstrated the type of responsiveness within the service sector which reinforces existing growth tendencies and which may act to stimulate still further growth. The manufacturing MLM's and small-size mixed-type places apparently respond in a limited and unpredictable way to growth stimuli. Finally, the government-associated and medical/educational MLM's, although relatively fast growing by virtue of rapid expansion in their export bases, have shown little tendency for growth to be amplified by secondary increases in service type employment.

The *third* analysis examines the applicability of the acceleration principle as an explanation of the forces determining the level of employment in the construction industry. The hypothesis is that employment in construction at the end of a decade is associated with change in MLM employment during the preceding decade. The latter variable is used as a surrogate for the demand for construction, since, according to the acceleration principle, the demand for increments to the stock of capital goods (i.e., investment) is determined by the *change* in final demand for the goods and services produced by the economic organization in question. The relationship examined was between the percentages of employment accounted for by construction in MLM's (the dependent variable) and the decadal rates of change in total employment (the independent variable).

An important finding was that shares of employment accounted for by construction varied relatively little among the 368 MLM's, indicating that maintenance requirements, building needs arising out of shifts within the urban economy, and other factors not closely related to local growth, combine to influence the level of construction employment to a significant extent. Nevertheless, the analysis showed that the share of employment accounted for by construction is associated to a significant extent with the decadal rate of change in employment.

8 THE COMPOSITION OF EMPLOYMENT CHANGE IN METROPOLITAN LABOR MARKETS: ANALYSIS OF SHARES OF JOB INCREASES AND JOB DECREASES

DATA ON the share of job increases and decreases provide a somewhat different type of information from that provided by the rate of employment change. Analysis of shares of job increases (decreases) makes it possible to measure the direct contribution of each industrial classification to employment expansion (contraction).

In this chapter, three types of analyses are undertaken: 1) examination of the extent to which shares of job increases in the individual industrial classifications vary among MLM's; 2) analysis of the average shares of job increases and decreases in selected industrial classifications for each of the various type–size MLM categories; 3) analysis of the average shares of job increases and decreases in selected industrial classifications for the 50 fastest-growing and the 50 slowest-growing MLM's.

IMPORTANCE OF VARIOUS INDUSTRIAL CLASSIFICATIONS AS A SOURCE OF JOB INCREASES

SHARES OF JOB INCREASES, BY INDUSTRY

To assess the importance of the various classifications as sources of job increases we examine arrays similar to those presented in Table 3.1. Table 8.1 presents for each of a number of industrial classifications the share of 1950-60 job increases at selected percentiles of a 368-MLM array.

For some classifications, a substantial share of job increases are found among a very large number of MLM's, whereas in other classifications, a substantial share of job increases are noted in only a relatively small number. The medical/educational classification is an important example of the first type. Not only does it account for more than a third of the job increases in the 90th percentile MLM and a fifth in the median MLM, but it also accounts for more than one-tenth in the MLM representing the fifth percentile. The total manufacturing category shows similar characteristics. It accounts for 27.2 percent of job increases in the median MLM, almost 17 percent in the 25th percentile. Below this point in the array, however, it accounts for a smaller share than medical/educational services.

Among the business services only FIRE is an important source of new jobs for any sizable number of MLM's. It accounts for 5.1 percent of job increases in the median MLM, almost 3 percent in the MLM representing the 10th percentile.

Among the consumer services, the retail category is second in importance to medical/educational as regards shares of job increases. For the median MLM, more than 8 percent of job increases are accounted for by retailing; for the MLM in the 25th percentile, more than 5 percent. Job increases in retailing are dominated by the other retail classification. For this classification the median MLM shows a share of job increases which is almost 7 percent; the MLM representing the 25 percentile, more than 4 percent.

A solid finding is that the share of job increases in recreation-type services is small, except in the case of a limited number of MLM's. For the MLM at the upper extremity of the range, the share is 31.1 percent; for the 95th percentile, less than 5 percent; for the median, well under 1 percent. Except within the extreme upper range of the array, the private households classification was of greater importance than that of recreation. In the 75th percentile, this classification accounts for 4 percent of job increases; in the median MLM, 2.1 percent.

TABLE 8.1

Analysis of Variations in Share of Job Increases, by Industry: Selected Percentiles, 368 MLM's, 1950-1960[a]

						Percentiles					
	1st	5th	10th	25th	33rd	50th	67th	75th	90th	95th	100th
Primary						1.3	.32	.51	1.9	3.5	33.7
Construction					1.3	2.6	4.1	4.9	7.6	9.4	26.9
Manufacturing	1.6	7.6	10.4	16.6	20.1	27.2	33.5	37.9	47.1	51.0	70.9
Utilities				.26	.47	.77	1.2	1.4	2.2	3.2	10.2
Mainly business services	2.0	5.1	6.2	8.0	9.3	11.3	13.5	14.9	18.5	21.3	32.2
Transportation					1.2	1.7	2.3	2.8	3.9	5.5	11.1
Railroads/railway express											1.2
Trucking/warehousing						1.4	2.0	2.4	3.4	5.0	11.1
Other transportation								.21	1.1	1.8	6.3
Communications							1.3	1.5	2.1	2.9	15.2
Wholesale						1.3	2.2	2.8	4.4	5.5	5.3
FIRE		2.5	2.9	4.0	4.4	5.1	5.9	6.5	8.2	9.5	20.1
Business/repair services						1.1	2.0	2.5	3.6	4.3	18.4

Mainly consumer services	20.1	22.9	27.6	29.5	32.8	37.3	40.4	47.4	52.8	76.1
Retail		2.3	5.3	6.5	8.5	10.3	11.3	14.1	15.8	22.3
Food/dairy stores						1.5	1.0	1.8	2.3	3.6
Eating/drinking places							1.9	2.9	3.3	6.6
Other retail		1.8	4.5	5.4	6.9	8.1	8.9	11.1	12.3	16.3
Recreation						1.7	2.2	3.6	4.5	31.1
Hotels/personal services						1.4	1.8	3.1	3.8	25.6
Entertainment/recreation									1.2	14.0
Private household	10.3			1.2	2.1	3.1	4.0	6.2	8.0	12.3
Medical/educational		12.3	15.0	16.7	20.1	24.4	26.1	34.1	39.0	62.6
Government		1.2		3.4	4.9	8.9	12.8	31.6	41.3	70.1
Administration			2.4	3.0	3.9	4.9	6.1	9.9	13.3	38.1
Armed forces						2.0	4.2	22.5	33.1	63.6
INR	1.1	3.0	5.2	6.1	9.1	12.3	14.5	21.5	25.0	44.5

[a] Percentages shown in each percentile are for lowest-ranking MLM in that percentile except in the 50th and 100th. In the 50th percentile we have shown the median value; in the 100th, the highest. Only values of 1 percent or more are shown.

The shares of job increases accounted for by direct government employment are large at the upper extremities of the array but small for the middle and lower segments. For the upper 10 percent of the MLM in their respective arrays, armed forces account for 22.5 percent or more of job increases; administration for 10 percent or more. The shares of job increases accounted for by armed forces below the 90th percentile were much smaller. For example, the share in the median MLM was less than .5 percent. Not unexpectedly, administration, which includes state and municipal as well as federal government employment, was of greater importance throughout the middle portions of the array: the share of job increases observed in the 75th percentile was roughly 6 percent; in the 50th percentile, 4 percent; in the 25th percentile, more than 2 percent.

Finally, Table 8.1 indicates the existence of bias in the job-increases and -decreases data arising out of the increased enumeration of workers in the INR-classification in the 1960 census. This failure to classify workers had the effect of causing 1960 employment in the appropriate classifications to be smaller than it otherwise would have been. The effect of the under-enumeration in the appropriate classification in 1960 was to reduce the number of job increases in those classifications in the 1950-60 period, and/or to increase the number of job decreases in the same classifications. For the MLM's in the upper ranges of the INR array, this type of bias appears to be substantial. In the 75th percentile MLM, more than 14 percent of the total job increases were accounted for by INR.[1]

---

[1] As an example of the degree of bias which might very easily exist in an under-enumeration classification we may note the extent of correction which would be necessary if we were to recompute for the MLM lying in the 75th percentile the shares of job increases for each classification assuming that the under-reporting reflected in the INR classification is distributed equally to job increases in all classifications (with no effect in job decreases). Under such an assumption the remaining 86 percent of jobs created in the 75th percentile city becomes 100 percent. The share of jobs created in each of the industrial classifications would need to be multiplied by 1.16 (i.e., $100 \div 86 = 1.16$).

AVERAGE OF SHARES OF JOB INCREASES
BY TYPE AND SIZE OF MLM's

THE CHANGING ROLE OF MANUFACTURING

Perhaps the most clear-cut finding concerns the change in the role of manufacturing as a source of employment expansion from the first to the second decade: average share of job increases due to manufac-

TABLE 8.2

Shares of Job Increases Accounted for by Manufacturing in Employment Expansion, by Type and Size of MLM

	Shares of job increases	
MLM's	*1940-50*	*1950-60*
Nodal	18.5	22.8
Small-size	14.9	21.3
Medium-size	19.3	23.7
Large-size	33.4	26.1
Manufacturing	42.7	36.5
Small-size	42.6	38.8
Medium-size	43.3	33.5
Large-size	39.4	28.1
Government	9.6	14.1
Small-size	9.4	11.9
Medium-size	10.0	19.6
Large-size	5.7	7.6
Medical/education	12.8	17.3
Small-size	12.7	18.1
Medium-size	14.1	11.9
Resort	8.6	16.9
Small-size	9.2	18.7
Medium-size	6.9	11.6
Mixed	23.6	29.3
Small-size	22.9	31.0
Medium-size	25.7	23.5
Large-size	27.3	31.1
All MLM's (median)	24.3	27.2
Total U. S.	28.3	27.7

turing declined in those places classified as manufacturing MLM's but tended to rise among the other type of MLM's.

Although significantly smaller in the second decade, the average share of job increases accounted for by the manufacturing classification continued to be larger for the manufacturing-type MLM's than for other types. In the large manufacturing places, the average share declined from 39.4 to 28.1 percent; in the medium-size, from 43.3 to 33.5; in the small-size, from 42.6 to 38.8.

Among the other types of MLM's, the rise in the percentage of job increases accounted for by manufacturing was impressive. For the fast-growing resort and government-associated MLM's, shares rose from 8.6 to 16.9 and from 9.6 to 14.1 percent, respectively. For the nodal (all sizes) and medical/educational MLM's, from 18.5 to 22.8 and from 12.8 to 17.3 percent, respectively; for the mixed-type MLM's (all sizes), from 23.6 to 29.3 percent.

Thus we see expressed here for types of metropolitan economies what was noted earlier (chapter 2) for regions: manufacturing became an increasingly important source of new jobs in those places where previously it was relatively unimportant, a less important source in the places which traditionally had specialized in this type of activity.

SHARES OF JOB INCREASES/DECREASES: SELECTED CLASSIFICATIONS

We shall not attempt to deal further with interdecadal comparisons, but rather shall observe for the most recent decade shares of job increases and decreases accounted for by the various industrial classifications, seeking to determine the typical patterns of employment change for the various groups of MLM's.

The average share of job-increase data (Table 8.3) highlight the findings. Taken along with the average decadal rates of employment change (Table 6.5) and with selected information relating to job decreases (Table 8.3) they provide a statement of employment expansion behavior in each group.

Nodal MLM's. The relatively fast-growing medium-size nodal places show a very high average share (18 percent) of job increases accounted for by business services. This finding must be interpreted carefully: the growth of business services has figured importantly in employment expansion at the same time that overall employment growth has been relatively rapid. Clearly, these nodal centers, which include such MLM's as Atlanta and Houston, are taking on additional business service functions as they assume a more important place in the American economy.

On the other hand, for these medium-size nodal places, shares of job increases in the consumer services and in manufacturing are slightly below the median levels for all cities. These observations must not be seen as indicating that the latter classifications have been unimportant as a source of employment expansion. Quite to the contrary, the fact that, under conditions of relatively rapid overall employment growth, the share of job increase accounted for by consumer services was only slightly below the median indicates that there was a healthy development of this sector. These places, most of which were already specialized in the rendering of services at the beginning of the decade, must be seen as continuing their nodal development with increasing emphasis on the business services. It will also be seen that the ratio of job decreases to job increases was relatively low for these MLM's and that roughly a third of such job destruction as occurred was accounted for by agriculture.

The small nodal places differ in several respects. Employment increase was at a slower rate, due in part to the fact that job decreases were higher relative to job increases. Once again the services category figures prominently as a source of employment expansion, but the share of job increase due to business services, though high relative to other groups, was not as high as for the medium-size nodal MLM's. The consumer services' share however, was higher, especially in the case of retailing, which had the highest average share (10 percent) of any group of MLM's except the resort-type places. The share accounted for by manufacturing was well below the median but was considerably above the average for government, medical/educational, and resort cities.

TABLE 8.3

Average Share of Job Increases and Job Decreases, by Type and Size MLM, 1950-1960[a]

	Nodal				Manufacturing				Mixed			
JOB INCREASES	Small	Medium	Large	Total	Small	Medium	Large	Total	Small	Medium	Large	Total
Construction	3.5	3.0	0.7	3.0	3.0	2.4	0.3	2.7	3.3	2.9	0.0	3.1
Manufacturing	21.3	23.7	26.1	22.8	38.8	33.5	28.1	36.5	31.0	23.5	31.1	29.3
Mainly business services	15.3	17.9	15.5	16.5	9.4	11.7	13.8	10.4	10.9	14.2	10.6	11.7
Transportation	2.4	3.0	1.9	2.7	2.1	2.2	2.1	2.1	2.0	2.1	1.3	2.0
Communications	1.5	1.2	0.4	1.3	0.6	0.9	0.4	0.7	1.0	1.4	0.7	1.1
Wholesale	2.1	3.4	0.9	2.6	1.0	1.5	2.1	1.2	2.0	2.2	0.9	2.0
FIRE	6.5	7.1	6.2	6.7	4.7	5.6	6.0	5.0	4.9	5.7	5.3	5.1
Business/repair services	2.5	3.0	6.0	3.1	0.8	1.3	3.0	1.0	0.8	2.6	2.1	1.3
Mainly consumer services	40.3	31.1	25.2	34.9	34.1	30.5	32.5	32.8	34.9	34.6	24.8	34.7
Retail	10.0	8.6	2.6	8.7	8.4	6.8	4.1	7.7	8.2	8.3	4.0	8.1
Recreation	2.1	1.4	0.3	1.6	0.8	0.4	0.1	0.6	1.3	1.4	0	1.3
Private household	4.7	1.9	0.4	3.1	2.2	1.2	0.7	1.8	3.5	2.6	0.0	3.3
Medical/education	23.3	19.1	21.8	21.3	22.6	22.0	27.5	22.5	21.8	22.1	20.7	21.9
Government	7.6	8.5	4.9	7.7	3.7	5.5	3.9	4.4	8.5	8.8	12.9	8.6
Administration	4.2	4.8	3.1	4.3	3.3	3.8	3.6	3.5	4.2	6.1	8.7	4.7
Armed forces	3.4	3.6	1.7	3.3	0.4	1.6	0.3	0.8	4.2	2.6	4.2	3.9
INR	8.2	13.2	26.9	12.1	9.4	15.3	21.0	11.9	8.5	13.5	20.1	9.8
JOB DECREASES												
Agriculture	44.0	33.2	7.5	36.0	38.7	26.1	10.1	33.2	50.6	29.3	14.7	45.1
Manufacturing	13.5	18.2	24.2	16.5	36.2	44.6	42.9	39.4	16.8	24.8	33.3	18.9
Transportation	22.5	32.5	22.6	26.9	10.6	15.2	20.8	12.6	11.8	20.3	21.6	13.9
Retail	3.2	2.5	14.6	3.9	2.4	3.7	6.7	3.0	3.6	3.4	8.8	3.6
Percent, net employment change, 1950-60	18.2	26.1	12.3	23.5	13.0	15.3	10.6	13.0	11.7	21.2	15.8	13.3
Job increase/job decrease ratios	.14	.07	.24	.11	.18	.20	.34	.20	.27	.09	.20	.18

	Government				Medical/education				Recreation				Median, all cities
	Small	Medium	Large[b]	Total	Small	Medium	Large	Total	Small	Medium	Large	Total	
JOB INCREASES													
Construction	4.1	4.8	1.2	4.3	3.2	3.2	3.4	3.2	6.9	10.4	7.7	7.7	2.6
Manufacturing	11.9	19.6	7.6	14.1	18.1	11.9	10.8	17.3	18.7	11.6	16.9	16.9	27.2
Mainly business services	8.0	10.7	15.7	9.0	9.7	10.8	9.8	9.8	14.7	21.0	16.3	16.3	11.3
Transportation	1.2	1.5	1.3	1.3	1.1	0.4	1.0	1.0	1.1	2.6	1.5	1.5	1.7
Communications	0.8	1.1	0.5	0.9	0.9	1.3	1.3	1.0	1.6	1.5	1.6	1.6	1.2
Wholesale	0.9	1.6	2.2	1.1	1.0	1.3	1.3	1.0	1.3	2.7	1.6	1.6	1.3
FIRE	3.9	4.9	5.4	4.2	5.3	6.4	6.4	5.4	8.6	7.5	8.3	8.3	5.1
Business/repair services	1.0	1.5	6.2	1.3	1.2	1.1	1.1	1.1	2.0	6.5	3.1	3.1	1.1
Mainly consumer services	27.8	27.9	33.3	28.0	54.1	43.5	52.9	52.9	35.6	41.6	37.1	37.1	32.8
Retail	9.4	8.7	5.4	9.1	7.6	7.9	7.6	7.6	12.4	18.2	13.8	13.8	8.5
Recreation	2.3	1.5	0.6	2.0	1.9	1.5	1.8	1.8	11.2	7.8	10.3	10.3	.8
Private household	2.7	2.0	0.7	2.4	3.2	1.3	3.0	3.0	1.5	3.8	2.1	2.1	2.1
Medical/education	13.3	15.6	26.3	14.3	41.3	32.6	40.2	40.2	10.4	11.6	10.7	10.7	20.1
Government	40.9	28.5	19.6	36.7	5.7	16.5	6.9	6.9	8.0	4.2	7.0	7.0	4.9
Administration	10.2	8.1	12.8	9.6	4.2	9.9	4.9	4.9	5.4	4.2	5.1	5.1	3.9
Armed forces	30.7	20.4	6.8	27.0	1.4	6.6	2.0	2.0	2.6	0	1.9	1.9	.4
INR	5.4	7.1	21.2	6.3	8.0	12.4	8.5	8.5	14.3	6.3	12.3	12.3	9.1
JOB DECREASES													
Agriculture	48.4	51.4	40.9	45.4	55.8	67.9	57.2	57.2	31.0	0	23.2	23.2	37.7
Manufacturing	19.5	14.3	.7	17.5	16.7	2.7	15.1	15.1	5.7	0	4.3	4.3	19.1
Transportation	14.6	18.7	57.1	16.8	9.2	19.5	10.5	10.5	31.0	100.0	48.2	48.2	11.3
Retail	1.0	1.0	1.1	1.0	5.7	8.9	6.1	6.1	3.1	0	2.3	2.3	1.3
Percent, net employment change, 1950-60	42.2	44.9	41.6	41.6				31.8				76.6	
Job increase/job decrease ratios[c]	.06	.04	.04	.04				.08				.04	.04

[a] Averages are unweighted and do not necessarily add to 100. [b] Washington D.C. [c] Urban-type employment, see Table 6.5.

The situation of the large nodal places is somewhat ambiguous due to the very large share of job increase found in the INR classification. Nevertheless several findings stand out. Growth was slow, due to an important extent to a high ratio of job decrease to job increase. The share of job increase accounted for by business services was relatively high, especially in the case of business/repair services, and the share accounted for by consumer services very low. The share due to manufacturing was only slightly below the median for all MLM's. At the same time, manufacturing's share of job decrease was well above the median. Here is evidence that a fairly high level of loss and rejuvenation in the industrial sector is taking place in these large metropolitan economies.

Manufacturing MLM's. The manufacturing MLM's show well-defined characteristics. The share of job increases within the business services is small (it does increase with size of place, however). The average share of job increase accounted for by consumer services in the entire manufacturing MLM category is the same as the median for all cities, but this is due largely to the effect of increased employment in medical/educational services. It is clear that relatively little of the growth in employment in these places is accounted for by services other than those in the medical/education classification. Roughly one-third of job increases which did occur was due to increases in manufacturing employment. This description throws into sharp focus the plight of these metropolitan economies: growth tends to take place at rates which appear to be well below the natural rate of increase of the labor force. The development process appears to be largely lacking in the dynamics by which gains are amplified and encouraged through expansion of the service sectors. Lacking this, even the manufacturing sector offers little opportunity for substantial job increase.

Mixed-type MLM's. Among the mixed-type MLM's we observe, as we did in chapter 7, that the medium-size MLM's appear to be developing as service centers. Shares of job increases accounted for by both business services (14.2 percent) and consumer services (34.6 percent) are above the median (11.3 and 32.8 percent). The share of job increase accounted for by manufacturing (23.5 percent) is approximately the same as for the medium-size nodal MLM's (23.7 percent).

On the other hand, the small-size mixed-type MLM's seem to resemble more closely the small manufacturing MLM's. The average shares of job increases accounted for by business services is small (10.9 percent) and the share due to manufacturing is large relative to that of other places classified outside the manufacturing category. Growth is slow and the job-decrease to job-increase ratio is high.

Government-associated, medical/education, and resort-type MLM's.
Observations relating to shares of job-increase and job-decrease patterns for these types of MLM's are consistent with the findings in the previous chapter. The government-associated and medical/educational MLM's show abnormally small shares of employment expansion accounted for by business and consumer services (with the exception of the medical/educational classification in the case of the medical/educational MLM's) and by manufacturing. Overall employment growth was relatively rapid in these places, but it was due largely to growth in those classifications which are the primary city-forming, or export base, activities. There appears to have been relatively little amplification of employment expansion as a result of growth in the services.

In view of this finding it is very interesting to observe such a substantial share of job increases accounted for by both business and consumer services in the resort places. Among the business services, shares of job increases contributed by FIRE and business/repair services are well above the all-MLM median. Among the consumer services, relatively large shares are contributed by retailing and recreation services.

The large-size mixed-type MLM's show small shares of job increases in business services relative to large-size MLM's in the other type-of-place categories. The principal difference lies in the business/repair service classification, where average share of job increase is 2.1 percent in contrast to an average 6.0 percent for the large nodal places. Shares are also somewhat smaller for transportation and for FIRE. Apparently the large-size mixed-type places are not developing as service centers for an outlying nonmetropolitan area or for smaller cities.

AVERAGES OF SHARES OF JOB INCREASES/DECREASES: 50 FASTEST-GROWING AND 50 SLOWEST-GROWING MLM's

The above analysis treats the patterns of job increases and decreases as they appear in the various size–type groups of MLM's without distinguishing between the fast-growing and slow-growing places. At least two interesting questions remain unanswered: If the metropolitan economies which grow very rapidly (or very slowly) are examined separately, are significant differences in patterns of job-increase or job-decrease shares observed among the various types-of-place categories? Will these patterns vary between the very fast-growing and the very slow-growing metropolises?

To shed light on these questions we have isolated the 50 fastest-growing and the 50 slowest-growing MLM's during 1950-60 for special study. It is important to note at the outset that these two groups vary widely in terms of the type and size groups to which they belong and the regions within which they are located:[2]

Such evidence reaffirms what was observed in chapter 6 (see Table 6.5). Growth has been fastest in the specialized government-associated and resort-type metropolises and in those places which provide nodal services in rapidly developing areas. On the other hand, metropolises which had little growth or an actual decline in employ-

---

[2] The regional distribution (not shown above) may be summarized as follows: Among the 50 fastest-growing MLM's, only 4 are in the New England, Mideast, Great Lakes, and Plains regions whereas 29 of the slowest-growing MLM's are in these regions. On the other hand, 29 of the fastest-growing and only 4 of the slowest-growing MLM's are in the Southwest, Rocky Mountain, and Far West regions. Finally, there were both 17 of the fastest-growing and 17 of the slowest-growing places located within the large Southeast region, reflecting wide variations in the pace of economic development within the region.

	50 Fastest-growing MLM's		50 Slowest-growing or declining MLM's	
	Number	Percent	Number	Percent
Nodal	11	(17)	4	(6)
Manufacturing	1	(1)	15	(13)
Government	20	(44)	—	
Resort	6	(75)	1	(12)
Medical/ education	1	(5)	—	
Mixed	11	(10)	30	(26)
	50		50	
Small-size	31	(13)	40	(17)
Medium-size	18	(16)	10	(9)
Large-size	1	(8)	—	
	50	(14)	50	(14)

Note: Figures within parentheses indicate percent of total MLM's in type or size category accounted for. For example, there are 11 nodal MLM's among the 50 fastest-growing MLM's, accounting for 17 percent of all nodal MLM's.

ment were most likely to specialize in manufacturing or primary production or to be economies which have failed to develop a major specialty.[3] The latter, which may include satellite cities, are classified within the mixed MLM's. All together, the manufacturing-type and mixed-type places account for 45 of the 50 slowest-growing places but only 12 of the 50 fastest-growing places. Only one manufacturing-type MLM was among the 50 fastest-growing places.

THE 50 FASTEST-GROWING MLM'S

Among the fastest-growing MLM's, there were relatively few job decreases. The average job-decrease to job-increase ratio for the 50 MLM's was 4 to 100. For this reason our attention is confined to analysis of job increases.

To a very considerable extent these various types of MLM's retain the same characteristic patterns of job-increase shares described

[3] A number of slow-growing mixed-type places show heavy concentration of employment in mining, a primary industry classification.

earlier in the chapter. If we examine simply the average shares of job increase the following patterns appear:

	Average Shares of Job Increases Accounted for by:				
	Mfg.	*Mainly business services*	*Mainly consumer services*	*Retail*	*med./educ. services*
Nodal	18.6	19.3	35.7	14.5	14.0
Government	11.9	9.5	27.0	9.4	12.4
Resort	10.3	15.9	45.7	16.9	12.3
Mixed, with nodal characteristics	18.6	15.9	33.0	12.2	14.8
Mixed, all	21.6	14.2	32.6	12.3	14.1
All 368 MLM's (median)	27.2	11.3	32.8	8.5	20.1

Among the nodal places the share of job increases accounted for by mainly business services was over twice as large as in the government-associated MLM's and well above the resort- and mixed-type MLM's. For these nodal places the average share of job increases within the mainly consumer services category was well below the share for the resort-type places, well above the share for government-associated, and slightly above the mixed-type MLM share. We observe once again that even in the fastest-growing nodal places, growth centers to a very large extent on the services with relatively strong emphasis on development of business services. The resort-type MLM's also give evidence of increasing their role as service centers but with greater emphasis on development of consumer services.

The mixed-type places included among the fastest-growing MLM's show only slightly smaller shares of job increases accounted for by business and consumer services than do the nodal places. These mixed-type MLM's apparently are also increasing their role as service centers.

As regards the government-associated MLM's, the evidence simply underscores the previous findings: the share of employment expansion accounted for by both mainly business services and mainly consumer services is well below the shares typically noted for the other types of places. Moreover, there seems to be little attraction for industrial growth. The average share of job increases accounted for by manufacturing in these high-growth government-associated MLM's is well below that for any of the other types of MLM's examined except the resort places.[4]

A finding which sheds light on the nature of job expansion within the consumer services sector is that retailing shares of job increases vary to a greater extent than do medical/educational services shares. Averages of shares of job increases accounted for by retailing in the various types of MLM's range from 9.4 to 16.9. Average shares accounted for by medical/educational services vary only from 12.3 to 14.0.

Business and consumer services as a whole play a disproportionately large role, and manufacturing a relatively small role, in the fastest-growing MLM's. In each type of MLM, except the government-associated places, the average share of job increases accounted for business and consumer services in the fast-growing MLM's is higher than the average share in all MLM's. For manufacturing, however, the reverse tends to be true.

Finally, the average share of job increases in medical/educational services is lower for the fast-growing MLM's in each of the type-of-place categories than is the average share of job increases in medical/educational services for all 368 MLM's. This reflects not so much a lack of importance of medical/educational services as a source of new jobs in the fast-growing places as the fact that it is one of the few consistently important sources of new jobs in the slow-growing places, and thus comprises a large share of such job increases as occur in these places. Accordingly, the average share for all 368 MLM's is above the average for the fast-growing places.

[4] This is not true of all of the fast-growing places which have been classified within the government-associated group, however. In San Diego, Pensacola, Sacramento, and Portsmouth the manufacturing category accounts for 20 percent or more of total job increases.

THE 50 SLOWEST-GROWING MLM'S

Rates of net employment change and the extent of transition are found to have varied to a considerable extent among the 50 slowest-growing places. For 40 of these MLM's the term "slowest-growing" was a misnomer since employment actually declined during the decade. For the entire group of 50 places, net employment change (1950-60) ranged from minus 17.3 percent to plus 1.8 percent.

For a number of places there was evidence of considerable transition. In 40 MLM's both the rate of job increase and the rate of job decrease were at least 10 percent, and among these 40 there were 9 in which both the job-increase and job-decrease rates were at least 15 percent. On the other hand there were a number of MLM's in which very little job creation took place to offset the forces of decline. In 5 MLM's rates of job decreases were above 20 percent while rates of job increases were less than 9 percent.

It will be recalled that the group of 50 slowest-growing MLM's was comprised largely (90 percent) of manufacturing and mixed-type places. It is hardly surprising that the major source of job decrease was the goods sector. Of the 10 MLM's with highest rates of net-employment decline, 7 were mining places in which the primary sector accounted for more than half of total job decreases. Within the entire group of 50 places there were 34 in which the share of job decreases accounted for by the goods sector was 60 percent or more, 47 in which the share was 45 percent or more.

If we exclude the railroad/railway express classification, in which there were sharp decreases in employment in many of the MLM's, the business services are found to have made almost no contribution to job decreases. There were only 12 MLM's in which the share of job decreases accounted for by the business services (excluding railroad/ railway express services) was greater than 10 percent.

Similarly there were relatively few job decreases accounted for by consumer services: in only 17 of the 50 MLM's were shares of job decreases accounted for by mainly consumer services as high as 10 percent. Among the individual consumer services classifications, retailing contributed the largest share of job decreases. In 41 MLM's retail services accounted for more than half of all job decreases within the mainly consumer services category.

We have observed that in a number of these declining or slow-growing places, job increases as well as job decreases were taking place to an important degree. Although there was considerable variation in the contributions of the various industrial classifications to job increase, these findings seem noteworthy:

1. The most important source of job increases was manufacturing. In 31 MLM's the share of job increases accounted for by this industrial category was 30 percent or above.

2. Consumer services provided the second most important source of job increases. These job increases were largely accounted for by the medical/educational classification. In 28 of the 50 MLM's, this classification accounted for 80 percent or more of the job increases occurring within the mainly consumer services category; in 45 of the 50 MLM's, it accounted for more than half.

3. The importance of business services as a source of job increases varied widely. Among 22 of the 50 places, the percentage of job increases accounted for by the mainly business services category ranged from 15 percent to a maximum of 20 percent. For the remaining 28, the percentages ranged downward to a minimum of 4.7 percent. For 17 of this latter group, percentages were 8 percent or less.

SUMMARY

The purpose of this chapter has been to measure the direct contribution of each industrial classification to job increase and job decrease in the various types of metropolitan economies.

In the first section we assessed the importance of the various industrial classifications by examining for each classification an array of percentages representing shares of job increases in the 368 MLM's. We observe that for some classifications, such as medical/educational services, the shares of jobs created do not vary greatly over a considerable portion of the array. In other classifications, such as recreation/ entertainment, however, the shares of job increases vary to a considerable extent. They are substantial at the upper extremity of the array, but below these higher percentiles they are quite small.

When average shares of job increases and decreases are examined for the various type–size MLM categories, the measures shed light on patterns of employment expansion and contraction. We observe, first of all, that the role of manufacturing as a source of job increase changed significantly from the first to the second decade, becoming an increasingly important source of new jobs in those places where previously it was relatively unimportant, a less important source in the places which traditionally had specialized in this type of activity.

Analysis of shares of job increases and decreases for the 1950-60 period substantiated the findings of chapter 7. The relatively fast-growing medium-size nodal MLM's showed very high shares of job increases in the business services category indicating that they were taking on additional business-service functions as they assumed more important roles as regional centers. In the small nodal places, shares of job increases in the consumer services were more important than in business services. Finally, in the large nodal places, shares of job increases in consumer services were quite low, but in business services they were high. These large places are continuing to increase their absolute and relative employment in these activities even though growth is slow. In the large nodal MLM's, as well as in the other large-size categories, there were relatively high ratios of job decreases to job increases, with manufacturing comprising a major source of the job declines.

Measures of the share of job increases reveal the difficult position of the specialized-manufacturing MLM's. Even under conditions of low growth, the shares of jobs created in the business and most consumer services were small. When growth occurs it is not amplified by accompanying increases in service employment nor does vigorous growth in the services provide locational attractiveness to new firms in the form of business service-type external economies or consumer service amenities.

Among the remaining groups of MLM's, a strong tendency for the medium-size mixed-type places and resort-type MLM's to evolve toward full-fledged roles as nodal centers was indicated by large shares of job increases accounted for by the service classifications. The government-associated and medical/educational MLM's, however, showed abnormally small shares of employment expansion accounted for by business services and by most of the consumer services.

Analysis of the 50 fastest- and 50 slowest-growing MLM's reaffirms that growth has been fastest in government-associated, resort, and nodal places, slowest in those which specialize in manufacturing or primary production or in unspecialized satellite places. Among the fast-growing MLM's, the nodal places show relatively strong emphasis on development of business services and the resort places in development of the consumer services. The fast-growing government-associated places typically do not show large shares of job increases in these services.

There was considerable transition among many of the slowest-growing places, though not among all. The major source of job decrease was the goods sector. Relatively small shares of job decreases were accounted for by either the business or consumer services. When significant job increases were noted, the most important source was manufacturing. Consumer services, largely the medical/educational services classification, provided the second largest share of job increases. Shares of job increases accounted for by the mainly business services category varied to a considerable extent but, in general, were relatively unimportant.

9 RELOCATION OF INDUSTRIAL EMPLOYMENT AND TRANSITION IN METROPOLITAN LABOR MARKETS

THUS FAR analysis of growth processes has dealt largely with the more residentiary industries. In the present chapter attention shifts to industrial employment changes which more closely relate to basic or export-type industries.[1]

Growth in the basic industries which comprise the export sector is a more complex process than is employment growth in the residentiary industries of the local sector, and the analysis must be carried out within a regional or national framework. Whereas growth in residentiary industries is dependent upon the overall growth of a metropolitan economy, growth in the export sector depends on national or regional changes in demand and productivity, factors primarily external to the particular metropolis. Growth depends also on the ability of firms within the export sector to compete with other firms in the metropolis concerned for labor, space, and capital.

The dynamics of metropolitan growth tend to bring about changes in the cost of those factors which influence the location decision of firms within an industry. As a result, firms may relocate, in many cases moving from one metropolis to another. In the process, metropolitan economies undergo considerable industrial transition as certain industries are added, replaced, or lost.

In this chapter, we consider factors affecting the geographical

[1] Eleven industries are classified as residentiary, 20 as basic. The basic or export industries accounted for 53 percent of employment in the U.S., 1960.

redistribution of industrial employment.[2] For a limited number of places, industrial transition (i.e., the offsetting of a decline in employment in one industry by an unemployment increase in another) in the exporting sector is also examined. Our findings indicate that the patterns of industrial relocation vary greatly by industry and that relocation takes very different forms. They also suggest ways by which the metropolitan planners may anticipate industrial transition and make appropriate policy recommendations.

THE ECONOMICS OF LOCATION AND INTER-URBAN ORGANIZATION

The question, "why do industries relocate?" should be considered within the framework of a general theory of location. Such a task is not within the scope of this study, but the following excerpt presents an excellent summary statement of the major considerations of such a theory:

Ideally, every location decision is a matter of balancing anticipated costs and receipts under different degrees of uncertainty. When potential savings from a move outweigh the additional costs entailed, net revenue is enlarged and, other things being equal, the rational entrepreneur will make the move; he *substitutes* new sets of revenues and outlays for his previous sets, his new location for his old. Some costs are, nevertheless, more significant than others in their effects on the overall spatial order. The differential advantages of possible locations at any time have their roots, broadly speaking, in three categories of costs:

1. *input costs:* labor, materials, fuel, water, taxes, insurance, weather conditions, political milieu, and so on (not all of which readily yield to the conventions of market pricing).

[2] In this discussion, the terms "redistribution" and "relocation" are used. The former is distinguished from the latter in that it is more inclusive term, being used to describe the effect of both growth differentials which act to alter the relative importance of regions or metropolises in an expanding industry and the transfer of establishments within an industry from one site to another, whereas the latter refers only to the transfer of establishments.

2. *transport costs:* the price of a composite input of services necessary to move labor, materials, equipment, and products.
3. *economies (and diseconomies) of agglomeration and deglomeration:* a set of relatively localized scale economies that may be (a) "internal" to the firm; (b) "external" to the industry at a particular location; or (c) "external" to the locality itself.

Among these sources of cost differentials, those having to do with distance are likely to be decisive in a spatial context. While all costs vary over time and space, only transport costs vary systematically with distance from any point, primarily because transport cost is some function of distance.[3]

The above suggests that firms will relocate if the move promises to result in an enlargement of profits. The theory does not, however, explain differential changes in the costs occurring in various metropolitan economies which underly the relocation decision. We hypothesize that since metropolitan growth varies by size and type of place, costs of doing business do not change at the same rate or in the same way in all places. It follows that the competitive position of a firm, particularly in a basic industry, will be affected by growth processes. The firm may outgrow the city or the city may outgrow the firm.

Growing firms often have to decide whether to make additions to their present facilities or build a new plant in another location. The larger the city, the more likely it is that certain types of firms will be forced to relocate. For example, a successful manufacturing firm, unable to expand its existing facilities in a large-size MLM, must relocate if it is to realize the economies of large-scale production.

Just how metropolitan growth will affect the costs or benefits to a firm is one of the uncertainties existing firms, as well as firms considering entering the market, have to face. As the metropolis grows, the competition for space increases. As property values increase, land is used more intensively and the vertical rise of structures becomes more commonplace. At the same time, the labor market becomes more competitive and labor more completely organized. Further,

[3] Eric F. Lampard, "The Evolving System of Cities in the United States: Urbanization and Economic Development," in *Issues in Urban Economics,* Harry S. Perloff and Lowdon Wing Jr., eds. (Baltimore, Johns Hopkins University Press, 1968), p. 89.

the differentials between costs of living and taxes in the large- and small-size MLM's, already considerable, widen. Certain industries, therefore, find it advantageous to relocate in areas with lower wage, tax, and rent structures. Other industries, however, can function more efficiently in larger places because of external economies and larger markets. For example, employment in business/repair services has grown in the larger cities at the same time that apparel and textile employment has declined. Cities which have grown up around specialized industries and have taken on new functions as growth occurs may find that some of their original industries are no longer able to compete. In some cases, only production activities may be affected, and though these activities are spun off, administrative activities remain and may even be expanded. The history of the motor vehicle industry in Detroit and the apparel industry in New York illustrates such a process at work.[4]

MEASURING THE GEOGRAPHICAL REDISTRIBUTION
OF INDUSTRIAL EMPLOYMENT

Changes in the geographical distribution of industrial employment are readily studied by comparing the geographical distribution of job increases with that of job decreases. It is important to distinguish our measures of geographical redistribution from those used by Fuchs and others who have studied changes in the location of industry.[5] In other

---

[4] Competition arising from urban growth will not necessarily force an industry to migrate *en masse* however. Instead, capital may be used to replace manpower and to increase productivity. This appears to be happening in retailing. While such employment has been increasing in the smaller places, it has been increasing at a much slower rate (or even decreasing) in the larger places.

[5] Victor Fuchs, *Changes in the Location of Manufacturing in the United States since 1929* (New Haven, Yale University Press, 1962); Harry S. Perloff et al., *Regions, Resources, and Economic Growth* (Pittsburgh, Carnegie Institute and Pittsburgh University Press, 1960); Lowell D. Ashby, *Growth Patterns in Employment by County, 1940-1950 and 1950-1960,* 8 vols. (Washington D.C., Dept. of Commerce, 1965).

studies, redistribution is measured in terms of employment growth in a region or state that exceeds the national growth rate of the industry. The underlying assumption in these studies is that there is no redistribution of employment if growth occurs at the national rate. Our measures of job increases and decreases offer an alternative approach. We take the position that all employment changes in labor markets are significant—not merely those job increases in excess of the industry's national rate of growth. Moreover, we feel that it is important to compare size and type characteristics of those labor markets where the industry is expanding with those where it is contracting. Use of the MLM and the NMC as the basic geographical units of study makes it possible to examine intermetropolitan changes rather than interstate or interregional changes as in previous studies.

FORM OF GEOGRAPHICAL REDISTRIBUTION

The redistribution of industrial employment may take different forms. Those considered here are decentralization, regional shift, and increasing centralization.

DECENTRALIZATION

Decentralization may be either *intraregional* or *interregional*. In the first case, firms may be moving out either to satellite or suburban areas near the original metropolitan concentrations or to places somewhat removed but still within the same region. In the second case, firms may be expanding into other regions previously underrepresented. Both cases imply that the industry was originally geographically concentrated. The first type of decentralization would suggest that the region's comparative advantages have not altered significantly, but that intraregional locational factors have changed considerably. The second type of decentralization implies that interregional locational factors have changed, altering regional comparative advantage.

Decentralization of the motor vehicle industry provides an excellent example of the first type. After a period of growth in the decade of the 1940s, employment in the industry declined during the 1950s. Following a net growth of 294,000 jobs in the 1940s, there was a net decline of 28,000 during the 1950s. In the first decade, the net change figure gave a relatively good picture of the changes occurring, since only 4,000 job increases were netted out by job decreases. In the second decade, however, 123,000 job increases were netted out (i.e., there were 123,000 job increases compared to 151,000 job decreases).

What makes this netting-out process particularly interesting is the concentration of the process within the Great Lakes region, which alone accounted for 58 percent of the job increases and 86 percent of all job decreases in the industry. Roughly 68 percent of the 129,000 job decreases in the motor vehicle industry in the Great Lakes region were netted out by job increases in other areas within the region at the same time. The region's share of national employment in the motor vehicle industry declined from 81 percent in 1940 to 74 percent in 1960. This relatively small decline of 7 percentage points in the region's overall share of motor vehicle employment is quite surprising considering that Detroit's share of national employment in the industry declined 18 percentage points (from 47 percent to 29 percent). Offsetting the 80,000 job decreases in the major auto manufacturing center, Detroit, were 71,000 job increases in smaller metropolitan areas and in NMC's in the surrounding region. Detroit accounted for 69 percent of the region's (and 59 percent of the nation's) total job decreases in the motor vehicle industry.

REGIONAL SHIFT

The best recent example of a shift of employment from one region to another is the apparel industry, where a substantial amount of employment moved from the large places in the Mideast region to the NMC's in the Southeast region. Between 1950 and 1960, 64 percent of the total national job decreases in the apparel industry took place in the Mideast region, while 65 percent of the job increases were located in the Southeast region. The remaining increases and decreases were distributed fairly evenly in the other regions.

The regional shift in the apparel industry was accompanied by a change in location in terms of size-of-place categories. This may be seen by examining differences in the sizes of places where the increases and decreases occurred. For all regions combined, 63 percent of the job decreases occurred in large MLM's and 68 percent of the job increases occurred in the NMC's. The major declining area was New York, which accounted for 44 percent of total job decreases in the apparel industry. A little over one-half of the job increases in the industry was located in NMC's in the Southeast.

INCREASING CENTRALIZATION

There are no clear-cut examples of increasing centralization in the data studied, but employment in the business and repair services category has been shifting from the NMC's to the largest MLM's in the nation. Of the 84,000 job decreases in this category, 75,000 of them were in the NMC's. Of the 381,900 job increases, 84 percent took place in the medium- and large-size places (47 percent in large-size places, including 13 percent in New York).

At least part of this shift actually reflects a changing mix within the industry category: employment in advertising and business services (primarily large city industries) grew much faster than employment in garages. Such being the case, it is not clear whether or not this is a valid example of industry centralization.

THE MEASUREMENT AND EXTENT OF
INDUSTRIAL RELOCATION

We have discussed employment change in a rather general way under the general heading of redistribution, which includes both increments to an industry's work force and the geographical relocation of that industry. Usually, analysis of employment redistribution ends at this point. For this reason, the terms "industry mobility," "regional shift," and "relocation" are so often used interchangeably in reference to geographic redistribution, whereas they are, in fact, different concepts.

The distinction between relocation and redistribution is now made because, though relocation is itself a type of redistribution, it presents special problems for those concerned with manpower planning. Relocation should be considered in industry manpower analysis because even under conditions in which there is no net growth in an industry, the relocation of existing jobs requires an adjustment to be made in all of the labor markets affected. The overall adjustment that must be made, of course, is not limited to the direct effect of the relocation since any autonomous change (either an increase or decrease) is amplified in the residentiary sector. Thus, should a firm employing 10,000 workers relocate, even if all those employed by the firm relocated with it, employment changes in the residentiary industries would be sizable in both places.

Industrial relocation may be approximated by comparing job increases to job decreases in an industry.[6] If total job increases are greater than total job decreases in an industry, it may be said that the job decreases which have been netted out actually signify the relocation of employment from one labor market to another. If job decreases exceed increases then it is the increases which are netted out and which, accordingly, represent geographical relocation of the industry's employment. It is interesting to note that where national industry data are studied, it is precisely that part of employment change which represents relocation which is netted out and cannot be analyzed. In the discussion that follows, we shall refer to this netting-out of job increase and job decrease within a single industrial classification, which provides a measure of geographical relocation, as "job increase-decrease offset," or JIDO.

We find that relocation of industry employment as represented by JIDO (indicated by an asterisk in Columns 1 and 2 of Table 9.1) is greater than net employment change (column 3) in six of the

---

[6] If an industry is not homogeneous, however, expansion in one sub-industry category in one labor market and contraction in another sub-industry in a different labor market would appear as relocations. Moreover, if such changes occurred in the same market they would offset each other and employment would appear to remain at a stable level.

TABLE 9.1
JIDO and Associated Measures by Industry: Total U.S., 1950-1960

	Job increases, 1950-60 (000's)	Job decreases, 1950-60 (000's)	Net growth of employment, 1950-60	JIDO AS % OF industry employment, 1960[a]	JIDO AS % OF Job increases	JIDO AS % OF Job decreases
Forestry/fishing[b]	15.3*	47.1	−25.5	16.4 (3.5)		32.5
Mining	103.8*	380.4	−29.7	15.9 (2.6)		27.3
Motor vehicles/equipment	123.0*	150.5	− 3.2	14.6 —		81.7
Apparel manufacturing	223.6	128.4*	9.0	11.1 (1.2)	57.4	
Lumber manufacturing	97.8*	220.7	−10.3	9.2 (4.6)		44.3
Entertainment/recreation	53.5	45.4*	1.7	9.0 (2.7)	84.9	
Other transportation	102.4	78.7*	2.8	8.9 (7.7)	76.9	
Textile mill products	77.7*	364.0	−23.1	8.1 (6.7)		21.3
Food/dairy product stores	107.7*	141.9	− 2.0	6.4 —		75.9
Business/repair services	381.9	84.4*	22.7	5.2 (6.1)	22.1	
Hotel/other personal services	177.8	97.9*	4.3	5.0 (2.0)	55.1	
Chemicals/allied products	247.6	42.4*	31.1	4.9 (2.0)	17.1	
Eating/drinking places	177.8	68.9*	6.4	3.8 —	38.8	
Armed forces	774.4	66.5*	69.0	3.8 —	8.6	
Communications	137.4	27.5*	15.5	3.4 (1.5)	20.0	
Construction	484.8	126.1*	10.4	3.3 —	26.0	
Private household	333.6	56.2*	16.9	2.9 —	16.8	
Utilities/sanitary services	138.2	24.9*	14.4	2.8 (4.0)	18.0	
Wholesale trade	290.3	59.2*	11.7	2.7 —	20.4	

Other manufacturing	1,017.6	128.8*	18.8	2.3 (9.9)	12.7	
Trucking/warehousing	227.8	19.0*	29.7	2.1 (0.9)	8.3	
Electrical/other machinery	1,031.7	60.6*	46.6	2.0 (4.8)	5.9	
Food/kindred products	436.3	27.9*	28.9	1.5 (9.8)	6.4	
Other transportation equipment	508.5	14.5*	102.3	1.5 (4.4)	2.9	
Agriculture	33.0*	2,694.0	−38.5	0.8 —		1.2
Printing/publishing	293.6	7.7*	33.4	0.7 —	2.6	
Other retail trade	944.8	42.6*	17.4	0.7 (6.9)	4.5	
Administration	712.1	23.5*	27.4	0.7 (0.7)	3.3	
Railroads/railway express	3.9*	450.7	−32.2	0.4 —		0.9
FIRE	778.8	4.9*	40.3	0.2 (1.7)	0.6	
Medical/other professional services	2,782.7	2.1*	58.0	0.0 (0.0)	0.0	

a Figures in parentheses are differences between JIDO (expressed a percent of total employment) estimated from 32 and from 118 industry categories, 113 MLM's.

b Italics indicate basic industries—those not classified or residentiary (see Table 3.1.)

* Indicates employment change not revealed in net employment change analysis (i.e., indicates job increase, or decrease, which is offset—JIDO).

thirty-one classifications examined (i.e., apparel manufacturing, motor vehicles and equipment, food/dairy product stores, hotels/other personal services, other transportation, entertainment/recreation.) The estimated number of jobs that are denoted as JIDO range from 128,000 in other manufacturing to 2,100 in medical/educational services. Their importance, measured in terms of the ratio of JIDO to industry employment (column 4), ranged from 16 percent in mining to less than 1 percent in medical/educational services.

Two factors stand out as important determinants of the extent of industry relocation: whether an industry is basic or residentiary; and whether the industry is fast or slow growing. Of the twelve industries where relocation was most extensive, ten were classified as basic, i.e., essentially export-type industries. In general, relocation is highest in the slow-growing or declining basic industries. Exceptions are found in two declining industries, railroads/railway express, and agriculture, where there are very few places in which employment of this type is expanding. There appears to be little relocation in fast-growing basic industries where growth pervades the entire national economy, e.g., printing/publishing and other transportation equipment.

In the residentiary industries, where employment expansion reflects primarily changes in local demand, JIDO takes a different form. As we have seen earlier (chapter 5), there is evidence that differences in productivity changes and labor supply conditions among size-of-place categories have resulted in job decreases in large MLM's and job increases in smaller places in the same industry. Such trends are probably most important in food/dairy product stores, eating/drinking places, and private household services, residentiary industries where JIDO was most important. Actual relocation of employment in residentiary industries is most likely to occur where there have been shifts in demand, i.e., relocation from declining communities to more rapidly growing places.

Any measure of employment relocation will be affected by the level of industry detail used. The analysis presented in Table 9.1 is for the thirty-two industry categories used throughout this study. Since some categories are less homogeneous than others, a similar analysis was done for 118 industry categories in the sample of 113 MLM's. The difference between the extent of relocation estimated on the basis of thirty-two and 118 industry categories in the 113 MLM's in the sample is placed in parentheses alongside the measure of relocation in column 4. Comparing these with JIDO figures we see that, when forestry and fisheries industries are combined, JIDO accounts for 16.4 percent of industry employment (in all MLM's) and that, when the two industries are considered separately (in the sample MLM's), JIDO accounts for an additional 3.5 percent of employment due to changes in industry mix. The category most affected is other and miscellaneous manufacturing. When the twenty industry categories comprising this category are considered separately, relocation accounts for an additional 9.9 percent of employment in the industry over and above JIDO of 2.3 percent calculated for all MLM's when the industries are treated as one category. On the other hand, in FIRE, the estimate of relocation is the same whether the industries are considered individually or combined. None of the subindustry classifications within the FIRE classification had significant employment declines offset by expansion in another subindustry classification in the same MLM.

INDUSTRIAL TRANSITION

Industrial transition occurs through a process whereby job increases in one industry are offset by job decreases in another, either within the same labor market, within a subregion (such as a megalopolis or Appalachia), a region, or the nation, or within a particular type of MLM. It should be noted that the geographical relocation of employment, i.e., the shift of an industry within a geographical unit, is usually part of the transition process and is included in the JIDO measures described below, which were devised for the purpose of analyzing industrial transition.

Summarized below are estimates of regional industrial transition, i.e., that part of employment expansion in a region that is offset by contraction, either in the same or in another industry within the region.

	Job increases, 1950-60 (000's)	JIDO, 1950-60[a] (000's)	JIDO as percent of 1950 employment	JIDO as percent of job increases	Intra-regional industry relocation as percent of JIDO[b]	Net growth of employ-ment, 1950-60
Southeast	3,449.9	1,949.2	16.4	56.5	19.5	12.6
Plains	1,021.5	717.1	13.3	70.2	27.7	5.7
Rocky Mtns.	434.2	140.0	11.1	32.2	40.1	23.2
Southwest	1,412.9	448.7	11.0	31.8	33.9	23.6
New England	786.1	309.3	8.4	39.2	20.5	13.0
Great Lakes	2,455.8	983.7	8.2	40.1	30.9	12.3
Mideast	2,470.4	941.6	7.0	38.1	27.7	11.4
Far West	2,488.7	226.5	4.0	9.1	52.2	40.3

[a] In every region JIDO is simply the number of job decreases since none of the regions had a net decline in employment.

[b] Increases in specific industries offset by decreases in the same industries in the same region expressed as a percent of total JIDO. Total JIDO includes shifts among industries as well as shifts within industries.

It will be observed that the measures of net growth do not pro-vide an indication of the importance of transition in the developmental processes of regional employment expansion. In the Plains, the slowest-growing region, 1950-60, the transitional process accounted for almost three-quarters of employment expansion (i.e., 70.2 percent of job in-creases were offset by job decreases). In the Southeast, the third slowest-growing region, transition accounted for over half (56.5 per-cent) of employment expansion. In contrast, transition in the fastest-growing Far West region accounted for only 9.1 percent of all the job increases in the region: roughly 90 percent of the 2.5 million new jobs in this region resulted from outright net growth. In the remaining five regions, however, transition, as measured by JIDO, accounted for over 30 percent of the job increases.

Intraregional relocation of employment in individual industries played a relatively minor role in regions where transition was most important. For the Southeast region, only 380,000 job changes were attributable to intraregional relocation of employment within individual industries, whereas total regional transition as represented by JIDO accounted for nearly 2 million jobs. Approximately four-fifths of the total transition in the Southeast occurred as a result of employment gains in one industry being offset by employment losses in other industries. In the Far West, where transition was relatively unimportant, however, over half of the transition was attributable to intraregional relocation of employment within industries.

The above are examples of the application of JIDO measures. Such measures may also be devised to show that part of national relocation (Table 9.1) which represents intra- and interregional relocation.

One of the major disadvantages of exclusive reliance upon the net change measure is that it leads to an overstatement of the role of individual industries or sectors as sources of employment growth. For example, the statement can be made that the net increase of employment in manufacturing in the Southeast accounted for 46 percent of net employment change in the region, 1950-60. One might, however, with equal validity have said that services accounted for 118 percent of net employment increase in the Southeast during the same decade. In short, since there were both negative and positive forces at work, the role of an industry in contributing to growth may be easily overstated by relating it to *net* change.

Such an overstatement would not occur if job increases were used as the basis for comparison. We would say that job increases in manufacturing accounted for 26 percent of all job increases in the Southeast, 1950-60, and job increases in services accounted for 69 percent. It is clear, therefore, that the developmental processes of employment expansion in a region cannot be described with the conventional measures of net employment change.

INDUSTRIAL TRANSITION WITHIN AN MLM

Industrial transition is a normal part of the metropolitan growth process. As a city grows it changes in terms of functions, productivity, wages, taxes, and amenities provided, causing some industries to contract and others to expand. Further, as an MLM grows, an overtaxing of its infrastructure will act as a constraint on further growth.

The most notable transitions occur, however, in those places where industries experiencing declines or major shifts dominate the local economy—in mining towns, textile towns, railroad terminals, lumber mills, and, to a certain degree, apparel centers. For these places expansion in other industries is necessary simply to prevent the labor force from contracting.[7]

Small decreases in the goods industries may be compensated for by increased employment in those services with strong upward national trends (e.g., medical/educational services) but any significantly large number of job decreases will require that new basic industries appear to take up the slack.[8]

MANCHESTER (N.H.): AN EXAMPLE OF
INDUSTRIAL TRANSITION

Manchester (N.H.) is a good example of a city that has undergone a simple industrial transition. During the decade of the 1950s, 14,548 jobs were added in the expanding industries, while 6,477 jobs were eliminated in the declining industries. Most of the transition can be attributed to the goods sector. Within this sector 5,957 jobs were

---

[7] Our measures may be used to identify those MLM's that have been successfully revived and those that have actually declined. A study of MLM's that have achieved a successful transition and those that have not been able to recover an eroding economic base should be helpful in identifying characteristics of those places or policies that are critical to a successful recovery from a major decline of one or more local industries.

[8] It should be noted that transition may be more important in terms of income than in terms of employment. The average wage level will probably increase significantly if the jobs lost are in low-wage industries and the jobs gained are in higher-wage industries. As the upgrading of employment in the goods sector increases relative income per employee, there will be an increase in the demand for both goods and services. Since most services are supplied locally, employment in the services sector will then increase even though the increased demand for goods may increase imports and the number of jobs in the local goods sector may not have changed significantly. The result will be an increase in demand for local services which will accentuate any trend toward structural change in the industrial mix favoring services caused by national trends in productivity and consumption discussed in chapter 2.

added in expanding industries and 5,672 jobs were lost in the declining industries. Of the job decreases, 4,078 were in textiles and 1,212 jobs in agriculture. Of the job increases, 4,123 jobs were in electrical/other machinery, 638 in printing/publishing, and 593 in food/dairy products.

It was in the services sector that most of the actual net employment growth took place; 6,459 jobs were added, (2,132 in medical/educational services and 1,062 in FIRE), while only 805 jobs were lost (in transportation, retail, hotels, and entertainment).

FURTHER EXAMPLES OF METROPOLITAN TRANSITION

Listed in Table 9.2 are 14 examples of MLM's where a large proportion of the employment increases were netted out by employment declines.[9] In addition, we include the large, fast-growing MLM, Los Angeles, where there was little transition, for purposes of comparison. Industry detail is given for increases and decreases in classifications where structural changes were greatest. In the first three MLM's, employment declines exceeded increases and total employment declined. In the next 11 places, arranged in descending order of the number of job decreases, employment expanded.

Almost all of the places listed have relatively high rates of job decrease. Structural change is greatest in the basic industries, with major declines limited to a relatively few classifications (i.e., mining, railroads, textiles, apparel, other manufacturing). Increases occurred primarily in electrical/other machinery, other transportation equipment, food/dairy products, printing/publishing, and other manufacturing. There was less transition in the more residentiary service industries. Job decreases were found primarily in railroad/railway express, armed forces, private households.

It is interesting to note that in New York, where the process of

[9] This type of netting out is actually an approximation of industrial transitions. Metropolitan growth occurring during the previous decade (1940–50) took place against a background of high national growth rates with the result that there was relatively little transition, i.e., netting out of job increases by job decreases.

TABLE 9.2

Selected Labor Markets Undergoing Extensive Industrial Transition: Total Job Increases and Job Decreases in Specified Industries, 1950-1960

(in thousands)

	Goods		Services		Total[a]		Specified industries			
	Increases	Decreases	Increases	Decreases	Increases	Decreases	Increases		Decreases	
Declining areas										
Johnstown (Pa.)	5.2	17.1	6.0	19.6	11.8	19.6	Misc. mfg.	2.2	Mining	14.9
							Apparel mfg.	1.4	Agriculture	1.8
Altoona (Pa.)	4.3	1.2	2.7	7.7	7.5	8.9	Misc. mfg.	2.0	Agriculture	.6
							Elec. mach.	1.3	RR/r'way exp.	6.7
Expanding areas										
New York	122.6	64.9	296.4	95.3	617.6	160.2	Elec. mach.	39.1	Apparel mfg.	55.9
							Misc. mfg.	22.0	RR/r'way exp.	14.6
							Print./pub.	19.7	Pvte. house.	14.0
							Trans. equip.	16.7		
							Food/dairy	16.1		
							Chem. prod.	5.2		
							Other trans.	8.6		
Detroit	71.0	96.1	133.6	10.0	242.3	106.1	Elec. mach.	30.6	Motor equip.	88.8
							Misc. mfg.	19.2		
							Print./pub.	8.7		
							Food/dairy	7.3		
							Pvte. house.	7.3		

City										
Chicago	84.6	28.4	156.4	64.7	377.7	93.1	Elec. mach. 40.9	Apparel mfg. 8.7		
							Construction 15.4	Agriculture 6.2		
							Misc. mfg. 11.4	Food/dairy 5.0		
							Chem. prod. 7.7	Lumber mfg. 3.6		
							Print./pub. 6.7	RR/r'way exp. 23.4		
							Armed forces 9.9			
							Truck./ware. 8.8			
Philadelphia	99.1	50.5	141.6	19.1	292.5	69.6	Elec. mach. 38.7	Textile prod. 30.3		
							Misc. mfg. 24.1	Agriculture 8.8		
							Chem. prod. 13.4	Construction 5.3		
							Food/dairy 10.4	RR/r'way exp. 7.1		
							Armed forces 15.6			
Pittsburgh	17.9	41.5	48.0	20.6	85.8	62.2	Elec. mach. 7.3	Mining 19.3		
							Print./pub. 3.3	Misc. mfg. 15.5		
							Food/dairy 3.1	Agriculture 4.1		
								RR/r'way exp. 11.2		
St. Louis (Mo., Ill.)	37.0	23.8	49.2	22.4	116.6	46.3	Trans. equip. 16.5	Misc. mfg. 7.9		
							Elec. mach. 7.2	Agriculture 6.7		
							Chem. prod. 6.2	Apparel mfg. 4.4		
							Truck./ware. 3.3	RR/r'way exp. 8.0		
								Armed forces 5.4		
Albany-Schenectady-Troy (N.Y.)	5.0	14.2	19.5	8.3	33.0	22.5	Misc. mfg. 1.7	Elec. mach. 6.9		
							Print./pub. 1.4	Textile prod. 2.5		
							Food/dairy 1.1	Agriculture 2.1		
								Trans. equip. 1.9		
								RR/r'way exp. 6.3		

TABLE 9.2 (continued)

	Goods		Services		Total[a]		Specified industries	
	Increases	Decreases	Increases	Decreases	Increases	Decreases	Increases	Decreases
Birmingham (Ala.)	8.1	12.9	21.9	7.1	35.5	20.1	Trans. equip. 3.1 Food/dairy 1.8 Misc. mfg. 1.4 Truck./ware. 1.4	Mining 10.3 RR/r'way exp. 3.8 Agriculture 1.3
Utica-Rome (N.Y.)	9.6	12.9	16.3	3.3	29.5	16.1	Elec. mach. 6.3 Trans. equip. 1.1 Armed forces 1.9	Textile prod. 7.0 Misc. mfg. 2.4 Agriculture 2.3 RR/r'way exp. 1.7
Erie (Pa.)	6.3	12.5	6.3	2.0	15.2	14.5	Trans. equip. 4.7	Elec. mach. 10.7 Agriculture 1.8 RR/r'way exp. 1.3
Tacoma (Wash.)	6.3	4.1	11.9	9.4	19.2	13.6	Trans. equip. 2.6 Misc. mfg. 1.2	Lumber mfg. 2.8 RR/r'way exp. 1.0 Armed forces 7.7
High growth (low transition) Los Angeles-Long Beach	327.4	5.6	354.5	5.1	788.2	10.7	Elec. mach. 102.2 Misc. mfg. 85.4 Trans. equip. 82.8 Food/dairy 14.6 Print./pub. 13.3	Agriculture 2.4 Forest./fish. 1.6 Mining 1.6 RR/r'way exp. 5.0

[a] Total includes INR classification.

job creation was almost as strong as in Los Angeles, the process of job destruction was much stronger. About 170,000 fewer jobs were added in New York than in Los Angeles, while 150,000 more jobs were destroyed.[10]

TRANSITION: A FACTOR IN METROPOLITAN PLANNING

Growth of the more residentiary industries is easier to project than growth in the more basic or export industries. Recognition of the particular type and size characteristics of a city should aid the planner in projecting the growth of the more residentiary industries. The more important these are in the local economy, the better grasp the planner may have of local employment growth processes. Nevertheless, employment in the basic industries will have to be projected before growth in the residentiary industries can be forecast.

The key to understanding the mobility of basic industries is the identification of the factors determining the location of activity in each. As the importance of one locational factor changes relative to another, or as the relative cost of one factor increases, the industry may decentralize, shift to another region, centralize, or shift from one size place to another size place. Further, the overall growth rate of the industry's output and productivity must be considered. Thus, knowledge of the economics of location in each industry is necessary if usable projections of local employment growth are to be constructed. The above analysis of metropolitan and industrial transition does not break new ground in location theory, but it does demonstrate that measures of job increases and decreases may be used to quantify metropolitan transition and to identify geographical changes on an industry-by-industry basis.

Transition within a metropolis occurs as a result of at least two types of causation. The first arises out of national and regional trends within the industries involved. As technology in an industry changes, so does the relative importance of the various locational factors. Simi-

[10] Job increases in New York numbered 620,000 compared to 790,000 in Los Angeles.

larly, technological changes in supporting industries (e.g., changes in transportation, industries supplying inputs, or even in finance and marketing institutions) may also affect the relative importance of location factors. Of course, where raw materials are important, the depletion of old resources or the discovery of more economical sources may dictate a move. A geographical shift of demand for the industry's output may also make it necessary for an industry to move to locate nearer its market.

The second type of causation originates in the growth dynamics of the metropolis itself; as already noted, the changing costs of the factors of production which accompany the growth of a metropolis affect its competitiveness as a site for industries. The cost advantages relative to those of other places will change as an MLM grows. A firm not requiring the benefits may choose to relocate in a lower-cost area, a firm requiring the benefits may be attracted to the metropolis. Sometimes the linkages between industries or firms are so strong that the locational factors affecting one industry may indirectly affect several ancillary industries.

Growth dynamics appear to differ by type and size of city. It should be possible therefore to anticipate the effect of metropolitan growth and development on the locational factors and to identify industries which are likely to be attracted or are likely to leave. Such information is critical to effective urban planning.

A metropolis competes with many other cities or both residents and industry. Its relative growth will indicate its competitive position *vis à vis* these other cities. Our findings suggest that competition differs in different type places. The nodal-type city competes within the framework of the regional or national system of cities while the specialized place competes mainly with other specialized places. Moreover, external economies and amenities appear to play a more important role in determining the competitive position of nodal-type cities than of specialized places.

10 PROSPECTS FOR GROWTH BY TYPE OF PLACE: THE INCREASING SIGNIFICANCE OF AMENITIES

In seeking to bring together the findings from the preceding chapters we are led toward certain additional conclusions which are less well substantiated but, at the same time, are more far-reaching. These conclusions have implications for manpower policy and suggest new directions for research.

Changing Emphasis on Locational Factors

A major question is the outlook for employment in the decades to come. Can past patterns be expected to continue or will there be significant changes in the factors which shape employment expansion in metropolitan places? Our answer depends on the interpretation given to the finding that there are very fundamental changes in the importance of factors affecting the location of new jobs.

In earlier years a major portion of the labor force was engaged in the goods sector. The location of most goods-producing activity was determined largely by industries' resource requirements and the availability of rail and water transportation facilities. To a large extent labor located where these sites happened to be—the farm, the mine, or the factory town. Today, however, the location of economic activity has increasingly come to be oriented toward markets and labor supply. As we noted in chapter 2 employment in the service sector has grown more rapidly than in the goods sector and now outnumbers the latter. Significantly, location of these service activities is oriented neither to transportation nor to natural resources.

Within the goods sector, two developments have worked to weaken older locational patterns. The first is that the sharpest decreases in employment have been in the primary industries where location of the production organization is dictated by natural resources. The second is that "footloose" manufacturing firms have come to have greater importance in American markets. The industries that have contributed the greatest number of new jobs in recent times have, typically, not been bound to locations near the source of their input of raw materials or even to final markets (e.g., electronics and aircraft manufacturers). Moreover, changing technology has tended to make most industries more footloose. The development of trucking, air passenger, and freight services has permitted the movement of people or goods in a fraction of the time formerly required; miniaturization has reduced bulk; air conditioning has permitted location in a variety of geographical areas previously considered undesirable; and the efficiency and virtual ubiquity of modern telephone communication has further loosened older locational ties.

The result of these changes has been that the desire of workers (and particularly of managerial personnel) for amenities has come to play an important role in determining the location of economic activity. The term *amenities* has not been clearly defined, but includes environmental factors such as favorable climate, attractive physical surroundings, and access to parks and recreational facilities, as well as the availability and quality of educational, medical, financial, entertainment, and retail services.

When worker and executive preferences are a major consideration, a business will find a strong inducement to locate its new plants or offices in amenity-rich areas. The promise of a job is not enough; the quality of life which accompanies it must be competitive with that elsewhere. Further, as skill requirements rise, businesses will have to give more consideration to the workers' satisfaction, not only to attract and retain desired personnel, but also to increase their productivity.

What, then, are the implications of the increasing emphasis which is being placed on amenities? First, amenity-rich places have an advantage over amenity-poor places and may be expected to continue to grow faster. Second, as amenities become increasingly important in the consumer's decision as to where to live, there will tend to emerge a new form of metropolis, evaluated primarily on the basis of the amenities it offers.

The implications are clear: for a metropolis to remain competitive and viable, amenities such as pollution-free air and water will have to be given equal or even higher priority than such time-honored demands of local industry as keeping taxes low. Of course, many amenities have a cost that results in higher tax rates, and firms that cannot afford this cost will be forced to migrate to areas with lower taxes and fewer amenities. Firms and consumers placing a high priority on amenities will converge in the amenity-rich city.

The reverse of the above is that amenity-poor places will tend to grow slowly or even to decline. We note that places where employment has declined over the last two decades were largely mining towns (resource-oriented industries) or railroad junctions. These places failed in earlier periods to develop local amenities, and the town declined with the industry. An example is a town built at the entrance to a mining shaft. When the mine closes, other industries have no reason to locate there. Such places could easily disappear from the map were it not for the inertia of the older population, which lacks the finances and initiative to move. If a community fails to build social infrastructure and improve amenities as it develops, it will be extremely difficult to superimpose all that is required to make it viable at a later date.

There may be places which are not worth rebuilding in a new form. For these places, costs relative to benefits will probably be much higher than elsewhere, or higher than they would be if new communities were built. On political and humanitarian grounds it may be desirable to perpetuate a mining town in which the mine is no longer operating, but on economic grounds the desirability of such a course will be difficult to establish.

PROSPECTS FOR GROWTH

We have seen that MLM's may be classified by functional specialization and that this specialization may be observed in the composition of the labor force. A further observation is that functional specialization tends to be reflected in the physical layout of the urban area—the urban form.

This is most clearly visualized in terms of the CBD, where the services tend to cluster. The importance of services should provide a good indication of the importance of the CBD. In a nodal city the CBD may be expected to dominate; in a manufacturing city it will be of much less importance.

It is likely that these relationships hold important implications for growth. The city with a large, well-developed CBD is more likely to be amenity-rich as well as rich in business services. Theaters, museums, good restaurants, night clubs, and public libraries tend to be found where the business and professional services flourish. Thus the larger and better developed is the CBD, the more services and amenities are found there and the more attractive the city becomes for the relatively fast-growing footloose manufacturing and service industries.

It follows, therefore, that our classification scheme, which recognizes the role of services, also tells us something about the importance of amenities and the urban form in the growth process.

Resort-type MLM's.   These places are amenity-rich. People seek them out because of climate and entertainment. Often, they are quite specialized, with the core of the area devoted to hotels and other consumer service facilities. For example, banking and other business services, which are developing rapidly in Las Vegas, are being expanded just outside the core in such a way as not to obstruct the city's main attraction. These services may eventually become more important than entertainment in the city's economy—witness the case of Miami.

Amenities that once were appreciated chiefly by visitors tend, in time, to attract new residents and new industry. Retired people become permanent residents, and industries are attracted to locate, since key personnel are readily induced to make their homes in such surroundings. As growth continues, these resort-type places will take on the characteristics of nodal, mixed, or, perhaps in exceptional cases, manufacturing MLM's.

Medical/education MLM's.   These places have a dominant service base that in certain cases may lead to growth and diversification. In general, however, college towns or medical centers seem to be specialized communities which lack the broad base of amenities required by a dynamic community. The location of a new major university or medical facility in a small rural town is often of questionable value. In contrast the location of a college medical complex in a growing nodal city will greatly enhance the community and at the same time serve the best interests of the institution by enabling it to attract superior faculty and students through the amenities offered by the community. In the latter case, the city will cross new thresholds, and the way will be open for still further development of services to be rendered to the community and its hinterland.

Government-associated MLM's.   Forty-five places were classified as government-associated MLM's. They are principally the sites of military bases or other major governmental installations. Because such installations frequently provide retail and recreational services at lower cost than could the community, relatively few amenities are provided commercially. Unless the major industry (government) expands its role, there is little ground to expect any growth in the community. A military base town may be compared to a mining town—amenity-poor and largely dependent upon a single activity.

On the other hand, state capitals were found to be, in most instances, nodal- or mixed-type places. If administrative functions were dominant in some early day, they have now been made secondary by the clustering of service-type and industrial firms. Existing services and amenities serve both governmental and commercial needs and add to the attractiveness of the city as a place for new firms to locate.

Nodal MLM's.   Among the three remaining types of MLM (i.e., nodal, mixed, and manufacturing), the nodal appear to have had the best growth performance and to promise the most favorable outlook for growth. As noted above, services dominate and amenities tend to be relatively more abundant.[1] Moreover, one may expect the CBD to be well developed along with the urban infrastructure (particularly a system of transportation providing access to the CBD from most points within the MLM). These attributes appear to be prerequisites for vigorous growth.

It is not surprising that employment expansion measured in terms of the regression analysis of chapter 7 was found to be relatively orderly in the nodal MLM's. In these places growth is in large measure an expansion of existing service activities. Business services are interdependent and mutually supportive. The particular patterns observed during the 1950s are unlikely to be duplicated during subsequent decades. Nevertheless, the observations made regarding past growth hold important lessons for the future. Even in nodal places, size is a significant variable. Patterns of growth (e.g., the importance of the business versus the consumer services as a source of job increase) are not expected to be the same in large-, medium-, and small-size places. Small-size places will be adding new service functions as they grow, with special emphasis on consumer services. Medium-size places often will be in the process of becoming regional centers, with consequent heavy increases in specialization in a number of business service activities. Large-size places will be under increasing constraints and will face increasing difficulties in expanding the infrastructure. They will tend to lose certain firms at the same time that they gain others. Above all, they will need to refine their specialization in activities in which they have a comparative advantage, as many of their functions are taken on by growing regional centers.[2]

---

[1] This generalization must be seen in terms of comparable sizes of place. Needless to say, a large manufacturing place, realizing economies of scale, is likely to be able to support a better theater, museum, or park system than a small nodal city.

[2] For example, New York City has retained its pre-eminence as an advertising and financial center by developing expertise and taking on more specialized functions at the same time that cities such as Atlanta and Dallas have developed as regional advertising and financial centers.

Manufacturing MLM's.   Manufacturing-type MLM's tend to be poor in amenities and poor in social infrastructure. This urban form is likely to lack a well-developed CBD, and, instead, to have an arrangement of industrial and residential structures which tend to form separate communities within the city—communities that reflect an earlier industrial specialization and product mix.

It is not unlikely that the transportation grid will be of a form that discourages easy movement of residents. Here the situation tends to differ significantly from that of a nodal city, where the transportation system has been specialized to permit ready access to the CBD from a variety of points inside and outside of the metropolitan area.

A possible result is that structural unemployment will be greater than in nodal places, where job openings are more readily filled because of the ease of commutation. Moreover, such amenities as do exist are inaccessible to many of the residents. Under such conditions the city cannot even make capital of its natural assets.

To the extent that an inadequate transportation network discourages movement through the city, the development of residentially oriented shopping centers will tend to be of greater importance. Although such shopping places may be relatively efficient in terms of cost, one may not conclude that they compensate for a lack of downtown development. To the contrary, these centers tend to draw business away from the central city, and, by substituting several market places for one central location, they limit the development of a wide range of commercial and public institutions, from specialty shops and theaters to museums and libraries.

The question of what is the most desirable urban form for manufacturing places must be left open, but the evidence at hand indicates that in the existing forms the CBD is not developed; there is a deficiency of services and a suboptimal functioning of the labor market because of its fragmented nature. If a transportation network could be established which would insure adequate linkage among various sectors of the MLM, the labor market would be made more efficient and a greater variety of amenities would become accessible to residents. It is an interesting thesis that the establishment of such a network might also tend to facilitate the development of the CBD and that the urban form would become more similar to that of nodal places of comparable size.

In view of all that has been said, manufacturing places would appear to face serious obstacles to growth. It is difficult to attract new firms into an MLM if the labor market is fragmented as a result of transportation facilities, if business services are poorly developed because they are internalized by the major firms, or if there is a paucity of amenities. For similar reasons the chances that new firms will be spawned by local entrepreneurs will tend to be restricted. It is not unlikely that existing industries will offer only limited prospects for new jobs.

The task of changing the urban form to one more attractive to the newer and expanding industries may well be too great for many manufacturing-type places. Major industries in these places have not found amenities necessary in the past and are not likely to be willing to share in their cost in the future. Their aim is to hold costs down. Some industries have threatened to take flight if taxes are increased and they are usually in an excellent bargaining position. Tax increases placed on workers will probably be reflected in higher wage demands being made upon local industries.

There is one great locational advantage which many manufacturing metropolitan economies offer, however: a supply of skilled or semiskilled workers who have become adjusted over at least a generation (frequently much longer) to the discipline and values of an industrial community. Within such an economy the natural rate of population increase alone makes available an attractive source of new labor for the manufacturing firm.

Given this special asset, but facing one or more of the limitations mentioned above, it would appear that renovation or rejuvenation of manufacturing places will require comprehensive planning and, very likely, considerable financial assistance from sources outside the metropolitan area. Benefits will accrue to both the national and the sub-economies involved if these places can be revitalized.

Mixed-type MLM's. The mixed-type MLM category is apparently the most heterogeneous of all and yields least rapidly to generalization. On one hand, these places are less industrialized than manufacturing cities. An attractive urban form should be able to emerge more easily here than in places where urban space has been more heavily committed to manufacturing. On the other hand, mixed-type MLM's may be satellite places whose service functions in the regional system of cities have already been preempted to a large extent by developed nodal centers. They may find themselves without the locational attraction of a supply of trained labor which a manufacturing place can offer and without the amenities or external economies of nodal places. The medium-size mixed-type places give evidence of fairly rapid development, but the small-size mixed-type MLM's are characterized by slow growth.

AMENITIES AND TYPE OF PLACE AS CONSIDERATIONS IN URBAN PLANNING

Urban plans usually encompass only the physical dimension of the city, its streets, transportation routes, parks, and zoning. But to really come to grips with the way a city is growing, and to identify the constraints which hold back its growth, the planner needs to understand the national trends affecting local industry, the relationships between the major sectors (the export sector and the local sector), the inter-industry relationships within these sectors, and the position of the city within the larger system of cities. Only when he is aware of the economics underlying these relationships can he draw up a plan that is compatible with the evolutionary tendencies dictated by the type and size of the city.

Moreover, the community may wish to exercise some discretion as to the kind of a city it is to become. It is not unlikely that a community has more control over the types of industry it attracts than has been considered possible in the past. For example, amenities that a community chooses to emphasize will influence the types of industry that it will attract. A high-skill, high-wage industry must locate in areas that provide the high standard of amenities demanded by its personnel. By upgrading its public services, a city may be able to attract such an industry, even though by so doing it may lose some employment in industries that cannot afford the increased cost.

The city may take the initiative in determining its future form rather than simply allowing itself to be a victim of circumstance. The consequences of not planning will increase with time, for people and industry are becoming increasingly mobile and cities are becoming more competitive. The surge in the construction, across the country, of museums, music centers, civic centers, convention halls, and stadiums, is just one manifestation of such competition. Even places rich in natural amenities (i.e., favorable climates or scenic beauty) may lose their advantage if the urban form is allowed to become unattractive. The special ambiance of a city must be cultivated. A community must be aware of what it is, know what it would like to be, and understand the economics involved before it can establish its objectives.

The Urban Economy Within a System of Cities

A city does not stand alone, but operates within the regional or national system of cities. Hence, growth of the city will depend upon its role in the urban system and the type of growth which is taking place in the larger regional context. This is especially true of nodal-type places. Each such city plays a role in its region's development and must be viewed as more dependent upon the regional system within which it lies than are specialized places. The latter are usually more sensitive to national trends influencing their specialized industries than to regional developments.

The dynamics of a regional system of cities have yet to be investigated. Our findings suggest, however, certain hypotheses concerning the growth of a region and the evolution of a regional system of cities. We have seen that the structure of certain services increases with an increase in the size of city and is higher in nodal than in specialized places. We have also seen that growth is more rapid in places well structured in services. The shares of employment in certain consumer services seem to be correlated with the shares of employment in certain business or producer services, but it is the role of the latter that is deemed most crucial to the growth process.

These observations suggest to us that regional development is partly a function of the availability of business services. Not only does the absence of certain crucial services mean that local funds will leak out of the regional economy as the services are purchased in other regions; it also means that the development process itself is slowed down, made more complicated and, probably, made more costly. As a consequence, the region is placed in a weak competitive position *vis-à-vis* other regions.

From these two observations, that services increase with city size and that regional growth increases with the availability of services, we tentatively conclude that the development of a region depends in part on the composition of the regional system of cities in terms of their function and size. In particular, the availability of services in a region appears to be determined partly by the size of the largest city in the region. This hypothesis has important implications for regional development policies. It raises the question of whether government policy should be designed to encourage development of a major regional center to accelerate growth in the region as a whole.

An example of such a policy would be that of locating as many government agencies as possible in the most strategically located regional center rather than dispersing them. Such a policy would add to the locational attraction of the regional center for private industry by increasing the size of the local market. Such an increase would make it possible for firms to realize economies of scale and make available certain external economies which would not exist otherwise. New firms locating in the regional center would enlarge the market still further and provide the basis for further external economies. In the process, the regional center would become the focal point of development, offering a greater variety of services and amenities to both the local residents and the hinterland.

SUMMARY

Type–size differences in the characteristics of MLM's go beyond the structure and growth of the metropolitan labor force. Urban forms and the availability of amenities appear to vary by type of place. They also appear to affect growth prospects.

The urban form of nodal cities seems most compatible with the national trends in employment expansion. The less-integrated urban form suggested by the dominant characteristics of manufacturing-type places appears to place a serious constraint on further growth in those places.

An urban or cities policy must confront the issues raised in this chapter. This appears to be especially true for those communities that are lacking in amenities, such as manufacturing-type places. It may be necessary to restructure certain urban areas both to make them viable and to make possible the development of the region within which they are located.

11 SOME KEY FINDINGS AND
THEIR IMPLICATIONS

FROM THE OUTSET, both theory and general observation have moved us to focus attention upon metropolitan places. There is, of course, abundant evidence that significant differences exist among regions, but these differences are, themselves, better understood once we have a clearer conception of the forces at work within the systems of metropolitan and nonmetropolitan areas which comprise each region. In the early chapters we have examined regional and national employment data, but only to the extent necessary to provide background material and to facilitate the analysis of employment structure and change within the metropolitan economies.

For the most part, the analyses has concentrated on two aspects of employment—structure and change. The first involved the examination of structural characteristics and the classification of each of the 368 MLM's. The second involved analysis of the processes of change, making use of this classification system. From these analyses have emerged a number of findings, some of the more important of which are set forth below.

STRUCTURE

1. When 1960 employment is analyzed in terms of a single criterion, size of place, well-defined tendencies for industrial composition of employment to be different in the different size categories are observed. The findings are best established for the business service classifications, in which, with only minor exceptions, percentages increase with size of place. For consumer services classifications, the tendency is for share of total employment to be highest in the small-size MLM's, second highest in the medium-size MLM's, followed by the NMC's and the large-size MLM's in that order. As regard percentage of employment in manufacturing, the size of place analysis reveals a tendency for the medium-size MLM's to have larger shares of such employment than the small-size MLM's and the NMC's, but there is no well-developed tendency for the large-size MLM category.

2. Analysis of inter- and intraregional differences in employment structure among the several size-of-place categories leads to a further observation: There are distinct regional differences in employment structure which are typically found in all size-of-place categories, except the large-size groups of MLM's. These differences take the form of smaller shares of employment accounted for by business and consumer services in those regions which are heavily industrialized than in those in which primary activities are relatively important. Nevertheless, differences among size of place noted for the nation are found also in most of the regions. Thus the relative structural difference among size-of-place categories is found to exist at the regional level in spite of the difference among regions in service requirements imposed upon the metropolitan economies by the regions' special needs. Changes in regional employment structures, however, were found to be converging toward the national structure.

3. Analysis of employment structure of MLM's reveals that there is a well-established tendency for agglomeration in most of the business and certain of the consumer services to occur in the same places. This is the major characteristic of nodality, and those MLM's observed to have such combinations of high services employment were classified within the nodal MLM grouping—one of the major categories used in our classification scheme. This category consists of metropolitan economies that exist primarily to provide consumer and business services to outlying areas (i.e., hinterlands). Cities which comprise this category are centers for shopping, wholesale, transportation, banking, and other service activities. Such a city may be relatively small, serving the needs of a limited area, or it may be of medium or large size, serving not only an outlying area, but also the special needs of smaller cities within an entire region or beyond.

4. The remaining places were non-nodal in character. Many of them were metropolises which specialize primarily in producing and exporting goods or some relatively restricted type of service. In this category we include manufacturing centers, resort centers, and cities which serve as the base for government installations or large medical/educational institutions. In addition, there were a number of places—mixed-type MLM's—which did not appear to be strongly differentiated as regards function. However, the provision of services to adjacent areas played a significant role in the local economy of roughly half of these places. In those remaining we found no distinguishing structural characteristics that were common to any sizable number of them.

Metropolitan economies vary in the extent to which services are important in their employment structure. The manufacturing MLM's have relatively small percentages of employment in business and consumer services, indicating that as they have evolved toward a heavy specialization in manufactures there has not been a need to develop the CBD sufficiently for it to play a major role in the metropolitan economy. Apparently, manufacturing firms have provided for their service needs from within the firm or from outside sources in distant headquarters cities. Internalized services make it more difficult for new firms to enter the metropolitan economy since they will also have to provide the required services from within.

Government-associated, medical/educational, and the mixed-type metropolitan places were found also to have relatively little employment within the service industries. On the other hand, the resort-type places showed high percentages of employment not only in most of the consumer services but also in a number of the business services.

GROWTH AND DEVELOPMENT

1. Among the size-of-place categories we observed fairly systematic differences in employment growth. The medium-size MLM's showed much the fastest rate of employment increase, with the small-size MLM's in second place. The large-size MLM's were found to have a higher rate of net employment change than the NMC's. The latter places were very frequently the scene of considerable transition from primary to manufacturing employment, however. The analysis makes clear that the net employment change data for these counties fail to reveal the extent of employment expansion that is taking place.

2. In the large-size MLM's, where net employment increases were relatively low, ratios of job decreases to job increases were relatively high. The story these ratios tell is that the large cities have faced major problems of manpower adjustment. Overall job opportunities opening up were relatively less than in the fast-growing medium-size places (i.e., rates of job increase were lower) and at the same time sizable numbers of traditional jobs were vanishing from the scene.

3. Regression analysis, in which employment change in a number of service-type industrial classifications was related to overall MLM employment change, revealed very different responses of the service sector among the various types of MLM's. The relationship between service and overall employment changes was best established in the nodal, medium-size mixed-type, and resort-type MLM's. For these groups of places the correlation was high, indicating that employment change in the services was associated with overall employment change in a consistent rather than erratic fashion. Moreover, the strength of this relationship as indicated by rate multiple values (i.e., coefficients of regression) was relatively high. For the manufacturing, government-associated, medical/educational, small-size mixed-type MLM's, as well as for the large-size MLM's taken as a group, the relationship was much poorer. It appears that exogeneous growth forces in these places are not amplified by endogenous growth in services as much as is the case in the nodal, medium-size, mixed-, and resort-type MLM's.

Additional insights on the amplification of employment expansion were provided by regression analysis in which employment change in each of fourteen service-type classifications was related separately to employment change in every one of the others. This analysis revealed that growth is a process of agglomeration in the nodal, resort-type, and medium-size mixed-type MLM's, i.e., that there are very strong linkages between employment changes in the various service-type classifications, whereas in the manufacturing, medical/educational, government-associated, and small-size mixed-type MLM's there were no clear interindustry growth patterns.

4. Another type of measure which sheds light on the processes of growth is the share of job increases and decreases accounted for by each of the various industrial classifications. Of all our measures these provide the clearest summary of the role played by each industrial classification in employment expansion and contraction within size–type groups of MLM's or within regions. A considerable variation in the patterns was observed. The nodal places were found to be developing in such a way as to increase the importance of the services, but there were considerable differences among sizes of place. Whereas the smaller places were building consumer services in an important measure, large places were showing no job increases in certain of these services although there were very large shares of job increases in certain of the business services. As a group the relatively fast-growing medium-size nodal places showed large shares of job increases accounted for by both business and consumer services. Clearly, most of these latter places were assuming major roles as service centers within their regions.

In stark contrast, the average slow-growing manufacturing places and small-size mixed-type places showed very small shares of job increases falling within the service sectors. Not only are these places typically lacking in services but there is no evidence of a catching-up process at work.

Among the remaining types of places, the resort MLM's showed large shares of job increases in both consumer and business services. The medical/educational and government-associated places showed little evidence of vigorous or well-rounded growth in the service sectors. We interpret these latter findings to indicate that the amenities-rich resort places tend to take on service funcions as new firms locate within their boundaries or nearby. The medical/educational and government-associated places show no such tendencies. The basic export activity grows, but there is little response evident in the service sector.

5. Still another type of insight into the processes of employment expansion and contraction was gained by examination of job-increase and job-decrease data. It was found that these measures serve to illuminate the extent of transition which occurs within the metropolitan economy, the region, or the entire nation. At the metropolitan level these measures indicate the extent to which employment growth has been closed out in some industrial classifications while employment opportunities are being opened up in other industries. At the regional and national levels, the JIDO measures can be used to measure the extent that employment in an industry is relocated or the extent of employment shifts between industries.

Specific examples of geographical redistribution are the decentralization of the motor vehicle industry, primarily within the Great Lakes region, the regional shift of the apparel industry from large MLM's in the Mideast region to small MLM's in the Southeast, and increasing centralization of business/repair services from the NMC's to medium- and large-size MLM's nationwide.

Relocation of employment within industries at the national level was found to be highest (ranging up to 85 percent of job increases) in the slow-growing (or declining) and basic industries. This type of employment change is not revealed in conventional analyses of industry trends. It is important, however, since relocation affects both the labor market to which industry has moved and the labor market from which it has departed.

Regional transition, the offsetting of job increases in one industry by job decreases in another, ranged from as high as 70 percent of the job increases in the Southeast (1950-60) to only 9 percent in the Far West. Regional relocation of employment within the same industry ranged from one-fifth to one-half the number of jobs involved in regional transition. Intrametropolitan transition, the offsetting of job increases and decreases, within MLM's was found to involve primarily the goods sector and in particular the manufacturing sector. There was very little transition as measured by JIDO within the service sector.

Further analysis of the patterns of geographical redistribution of employment would be helpful in understanding the dynamics of employment growth in MLM's. What would be most helpful would be the identification of the factors contributing to either centralization or decentralization of an industry. Urban planners could well use some general guides as to the factors which most affect the mobility of their basic (export) industries.

EVIDENCE OF A REGIONAL AND NATIONAL SYSTEM
OF METROPOLITAN ECONOMIES

It has long been recognized that there is a size hierarchy of metropolitan places within the nation. The information gained from the analysis of employment structure and the resulting classification of MLM's suggests that there are also regional systems of metropolitan economies which, taken together, form a national system. It is the nodal places which appear to form the major framework of this system. Each serves a hinterland which may include smaller nodal centers as well as non-nodal places. Where the region is strongly oriented to the production of primary goods, these nodal places tend to be small or medium sized; no large regional centers have developed in these regions. Where the region is industrialized there are a few large nodal centers but very few small- or medium-size ones.

The non-nodal places play a different role in the regional organization. They exist principally to export specialized goods or services to other places within the region, to the national market, or to overseas markets.

The information gained from analysis of employment change provides still further insights regarding this system of nodal and non-nodal places. We see that, as regions have grown, the nodal places have grown somewhat faster and have taken on new roles. The medium-size places such as Atlanta, Dallas, and Denver have developed their service sectors very rapidly, taking on certain banking, advertising, consulting, and other high-order functions previously performed in the large nodal centers, such as New York and San Francisco. At the same time, the large nodal centers have become even more specialized in business services such as advertising, international finance, and corporate headquarters. At lower levels in the system, the small metropolises have built their consumer services and certain of their business services, while the nonmetropolitan counties have gained in manufacturing and in certain consumer services.

In short, there appears to have been a passing down of functions within a system of nodal places and their hinterlands. At the same time that this has occurred, the non-nodal places have grown or declined depending upon their success in attracting and holding specialized goods and service-producing activities.

IMPLICATIONS

The major lesson to be drawn from this study would seem to be that an understanding of the basic size–function characteristics of a metropolitan economy is necessary for analysis of the problems which the metropolitan and regional economies face and for formulation of policies which will enable them to remain economically healthy and to prosper in the years to come.

POLICY IMPLICATIONS AT THE METROPOLITAN LEVEL

At the local level it is essential to recognize that the problems of large places differ from those of small- and medium-size places. The large-size metropolis must build upon the attractions offered by its great army of workers, technicians, and professionals with their varied skills and training, its external economies, its position within the transportation network, its urban amenities. As the nation grows and regional and subregional markets become large enough to permit functions to be "passed down" to smaller places, the large-size metropolis must take on even higher order functions, must enhance its urban amenities, must "spawn" new firms (both manufacturing and service) better suited to the urban environment than those forced to leave by space restraints and other cost considerations.

On the other hand, problems of the small- and medium-size metropolitan economies involve shaping the urban form to maximize their locational appeal, building appropriate infrastructure, and encouraging the development of external economies and amenities.

The opportunities and problems relating to urban development will vary greatly by type as well as by size of place. For example, we have argued that the nodal MLM will tend to have an urban form better suited for growth than most manufacturing MLM's, since its

CBD will probably be better developed both spatially and in terms of the business and consumer services which it offers. Moreover, its transportation system is more likely to facilitate movement both within the city and from outside its boundaries. The manufacturing city frequently offers a basic locational attraction due to its supply of trained labor, but may be expected to have a poorly developed CBD and is likely to be lacking in both business services and amenities that would attract new firms or facilitate the spawning of new firms.

POLICY IMPLICATIONS AT NATIONAL AND REGIONAL LEVELS

Throughout the postwar period there has been a heavy emphasis on broad macroeconomic analysis and policy formulation. Such analysis has been extremely useful and must be continued. Yet there are disadvantages, even dangers, in excessive dependence on the national data to the neglect of analysis of changes which are occurring at the regional and urban levels.

An example of the dangers inherent in aggregate analysis may be found in the lively current interest in the trend toward an even larger service sector. Extrapolation of the national data leads to the prophesy of a society in which future additions to employment will be largely in the service sector. Yet examination of the data for the two decades under study indicates that the expansion of service employment was principally in the medical/educational classifications and in certain relatively small but strategically important business service classifications. There were negative trends in some service classifications and relatively small gains in others, such as recreation/entertainment and retailing.

We see, moreover, that expansion of employment in the services has by no means been evenly distributed geographically. Expansion in retail services has tended to be concentrated in the smaller places and the NMC's. Expansion in recreation services has occurred mainly in resort-type and fast-growing nodal places. Business services employment has tended to grow most rapidly in those places which are developing their nodal (service center) functions.

It is not the purpose of this study to determine whether or not the trend toward an enlarging share of employment in the service sector will continue unabated. It is clear to us, however, that goods production remains an important sector and that manufacturing has increased in importance as a source of employment in the more rapidly developing areas. An across-the-board program for training manpower for a largely service economy will surely fall wide of the mark in the years immediately ahead. It is only when the situation is studied within the framework of a developing system of regions and urban places and when the very significant differences which exist in outlook and requirements in different types and sizes of places are recognized that national policies may be better designed to meet our national objectives.

In examining the industrial sources of growth in regions, the measures of job increases and decreases make it possible to give a more accurate description than can be given with the conventional measures of net employment change. For example, one may say either that manufacturing accounted for 46 percent of net employment change in the Southeast (1950-60), or 26 percent of job increases. The publication of these measures of job increases and decreases should be highly useful to those who wish to understand the dynamics of a region's or industry's employment growth.

IMPLICATIONS FOR PUBLIC INVESTMENT

A further example of the need for analysis at the regional and urban levels can be offered in the area of public expenditure designed to stimulate national growth. Growth in the overall economy is the sum of growth in the regional, metropolitan, and submetropolitan economies which comprise it. The location of specific social investment may affect the overall development of the region or nation. For example, if it is true that the growth of an area tends to center around and to be encouraged by the vigorous development of a nodal metropolis, then the location of public expenditures for highways, urban renewal, and institutions of higher learning and manpower training should be focused upon such centers and their environs.

To us the fundamental observation is that a dollar of federal funds spent in one place does not necessarily have the same impact upon growth and development as a dollar spent in another. The nation will enjoy the greatest prosperity when growth unfolds in the regions and urban places in such a way as to best realize the potentialities of each. Expenditures must be properly allocated not only to the most effective types of programs (e.g., to public education, highways, research and development), they must also be allocated to those points within the system of cities where growth and development opportunities are greatest.

There are no simple criteria for selecting growth centers. Neither the "worst first" policy, which leads to the selection of areas that are growing the slowest or that have the highest rates of unemployment, nor the use of a simplistic size-of-place criteria (often referred to as "optimal" size of place) for making social investment can be expected to succeed. Each urban place is a point in a regional system and the impact of a policy will vary depending on the industrial composition and the position of the place within the system. The spatial structuring of the national economy changes over time—some areas expand, some decline, and often are "left behind" at the interstices of regional systems. In the latter case (Appalachia being a prime example), it is questionable whether the present policy of redeveloping the area as a special region is defensible on economic grounds.[1]

IMPLICATIONS FOR MANPOWER POLICY

All that has been said above simply underlines the observation that regions differ and that cities have different structures and growth characteristics depending upon their size and the functions which they perform. Manpower requirements will vary widely among cities and among regions. Programs for training, recruitment, and guidance must be dictated by the unique requirements of each labor market. The more completely the local requirements are assessed, the more effective these programs will be.

[1] See Niles H. Hansen, "Urban and Regional Dimensions of Manpower Policy," prepared for the U.S. Dept. of Labor Manpower Administration (June, 1969), ch. 12.

New and better theory is needed as well as more effective tools of analysis. Our efforts at classification of metropolitan places and our techniques for analysis of employment growth and transition are only preliminary; they need refinement. We hope, however, that they have been of assistance toward improving understanding of the structure and dynamics of the metropolitan economy.

Appendix A DEFINITIONS AND
LIMITATIONS OF THE
CENSUS MATERIAL

SINCE THIS STUDY is based almost entirely upon analyses of Census of Population estimates of the employed labor force for the three years 1940, 1950, and 1960, the accuracy and reliability of the measures are limited by the data upon which they are based. If the enumeration of the employed work force is not comparable in the three years, if the industrial classifications are inappropriate, or if there are inaccuracies in the estimates, the story which the data tell will be to some extent distorted.

COMPARABILITY OF THE TWO DECADES

There is reason to question the comparability of the estimates of the employed work force for the three census years. In 1940 the nation had not fully recovered from the depression and had not reestablished itself on the trend line of long-term growth along which it has tended to move since the middle of the nineteenth century. The unemployment rate stood at 14.5 percent of the work force, in contrast to rates of 5.3 percent and 5.6 percent which were to exist in 1950 and 1960.[1]

From 1940 to 1950 the level of total output rose sharply. The economy was brought up to full capacity operation following the outbreak of the war, expanded further to fulfill the needs of our own and our allies' forces, and, finally, was shifted over to a peacetime basis. In manufacturing the emphasis was on durable goods production; during the first half of the decade to meet the demands of war, during the second, the requirements of a people eager to purchase automobiles and other consumer goods. These years saw also an economic dynamizing of great areas of the South and West, brought about in a large measure by the location of military centers and of new industry in these states.

The second decade brought the nation far along into the postwar era.

[1] U.S. Department of Commerce, *Business Statistics 1963*, p. 65.

Industrial equipment and plants were modernized and increased, as was the stock of residential, educational, and medical facilities. A continued increase in output per worker meant further increases in income per capita; and rising income favored the growth of banking, medical, educational, travel, and governmental services. Moreover, by 1960 the "war baby" generation had begun to establish its importance as an economic force. For these reasons, and others as well, a very new and different assortment of consumer and governmental requirements began to guide the allocation of resources in the market place.

But growth was not as rapid in the second decade. Inasmuch as the economy had returned to the long term path of growth by the end of the 1950s, increases in output were once again limited on the supply side by manpower, capital, and technological considerations. From 1940 to 1950 the Census of Population data show a net increase in employment of 26.7 percent; from 1950 to 1960, a net increase of 15.5 percent.

This basic difference in the rate of growth calls into question the comparability of the three census years and of the decadal changes which occurred between them. Our position is that comparison between 1940 and 1950 is not completely satisfactory. Not only was unemployment far higher in 1940 as a percentage of the labor force, but also the labor force was itself smaller in relation to the population eligible for employment. In 1940 the labor force participation rate was 55.9 percent. In 1950 it was 58.9 percent.[2] Thus the employment expansion of the 1940s may be looked upon as due, to a substantial extent, to the reduction of underemployment in the labor force coupled with a structural change in the labor force resulting in increased employment of women. Moreover, it is probable that part-time employment was of less importance in the labor markets of 1950 than it had been in the slack labor markets of ten years earlier. Those industries most affected by reduction of part-time employment would be those such as agriculture and private household services where traditionally there has been a large amount of such employment.

In the years 1950 and 1960, however, the unemployment rates were approximately the same, and the labor force participation rates were equal. Both years may be regarded as years of cyclical expansion: 1950 was the first full year of recovery following the recession of 1948-49; and 1960 was the second year of recovery following the recession of 1957-58.[3] It is

[2] *Ibid.*

[3] Although it was also a year in which the mild recession of 1960-61 began, the census enumeration (principally in April) occurred at least one month prior to the peak (May) of the expansion.

our judgment that these two years are, therefore, acceptable for purposes of measuring employment expansion.

We do not regard the two decades, 1940-50 and 1950-60, as being completely comparable for purposes of analyzing changes within the employed work force. The decade of the 1950s is much to be preferred both because it is more recent and, therefore, more relevant to the present, and because the two census years from which the decadal changes are prepared are more comparable. For these reasons we place greater emphasis upon the second decade than on the first. Nevertheless, the measures available from inclusion of the 1940 census materials provide important information, and we find frequent occasion to examine them.

DEFINITION OF EMPLOYMENT AND
METHOD OF ENUMERATION

Census employment data accounts for the fully and the partially employed but not the unemployed. "Employed persons" are defined as follows:

> All civilians 14 years old and over who are either (a) "at work"—those who did any work for pay or profit, or worked without pay for 15 hours or more on a family farm or in a family business; or (b) were "with a job but not at work"—those who did not work and were not looking for work but had a job or business from which they were temporarily absent because of bad weather, industrial dispute, vacation, illness, or other personal reasons.[4]

In addition to employed persons in the civilian labor force, the data we have used include members of the armed forces.

Census employment data are based upon enumeration at place of residence rather than at place of work. Change of residence within a metropolitan market will not be observed in the data. Since all of the reporting units are defined in such a way that the geographical boundaries tend to include both place of residence and place of work (except in those instances where the reporting unit underbounds the labor market), it would appear to be largely a matter of indifference whether enumeration has been carried out on one basis or the other.[5]

[4] U.S. Bureau of the Census, *U.S. Census of Population: 1950, General Social and Economic Characteristics, United States Summary* (Washington D.C., 1962), p. xxvii. Note: minimum age is now 16 years.

[5] For the study of employment amplification, however, data by place of residence is preferred. This is because many "residentiary" industries, such as retailing, are oriented to consumer needs and located near points of domicile.

APPROPRIATENESS OF THE INDUSTRIAL
CLASSIFICATIONS USED

In compiling its published county data on the Regional Economics Division, staff of the Department of Commerce found it necessary, "in order to achieve a high degree of comparability from one census to the next," to combine certain industrial combinations which had previously been published separately.[6] In discussing the effect of such combination, they note:

> Incomparabilities in industrial categories published in the several censuses of population arose from two sources: First, the structure of industrial detail presented had changed from one census to another, and second, the industrial classification of some economic activities had undergone change between censuses. While the industrial combinations made for this publication have corrected most of the incomparabilities arising from the first source, some remain attributable to the second. Caution should therefore be exercised in placing great stress on the significance of small change in industrial sectors over time.

The thirty-two derived industrial classifications may be observed in Table 3.4. The most important categories not included in the thirty-two classifications but published on a county basis in the 1960 Census of Population are indicated in the right-hand column below:[7]

Classification used in present study	1960 Census of Population component categories (published by county)	Percent[a]
Miscellaneous manufacturing (32% of manufacturing)	Primary metal industries	22
	Fabricated metal industries (incl. not specified metal)	23
	Other durable goods (incl. not specified)	30
Business/repair (16% of mainly business services)	Business Services	47
	Repair services	53

[a] Percent of industrial classification in left column.

[6] Lowell D. Ashby, *Growth Patterns in Employment by County, 1940–50 and 1950–60,* 8 vols. (Washington, D.C., U.S. Dept. of Commerce, 1965), p. xiv.
[7] *Ibid.,* Appendix, Table A.

Medical/education	Hospitals	34
(35% of mainly consumer services)	Education services: government	33
	Education services: private	11
	Welfare, religious, and nonprofit	8
	Other professional and related services	14

THE TREATMENT OF GOVERNMENT-ASSOCIATED WORK

Another characteristic of census employment classification is that only persons in administration and in the armed forces are treated as employees of government agencies. For example, physicians and teachers in governmental institutions would be classified along with persons of the same professions who are employed by private firms, in private practice, or in nongovernment institutions.

ACCURACY OF THE DATA

For the nation as a whole or for large aggregations such as regions, the census materials provide reasonably accurate measures of employment structure and change. When the data are examined at lower levels of aggregation (e.g., the individual MLM) opportunities for error because of under- or over-enumeration or industry misclassification are greater than at higher levels of aggregation, where random errors may offset one another. Accordingly, findings based on data relating to detailed classifications or small aggregations of reporting units must be assessed cautiously.

There is one source of error which deserves special mention, that which arises out of the increase in the relative size of the INR classification in the 1960 census. In Appendix B we analyze the significance of over-enumeration of workers in INR and conclude that the increase in the INR category makes for a downward bias in the job increases and net change data for individual industrial classifications and an upward bias in the job-decrease data. This bias probably extends over most of the industrial classifications. We know of no way to make defensible statistical adjustment and present the data in the form made available by the Department of Commerce. Clearly, the 1960 underenumeration of the industrial classifications which resulted in an increase in the INR category demands a greater measure of caution in interpreting our results than might otherwise be required.

THE 113-MLM SAMPLE

In many cases, where the need for a finer breakdown of industrial classifications arises, we are able to make use of unpublished data for a sample of 113 MLM's. The employment estimates for these MLM's are comparable to the estimates which appear in the published material except that they are available for 118 industry classifications.[8] From these data it is possible to observe changes in small but interesting categories such as the highly dynamic "miscellaneous business service" classification or "legal, engineering, and miscellaneous professional service."

The principal limitation upon the use of this data source is that it contains no metropolitan counties other than officially defined SMSA's (i.e., counties which we define as metropolitan counties but which are not defined by the Department of Commerce as SMSA's are omitted) and only one of the MLM's in the 50,000 to 100,000 population category. This will be clear in the tabulation below:

TABLE A.1

Number and Percent (in parentheses) of MLM's Represented in the 113-MLM Sample in Each Size Category, by Region

	Small-size[a]		Medium-size	Large-size
New England	b	1 (25)	2 (29)	d
Mideast	c	2 (100)	15 (79)	4 (67)
Great Lakes	b	8 (41)	16 (76)	2 (67)
Plains	b	6 (86)	4 (67)	d
Southeast	b	9 (53)	22 (69)	c
Southwest	1 (14)	22 (28)	7 (54)	c
Rocky Mountain	b	c	1 (50)	c
Far West	b	c	10 (77)	d
Hawaii	c	c	1 (100)	
Alaska	c	c	c	c
All U.S.	1 (5)	30 (46)	76 (67)	6 (46)

a No MLM's in the 25,001—50,000 category are represented in sample.

b Not represented in sample.

c These regions or states have no MLM's in size category.

d New England and Plains have one large MLM, Far West has two; none of these three MLM's are represented in the sample.

[8] These data, of course, have the same limitation arising out of excessive classification within the INR category as the published data.

If we exclude the 25,001 to 50,000 and 50,001 to 100,000 population categories of small MLM's the sample is generally representative not only for the nation but for each region. For the medium-size MLM's the sample is as small as 29 percent for only one region, New England. It is somewhat less representative of the large-size MLM category since it does not include Boston, St. Louis, or the two Far West major metropolises, Los Angeles and San Francisco. It does include New York and Chicago, however, as well as a variety of other large places, such as Washington, Detroit, and Philadelphia.

Appendix B THE SIGNIFICANCE OF OVERENUMERATION OF WORKERS IN INR AS A SOURCE OF ERROR

THERE is one industry category, INR which requires special comment because rather than representing a specific industry, it represents employment in many industries not classified at the time the census was taken. Had the importance of this category remained at its 1940 or 1950 level of approximately 1.5 percent of total employment, it could be disregarded. But in 1960 its share of employment jumped to almost 4 percent (roughly 2.6 million jobs), thereby giving rise to significant underreporting among the remaining industrial classifications.

So far as we have been able to determine, the reason for this substantial increase in unclassified employment is that in 1960 a new type of enumeration, the marked questionnaire, was introduced to secure more accurate information relating to employment. In the absence of an on-the-spot interviewer who would insist that the respondent give some answer to each question, many respondents failed to designate the industry of their principal employment. It is important to establish, therefore, whether these new reporting procedures introduce any discernible biases into the census employment statistics for regions, size- or type-of-place categories, or industrial classifications.

EFFECT OF INR ON EMPLOYMENT STRUCTURE AND ON JOB-INCREASE/JOB-DECREASE MEASURES

An increase in the INR category due to nonclassification of workers in one or more of the industry categories results in a lower employment figure in the industries concerned. As a result, the shares of employment accounted for by the underreported industrial classifications are inappropriately small. Moreover, the net rate of growth and the rate of job increases of an underreported industry are biased downward, and the rate of job decreases in those instances where the industry has declined is biased upward.

The nature of the effect on employment structure is readily understood, but the nature of the bias in the job increase, job decrease, and net measures of employment change is more complicated. For MLM, regional, or national totals *both* the total of job decreases, and the total of job increases will be biased upward. The total of job decreases is biased upward for the reason noted above, i.e., that wherever actual job decreases occur in specific industries, such decreases will be augmented by an increase in underreporting. The total of job increases is biased upward because the entire number of jobs underreported is recorded in the job-increase column for the INR classification.

This is illustrated in the following example of a labor market in which there are two industrial classifications and a rise in employment classified as INR from zero in Year 1 to 20 in Year 2. Job decreases are seen to be overstated in industry B (the declining industry) and for the labor market as a whole. Job increases are understated for industry A (the industry with rising employment) but are overstated for the entire labor market.

Industrial Classification	Employment[a]		JI[a]	JD[a]	Underreporting
	Year 1	Year 2			
A	(100) 100	(110) 105	(10) 5		5
B	(100) 100	(95) 80		(5) 20	15
INR		20	20		
Total	(200) 200	(205) 205	(10) 25	(5) 20	

[a] Numbers in parentheses show the data as they would have appeared had there been no underreporting. Numbers without parentheses are the recorded employment data and are in error to the extent that underreporting occurred.

An additional observation is that the rate of growth of the MLM or of the region is important when considering the effects that INR changes have on the measures used in this study. If an MLM or a region is growing rapidly, total job increases will be relatively large and the share of job increases accounted for by INR tend to be small, whereas if the MLM or the region is growing slowly, job increases in INR taken as a share of total job increases (which will be relatively few) will tend to be high. For example, the share of 1960 employment accounted for by INR is third highest in the fast-growing Far West, but the share of 1950-60 job increases accounted for by INR ranks sixth. The principle also holds in individual labor markets. In 1960 for example, INR in Sarasota, a very fast-growing area, was 8.4 percent of MLM employment, but in Jersey City, an MLM with declining employment, it was only 4.8. Yet during the 1950-60 period, job increases in INR in Sarasota were 13 percent of total job increases compared to 44 percent in Jersey City.[1]

EXTENT OF UNDERREPORTING IN
INDUSTRIAL CLASSIFICATIONS

Before assessing the extent to which our findings may have been affected by underreporting, it is desirable to know whether or not such underreporting tended to be concentrated in certain industrial classifications or whether it was more or less evenly distributed among the various classifications. If underreporting was heavily concentrated, errors in the employment data for affected classifications are likely to have been large. Under such conditions we would have less confidence in the findings relating to these classifications than would otherwise be the case. If the underreporting was more or less evenly distributed among the various classifications, however, the distortion of the measures is reduced and the likelihood of serious biases appearing in the findings is minimized.

Fortunately, a special Census Bureau study is available in which industrial classifications reported in the 1960 Census of Population have been *matched* with classifications reported by the *same persons* in a 1960 Census Population Survey.[2] Industrial classifications are shown for 345,000 of the jobs classified as INR in the 1960 Census of Population.

In general, these jobs reclassified from INR (Census of Population) to specific industrial classifications (Census Population Survey) tend to be distributed among the industrial classifications in roughly the same proportions as those found for the entire U.S. employed work force in the Census of Population data (Table B.1). For example, wholesale and retail employment accounted for 3.8 and 12.9 percent, respectively, of the redis-

[1] The 1950 INR percentages in the two places did not differ greatly. In Sarasota it was 1.0 percent, in Jersey City, 1.3 percent.

[2] U.S. Bureau of the Census, *Accuracy of Data on Population Characteristics as Measured by CPS—Census Match,* Series ER 60 #5.

TABLE B.1

Industrial Classification of 345,000 Persons Reported in INR, 1960 Census of Population

	Redistribution of INR employment[a]		Total U.S.,[b] 1960
	Number	Percent	Percent
Total INR jobs redistributed	345,000	100.0	100.0
Agriculture, forestry, fisheries	49,000	14.2	6.5
Mining	7,000	2.0	1.0
Construction	20,000	5.8	5.8
Manufacturing	76,000	22.0	26.4
Transportation	13,000	3.8	4.1
Communications, utilities	—	—	2.6
Wholesale trade	13,000	3.8	3.3
Retail trade	48,000	13.9	14.4
FIRE	24,000	7.0	4.1
Business/repair services	13,000	3.8	2.4
Personal services[c]	43,000	12.5	
Private household	(29,000)	(8.4)	(2.9)
Other	(14,000)	(4.1)	(2.9)
Entertainment/recreation	6,000	1.7	0.8
Professional/related services[d]	19,000	5.5	11.4
Administration	14,000	4.1	4.8
Armed forces[e]	—	—	2.6
INR[e]	—	—	3.9

[a] 345,000 employees classified as INR in the census data as found to be distributed among industry categories in the 1960 census match study.

[b] *Census of Population* estimates.

[c] Includes hotels/personal services.

[d] Includes medical/educational services.

[e] Not included in industry groups of persons surveyed.

tributed INR employment, and 3.3 and 14.4 percent, respectively, of the total employed work force according to the 1960 Census of Population estimates.

There were variations from the national pattern in several industries, however. A disproportionately large share of the INR jobs were found to be in the primary, FIRE, business/repair service, private households, and entertainment/recreation service industries. Among them, variation in private households was largest: 8.4 percent of the INR jobs that were matched were found to be in this industry compared to 2.9 percent in private households according to the Census of Population data for total national employment. On the other hand, the representation of professional and related services was disproportionately low, 5.5 percent compared to 11.4 percent nationally.

The above findings provide some basis for speculating as to the causes of increase in the INR category in 1960. Of course, the fundamental reason for the increase in INR appears to be the increased use of the mailed questionnaire, but two other factors may have also contributed. The first is that many people who work in more than one industry simply do not know how to classify themselves according to the industry in which they work. This could be true for a secretary, a laborer, a driver, a handyman. Such persons, when filling out a census form by themselves, would tend to leave unanswered a question regarding industrial classification, whereas if the census taker were present, a choice would have to be made. If this is the reason for the increase in non-reporters from 1950 to 1960, then the INR category may well be reflecting the increasing inappropriateness of the industry categories used, or conversely, the increasing importance of certain people who have high mobility among industries. Moreover, in a following section evidence is presented to show that INR increases with city size. This suggests that job mobility also increases with city size, since many of the activities of different industry categories become more similar in large places (e.g., office headquarters activity is similar in insurance and manufacturing).

The second possible reason for differences in rates of non-reporting among industries relates to the status associated with the type of work involved. For example, the status associated with working in private households is very low, whereas the status of working in the professional and related services is high. If this influence is significant we would expect the percentage of non-reporters to be disproportionately high in the low-status categories and disproportionately low in the high-status categories. Our findings above support this hypothesis with the possible exception of FIRE. Although, in general, job status would appear to be high in this white-collar industrial classification, there are many clerical-type positions that have relatively little status. The existence of such positions may explain the high proportion of non-reporters found in this classification.

There are two major ways by which the excessive classification of employment within the INR category may influence the analysis of employment
structure in this study. The first is to change the employment structure
characteristics by size of place discussed in chapter 4. The second is to
bring about changes in employment structure of individual MLM's which
are sufficient to alter their classification by type of function (e.g., as nodal
or manufacturing places).

Size-of-place categories.   When we examine the census employment data
the most distinct pattern that can be discerned from an analysis of the
importance of the INR (measured in terms of percentage of the employed
labor force) is that the incidence of INR increased with the size of the
labor market. This pattern, which did not exist in 1940 or 1950, is quite
apparent in the data for 1960 shown in Table B.2. The importance of
INR is found to have increased with each increase in size-of-place category,
not only for the nation as a whole but for every region.

 Clearly, the significance of this well-established pattern is that there
is a tendency for percentages of employment in the various industrial categories to be increasingly understated as we move from the small- to the
medium- and large-size MLM's. This means, of course, that the downward
bias in those industrial classifications, which arises as a result of improperly
classifying workers within INR, tends to increase with size of place.

 It seems likely that INR acts to mute the differences in structure
which exist among size-of-place categories of MLM's at least as regards
the increasing importance of business services with increases in size of
place. For example, both FIRE and INR increase as a percentage of
employment with size of place. Moreover, according to the Census matching survey (Table B.1), underreporting was disproportionately high in
FIRE. It would seem to follow, therefore, that if there were no INR, the
structural differences between large places and small, in so far as they relate
to FIRE, would be more pronounced.

 In an effort to make a crude adjustment for this bias for the year
1960, we redistributed the INR employment among the remaining thirty-
one industrial classifications in each of the regional size-of-place categories.
In making these adjustments within each regional size-of-place category,

TABLE B.2

Percentage of Total Employment (1960) and Job Increases
(1950-1960) Accounted for by Size-of-Place Category,
Regional and National

Region		INR as percent of total employment				INR share of job increase (total)
	NMC	Small-size MLM's	Medium-size MLM's	Large-size MLM's	Total	
New England	3.29	3.24	4.36	5.14	4.33	17.22
Mideast	3.21	3.58	3.86	5.43	4.76	20.90
Great Lakes	2.72	2.98	3.93	5.31	4.01	15.42
Plains	2.25	3.01	4.35	5.56	3.33	10.47
Southeast	2.25	2.91	4.37	—	3.16	7.57
Southwest	3.02	2.92	4.79	—	3.92	9.70
Rocky Mountains	2.29	2.44	3.48	—	2.72	5.82
Far West	2.45	3.72	3.33	5.13	4.06	10.17
Total U. S.	2.56	3.08	4.08	5.33	3.93	12.44

it was assumed that those workers classified in INR should be redistributed among the remaining thirty-one industrial classifications in proportion to the employment falling within these classifications. This assumption seems to be justified in view of the census study which matched classifications as mentioned above. For example, if 30 percent of the total employment (excluding INR) were found to be in manufacturing, then 30 percent of INR in that size-of-place category would be added to employment in that industrial category. This exercise provides us with only a rough approximation of adjusted industry employment, but the adjusted figures do give an indication of the direction and possible bias in our measurements.

After making these adjustments to the data we ranked size-of-place categories for each industrial classification within each region using the ranking system described in chapter 4. The rankings based on the adjusted data are shown in parentheses in Table 4.4 in those cases in which such rankings are different from those based on unadjusted data. Since in most regions the extent of INR overreporting was relatively larger in the larger-size MLM's, the effect of the adjustment was to increase the percentages of employment in non-INR industrial classifications to a greater extent in the larger than in the smaller MLM's.

The most striking finding is that there are very few changes in rankings. In the mainly business services category there are none and, among the large majority of component individual business services which make up this category, there are also no changes.[3] In those few instances in which changes in rankings occurred within individual business service classifications, the altered rankings in no way damaged the essential findings set forth in chapter 4. In general, the effect of the adjustment was to reinforce the finding (based on unadjusted data) that the share of employment in the business services increases with size of place.

In the mainly consumer services category there was only one change in ranking among the eight regions, a change which indicated the possibility of somewhat greater importance of consumer services in the medium-size MLM's of the Southeast than had been indicated by the unadjusted data. Inspection of Table 4.4 indicates no significant changes in ranking in the two major consumer services categories, retailing and medical/ education services, however.

There is little reason to comment in detail on the changes in ranking in the remaining categories—construction, manufacturing, and government (administration and armed forces). Table 4.4 indicates no changes which significantly alter the earlier findings.

Type-of-function categories. To assess the possible effect of overstatement of INR on the type-of-function classification of MLM's we have attempted to make a rough estimate of the extent of bias in the national employment data. This we have done by making a very exacting redistribution of INR · employment among the thirty-one regular industrial classifications for 1960. In this adjustment INR employment has been redistributed separately in *each of the 368 MLM's* rather than in each regional size-of-place category as was the case in the adjustment process described above. After employment was adjusted for each MLM, the data for each industrial classification were totaled for the nation and shares of employment computed.

Among the various service-type industrial classifications which were analyzed in classifying nodal places, the adjusted 1960 data exceed the actual (Table B.3) by not more than 8 percent in any case.[4] No doubt

---

[3] These component classifications are not shown in Table 4.4.

[4] The actual share of total employment was changed by .2 of 1 percent or less in all but three industries: miscellaneous manufacturing and other retailing, which increased by .4 of 1 percent, and medical/educational services, whose share of total employment rose by .5 of 1 percent.

TABLE B.3

Reported Employment, and Employment Adjusted to Reflect Redistribution of INR Employment, 368 MLM's, Total U.S., 1960[a]

	Reported employment		Adjusted employment		Ratio[b]
	Number[c]	Percent	Number[c]	Percent	
Primary					
Agriculture	1239.0	2.5	1286.3	2.6	1.040
Forestry/fisheries	36.6	0.1	38.0	0.1	1.000
Mining	269.9	0.5	280.6	0.6	1.200
Construction	2780.8	5.6	2907.5	5.8	1.036
Manufacturing					
Food/dairy products	1402.0	2.8	1466.4	2.9	1.036
Textile mill products	564.0	1.1	586.1	1.2	1.091
Apparel manufacturing	850.5	1.7	894.2	1.8	1.059
Lumber/wood products	485.3	1.0	505.6	1.0	1.000
Printing/publishing	994.6	2.0	1043.4	2.1	1.050
Chemicals/allied prod.	714.3	1.4	748.5	1.5	1.071
Electrical/other mach.	2640.2	5.3	2765.1	5.5	1.038
Motor vehicle equip.	769.4	1.5	801.0	1.6	1.067
Other transp. equip.	880.1	1.8	920.6	1.8	1.000
Other misc. mfg.	4719.6	9.5	4931.4	9.9	1.042
Utilities	680.7	1.4	711.9	1.4	1.000
Mainly Business Services					
Railroad/railway exp.	712.4	1.4	744.2	1.5	1.071
Trucking/warehousing	701.3	1.4	733.6	1.5	1.071
Other transportation	763.3	1.5	802.7	1.6	1.067
Communications	677.2	1.4	709.3	1.4	1.000
Wholesale	1845.8	3.7	1933.6	3.9	1.054
FIRE	2342.9	4.7	2457.4	4.9	1.043
Business/repair	1316.1	2.6	1379.6	2.8	1.077
Mainly Consumer Services					
Food/dairy stores	1255.1	2.5	1312.8	2.6	1.040
Eating/drinking places	1366.7	2.7	1430.1	2.9	1.074
Other retail	4595.0	9.2	4805.6	9.6	1.043
Hotels/personal	1500.7	3.0	1570.9	3.2	1.067
Entertainment/recreation	417.2	0.9	437.1	0.9	1.000
Private household	1327.9	2.7	1387.1	2.8	1.037
Medical/education	5859.1	11.8	6128.7	12.3	1.042
Government					
Administration	2588.3	5.2	2708.9	5.4	1.038

TABLE B.3 (*Continued*)

Reported Employment, and Employment Adjusted to Reflect Redistribution of INR Employment, 368 MLM's, Total U.S., 1960[a]

	Reported employment		Adjusted employment		Ratio[b]
	Number[c]	Percent	Number[c]	Percent	
Armed forces	1382.9	2.8	1434.6	2.9	1.036
INR	2189.5	4.4	0.0	0.0	—
Total	49868.2	100.0	49862.6	100.0	—

[a] INR employment was distributed among the remaining industrial classifications separately in each of the 368 MLM's. Redistribution was proportional to reported employment in these classifications. Adjusted employment estimates were then totaled for the entire U.S.

[b] Adjusted to reported employment.

[c] In thousands.

the adjusted measures for individual MLM's vary to a greater extent than is indicated in the national data, but it seems unlikely that the effect of more variations could have worked to change the classification of individual MLM's in more than a few instances. It will be recalled that in order to be classified as nodal an MLM must be within the top quartile of four out of six specified industrial classifications (see chapter 6). To the extent that INR should be redistributed more or less proportionally among the industrial classifications (which Table B.1 indicates to be the case) such redistribution would not alter an individual MLM's relative position, i.e., its position in terms of rank in a given industrial classification. Moreover, if an MLM were found to rank relatively high in as many as four out of six classifications using unadjusted data, it is probably because it is essentially nodal in character.

It would seem even less likely that classification of other types of MLM's was influenced significantly. Essentially, the strategy employed in classifying specialized MLM's was to set up fairly "hard" tests to be met and to leave a large number of MLM's in a residual, mixed group. We doubt, for example, that more accurate information regarding those persons reported in the INR category would result in a change in the list of resort-type MLM's. These places were found to be much more heavily structured in the combined recreation and entertainment classifications than others. Moreover, even if a few MLM's were reclassified it is unlikely that this

would significantly influence our findings regarding the structural characteristics of a given type of MLM, since the findings were based on analysis
of the entire group of places.

Measures of employment change in MLM's. The real test of the effect
of the INR reallocation is an analysis of the sensitivity of job-increase and
job-decrease measures, which are changes at the margin. The result of
distributing the .5 million unclassified jobs in 1950 and the 2.2 million
unclassified jobs in 1960 among the thirty-one industry categories in the
manner indicated in Table B.3 was to increase the shares and rates of job
increases (1950-60) among the individual industrial classifications and to
reduce rates of job decreases. Shares of job decreases increased in some
industries and decreased in others. The rates of job increases rose by as
much as a fourth (other transportation) and by more than a tenth in
twenty-six of the thirty-one industries. The rates of job decreases are much
more sensitive to the adjustment procedure; they were reduced by up to
70 percent, from a rate of 0.7 percent to 0.2 percent in the other retailing
category (an actual decline from 27,000 to 7,000 job decreases).

These changes do indicate the sensitivity of the different measures
used and thus will serve as a useful guide to anyone wishing to use selective
statistics. The most sensitive measures are the measures of job decreases.
The measures of job increases are also significantly affected but the
measures of industry structure are only minimally affected.

Analysis of shares of job increases by size of place. When we turn to
size-of-place categories we find considerable differences in the importance
of INR measured in terms of share of job increase. For the nation as a
whole, INR comprised the following proportions of total job increase in
the four size categories:

NMC's	4.9
Small-size MLM's	8.1
Medium-size MLM's	12.2
Large-size MLM's	23.1

Among individual MLM's the share of job increases comprised by INR
ranged widely, from 44.5 percent (Table 8.1) to zero in a number of
places.

We were not able to rerun our analyses with data adjusted on an individual MLM basis to remove the effect of excessive classification within the INR category, but we did make a very crude adjustment of the 1950-60 job-increase data for each of the regional size-of-place categories. This was done by allocating the job increases in INR to the remaining industrial classifications in proportion to their share of job increase as indicated by the unadjusted data. Such an adjustment fails to recognize that in some instances job increases in the INR classification were accompanied by excessive job decreases. Accordingly, INR should be redistributed in such a way as to reduce job decreases in certain of the other industrial classifications rather than simply to raise job increases. More important, the assumption that job increases in INR should be distributed among the remaining classifications in proportion to their shares of job increases computed from the unadjusted data is not necessarily valid. Overenumeration in INR may cause the reported job increases in some classifications to be unduly small. Such classifications will not receive a proper allocation of job increases when the INR job increases are redistributed.

Nevertheless, the redistribution involves very substantial adjustment of the data and permits us to observe whether our findings based on the unadjusted data would be readily altered by revisions of the data such as would be occasioned by introduction of employment estimates free from the INR overenumeration.

In this analysis we have used the same type of procedure as was described in the adjustment of the regional size-of-place structure data. The results are shown in Table 5.3. Following the adjustment of data, the size-of-place categories in each region have been ranked for each industrial classification. Where ranks were different from those in the unadjusted data the adjusted ranks are shown in parentheses.

Although the INR share of job increases is large and the adjustments quite sizable the results of this analysis are similar to those described for the analysis based on adjustment of regional size-of-place structure data. Not one of the rankings for the mainly business services category is changed. In the mainly consumer services category, none of the rankings are changed sufficiently to alter the findings in chapter 5 except in the case of the large-size MLM's. Here the position of four of the five large-size MLM categories is changed. In two regions, New England and the Mideast, the ranking of the large-size MLM's rises from third or fourth to first. In the remaining two, the rankings changed by only one place (from fourth to third).

We should note, however, that in the two most important consumer service classifications, retailing and medical/education services, there were no significant changes in rankings. In spite of the fact that the adjustments work to distribute relatively more INR job increases to the larger than to the smaller places, there were no changes in the large-size MLM and the NMC rankings in retailing and no significant changes in the small- and medium-size MLM categories. In the medical/education services classification there were no changes of significance (the large-size MLM ranking changes from second to first place in the Great Lakes region and from third to second in the Far West. In the Plains, the NMC and medium-size MLM rankings changes by one position.

Even more striking is the fact that in the remaining classifications shown in Table 5.3 (construction, manufacturing, administration, and armed forces) there were no significant changes in rankings.

Our interpretation of this evidence is that the share of job creation characteristics are shown to be very well established. Although the adjustment, itself, does not serve to provide us with accurate job-increase estimates it does involve quite sizable changes in the data. Since such changes do not alter our basic findings, we suggest that they are generally reliable, in spite of the unfortunate overenumeration of INR employment.

INDEX

Acceleration principle, 66-67; in construction, 65-67, 179-84, 186-87; defined, 182*n*

Administration, *see* Government services

Agglomeration, 117-25, 210, 242

Agriculture, 24, 77-78, 98-100, 223, 263; *table,* 263

Alternate classification of MLM's, 138-39

Amenities: defined, 230; significance in employment growth, 230-38, 240

Amplification of change in employment, 62-73, 255*n*

Amplification process, *see* Income multiplier

Armed forces, *see* Government services

Ashby, Lowell D., cited, 7, 74, 211, 256

Atlanta, example of use of data, 8, 10, 14; *table,* 9

Basic (export) industries 49, 65, 77, 208*n*; defined, 50; *see also* Export activity

Berry, Brian, cited, 6, 55

Business services, xi, 25; job increases, 26, 30, 33, 35, 38, 45, 101-9, 114, 189, 195, 198-99, 202, 203, 205, 245, 271; job decreases, 32, 33, 101-7, 113, 195, 204; normalized values of, 42-43; and coefficients of variation, 54, 55, 92; and size of market, 67-68; and external economies, 69; and size of place, 79, 80-83, 86, 89, 241; and quartile analysis, 119, 120-22; and nodal classification, 128, 139, 149; employment growth in six, 158, 168-73, 175-76; in 50 fastest-growing MLM's, 202, 203; *tables,* 9, 10, 22, 23, 27, 36-37, 40-41, 42, 52-53, 81, 84-85, 90-91, 102, 110-11, 148,

166-67, 171, 174, 177, 190-91, 196-97, 268

Capitals, state, 146-47

Censuses, 3*n,* 253-59; *see also* U.S. Census of Population

Central business district (CBD), xiii, 57, 232, 234, 235-36, 243, 249

Centralization, in employment, 214

"Central place" theory, 55-56

Change, measures of, 5; *see also* Employment change; Unassociated change

Classification of MLM's, 111-56; criteria for, 125-27; problems in, 127-31; alternate classifications for 11 cities, 138-39; and size-of-place categories, 75-95; *tables,* 76, 132-37

Coefficients of correlation, 89, 92-93, 160, 169, 172-73, 175-76, 178-79, 181, 184; *tables,* 162, 166-67, 174, 177

Coefficients of variation, 51, 54-55, 67, 181

Competition, among cities, 69, 103-4, 211; *see also* Amenities

Construction: and employment growth, 24-25; acceleration principle in, 65-67, 179-84, 186-87; and size of place, 87-88; and quartile analysis, 123, 124; *tables,* 9, 22, 23, 26, 27, 36-37, 40-41, 52-53, 81, 84-85, 110-11, 120, 190-91, 196-97, 216-17, 263, 268

Consumer services, xi; job increases, 25, 26, 28, 29, 33, 35, 38, 45-46, 101-7, 109, 189, 195, 198, 202, 203, 207, 271-72; job decreases, 32, 101-7, 113, 114, 204-5; normalized values of, 43; export of, 54-55; and size of place, 80, 86-87, 89; and coefficient of correlation, 93; and quartile analysis, 119, 120-22; and nodal classification, 128; employ-